A SOCIAL AND ECONOMIC
HISTORY OF ENGLAND
FROM 1700 TO 1970

A

A Social and Economic History of England From 1700 to 1970

by A. H. STAMP

RESEARCH PUBLISHING CO.
52 Lincoln's Inn Fields · London

© A. H. STAMP, 1979
ISBN 0 7050 0070 2
Made and Printed in Gt. Britain for The Research Publishing Co.
(Fudge and Co., Ltd.,) London.

CONTENTS

CONTENTS (continued)

6

PLATES

PREFACE

This text book has been designed for C.S.E. and G.C.E. candidates, and covers fully the social and economic history of England from 1700 to 1970, as required by the various examining Boards. I have tried to present each topic in as interesting a way as possible.

Grateful acknowledgment is made to Clive Holmes Esq. for the drawing of Kay's 'Flying Shuttle', and to S. Grant Esq., for illustrations provided.

For the use of copyright material as indicated, grateful acknowledgment is also made to the Science Museum, London; the National Portrait Gallery; Mansell Collection; the Wellcome Trustees; Radio Times Hulton Picture Library; Rochdale Art Gallery Committee; Pictorial Education; and to R. Barnard Wray, author of *The Story of British Locomotives*, published by Methuen and Co., for the illustration of Blenkinsop's Railway, and to A. & C. Black Ltd.

A. H. STAMP.

PART ONE

AGRICULTURAL AND INDUSTRIAL REVOLUTIONS

Chapter I

Life in the
Eighteenth Century

He was a 'beau' — or, as we should now say, a dandy — one of the
most typical figures of the 18th century, and we must not delay, therefore, to make his acquaintance. Indeed, we could not have found a
better opportunity than the present one, for at this very moment he
was preparing for the usual routine of his daily life.

The time was half-past nine in the morning, and from the large
four-poster bed with its purple silk hangings, where he had spent a
warm but stuffy night, the beau was slowly arising. Clad in a magnificent
dressing-gown, he consumed a light breakfast of toast and of coffee
flavoured with mustard.

After thus refreshing himself, he commenced the most serious
business of the day. This took a very long time, but it was certainly
well worth all the care and energy expended, for when the beau emerged
from his house, he represented, without doubt, the final word in fashion.

Here, then, we must pause, and consider in closer detail this con-
noisseur of 18th-century elegance.

Upon his head reposed a black felt cocked hat with wide and flapping
brim, and beneath this, a very expensive wig carefully powdered with
scented flour. His beautiful silk neckerchief was arranged with deliberate
carelessness so that it exposed to view one of the dozen or so different
shirts he wore every week. His coat was of blue silk, heavily em-
broidered, and with silver-edged button holes for the silver buttons;
his long waistcoat, reaching to the thighs, was of green silk; and his
breeches were of black velvet. We had thus a blue coat, a green waistcoat
and black breeches — blue, green and black. But such was not all. His
silk stockings were shining white, with gold-braided gaiters below the
knees, and his shoes had magnificent silver buckles. From his left side
hung a silver-hilted sword; in his right hand he held a cane, while his
left hand carried an ivory snuff box and handkerchief. To complete

the dazzling picture, his hands and face had been carefully scented —
most carefully indeed, for this was required to disguise the fact that he
had not washed for some time.

The beau.

Thus attired, the beau emerged at last from his home. Not even
Solomon in all his glory . . .

With a dignified pace, he made his way along the street. There was,
in fact, rather a chill wind, and he wished that he had put on an outdoor
coat, as several other gentlemen he met had decided to do. However,
to keep warm, he slightly quickened his steps, but was then halted, only
a few yards further on, by the interesting struggles of a lady trying to
enter her carriage. Desperately she endeavoured to manoeuvre herself
through the carriage door, while the coachman, two grooms and an
ostler reinforced her efforts. To be truthful, however, it was not the
fault of nature that she was too wide to achieve success. It was, instead,
the fate of fashion, for at this period it was the custom of the upper class
ladies to wear huge hoops of whalebone around their waists beneath
their dress. So monstrous were these hoops that it became very difficult
for the wearers to sit on a chair, enter a carriage, or even to pass each
other in a fairly narrow street.

Fortunately, fashions change, and after the middle of the 18th century, the hoop disappeared, and was replaced about 1780 by the head-dress — an even more remarkable phenomenon. First of all, the hair was piled up into a column about three-foot high. Then, in order to support such a mass, it was stuffed with wool, tow (rough flax) and hemp, and in order to keep it firm, it was plastered with lard, meal (a kind of flour) and clotted cream, which duly turned sour until the good lady smelt like a walking refuse heap. The whole fantastic super-structure was then decorated with gold ornaments, jewels, ribbons and lace. At night, the wearer slept with a strong wire cage about her head-dress to prevent the mice getting in, yet even then, when the erection was dismantled after every two months or so, goodness knows what might emerge.

But the demands of fashion were still not satisfied even with such a head-dress. Further to increase the outline beauty of the female figure, it was usual to wear false bosoms and false rumps as well, so that the ladies of those days blossomed forth most startlingly, both in the front and to the rear.

Once more, the beau resumed his walk, though by this time he found that the streets were becoming very crowded indeed. Gentlemen in dress similar to his own; ladies in rich silks and heavy brocades be-spangled with diamonds, and both sexes with small black velvet patches gummed on the faces for decoration; merchants in more sober clothes — though an unusual dye, a fur collar or a gold braid gave a hint of the wealth they possessed; a doctor carrying a cane, the knob of which contained a disinfectant for him to sniff; a lawyer in black silk garments; artisans wearing linen coats and leather breeches; men of different trades and professions — all were making their way along the same road.

And here, indeed, came a soldier — a soldier of the Life Guards, to judge by his uniform. The Life Guards, founded in 1660, were the oldest regiment of the British Regular Army, and in the 18th century were to have the battle honours of Dettingen, 1743, to their name. Thus it is not surprising that the trooper bore himself so proudly, even though his uniform alone was a sufficient cause for pride. What a brilliant uniform it was, indeed! The age of full armour had long since passed away in the Middle Ages, and though three-quarter armour (to the thigh) and half-armour (to the waist) had lingered on in the 16th and 17th centuries, by the 18th century, metal suits were no longer of use. The reason was that guns and gunpowder had gradually improved in quantity and efficiency as the centuries passed, until they ruled the battlefield. True, it was possible to make armour sufficiently strong to withstand a bullet, but such an overall protection would have been far too heavy to wear.

So the trooper of the Life Guards moved smartly down the street, clad, not in shining armour, but in even more brilliant cloth. Upon his curling wig was a dark, gold-brimmed three-cornered hat. Then a bright scarlet coat, glittering with gold braid and a gold belt, reached to his knees. The corners of the coat skirt were turned back to form a triangle at either side, and thus display the brilliant royal blue of the inner lining . . . Also, as the coat was open down the front, it revealed the white, gold-bordered waistcoat worn beneath. The breeches, too, were dazzling white. Gauntlets over broad blue-and-gold cuffs, and dark cavalry boots reaching to the thighs and fitted with cruel wheeled spurs called rowels, completed the picture. It was certainly a brilliant uniform, designed to attract anything from recruits to fair ladies. But after five minutes of the blood and the mud of the battlefield, what then of the glitter and the sheen? So the soldier passed on his way.

But above all, the street was crammed with hawkers and pedlars, who thus sold most of the articles which we should now buy in shops — dairy produce, chickens, rabbits, fish, vinegar, fruits, herbs, scissors, tools, pots and pans, brooms, etc. Bakers carried bread in huge baskets; milk sellers carried buckets hanging from wooden yokes on their shoulders and it was interesting to watch them as they openly diluted the milk from the street pump as they passed. Indeed, the street pump was known as the 'Black Cow'. There were apple-sellers, tinkers, chair menders, knife grinders, ballad sellers, and chimney-sweep boys with brushes and bags of soot, as well.

And the whole of this mob fought its way fiercely down the street. The 18th century was, above everything else, an age of brutality. No wonder the beau carried a sword. At any moment, he knew he might be compelled to use it. The slightest insult, real or fancied, that passed between gentlemen was settled by a savage duel there and then in the street. If such was the example of the gentry, the lower classes were only too swift to copy it in their own far rougher fashion. Apprentice fought apprentice as they sold their masters' wares; coachmen, unable to pass on the road, battered each other with their fists to decide who should give way; women fought women with no less savagery than men — for even in the most respectable of society, though women might swoon and languish, they could also spit and swear. And around every fight, whether it was two gentlemen duelling with swords, or a couple of gutter urchins with grimy fists, the crowd gathered in eager appreciation, enthusiastically cheering the sight of bruises and blood.

Perhaps one of the reasons for this age of brutality was the curse of drink. It was a recognised fact that at any party or social function, you should become drunk — failure to do so was an insult to the host, for it meant that there was definitely something wrong with his hospitality. Everyone drank liquor without restraint — ladies, clergymen and children included. Judges were known to arrive in court, try cases and pass sentences, while all the time in a state of semi-intoxication. Ministers of the Crown staggered drunkenly in the presence of Queen Anne. The rich became drunk on port wine and burgundy, while for the poor there was not only beer, but an even deadlier liquid — gin. The effects of this grain-distilled spirit were revolting in the extreme. It dragged human beings to the lowest level of existence; it made them worse than brute beasts in their habits and customs. And worse still, it was cheap. The gin shops used to display the advertisement 'Drunk for 1d., dead drunk for 2d., clean straw to lie on for nothing.' Is it to be wondered, therefore, that millions of gallons were consumed every year — in 1742, for example, no less than 19 million gallons. Is it to be wondered, therefore, that one-eighth of the adult population of London died from drink?

So past the fighting, drunken mob, with his ear-drums deafened by the shouts of the hawkers and pedlars, the clatter of the horse-hooves and carriages, and the cracking of coachmen's whips — past all this the beau continued on his way till he reached the most typical institution of the 18th century — the coffee house. These had become so famous and popular that they had developed into clubs where every man might find one according to his taste. In London, members of the political party known as the Whigs (which later became the Liberal Party), met at St. James's; the Tories (now the Conservative Party) met at the Cocoa Tree; gamblers met at White's, underwriters at Lloyd's, churchmen at Truby's. But indeed, there were clubs for men of all types. There was the Fat Men's Club, whose qualification for entry was the inability to get through a door of a prescribed size. At one time, its fifteen members weighed over three tons altogether. Its rival was the Scarecrow and Skeletons' Club.

Here, in the coffee house, the beau read the latest news. In 1702, the first English daily newspaper, the *Daily Courant*, was issued. Its information was contained on sheets 14 x 8 inches, at first printed on one side only, later both. Some editions contained a blank sheet, so that Londoners could write a letter thereon, and send both national and personal news at the same time to their friends in the country. The *Daily Courant* lasted till 1735, but by then there was also in existence the *Daily Post*, commenced in 1719. The first English Sunday newspaper appeared much later, in 1780 — the *British Gazette and Sunday Monitor*. In 1785, the *Daily Universal Register* appeared, whose name was later changed to *The Times*. There were magazines available, too — the *Tatler* 1709, the *Spectator* 1711, the *Gentleman's Magazine* 1731. So the beau sharpened his knowledge ready for conversation on the topics of the day.

More likely, however, he spent his time gambling at cards, and when we say that he gambled at cards, we mean that this was a really serious occupation. The beau, indeed, gambled thoroughly, passionately and expensively. For hour after hour, he shuffled, dealt, staked and played in an atmosphere of the most intense concentration. Not even a meal-time was permitted to interfere with his game — indeed, the Earl of Sandwich placed a piece of meat between two pieces of bread and ate it as he played rather than delay the contest — thus, incidentally, giving his name to that item of food. Not even news of peace or war, of earthquake or cloudburst, could disturb the fanatical interest with which the cards were dealt and delivered.

There can be no doubt whatever that this was an age of mad and uncontrolled gambling. A man would gamble away his fortune as hour succeeded hour. Then, bankrupt and penniless, he would gamble away his cloak, his coat and his waistcoat, and still the passion drove him on. So he gambled away his cravat, his shirt, then his shoes and his stockings, until finally he stood in a corner of the room, alone and forlorn, in nought but his little silk breeches.

Should the beau be not too skilful at cards, however, there were numerous other ways to satisfy his gambling fever. The race-course, for instance, provided a very welcome alternative to the card tables, and in this century, many of the great present-day racing events were founded — Ascot 1711, the St. Leger 1776, the Oaks 1779, and the Derby 1780. It was at this time, too, that there lived the greatest race-horse ever known — the chestnut-hued 'Eclipse'. He commenced his career at the age of five in 1769, and during the whole of his time of three years, was never once defeated. The climax really came in 1770 at the King's Plate race at Newmarket, when he walked triumphantly round the course to victory, for no-one dared to enter a competitor against him. Yet neither whip nor spur was ever used upon him.

Other amusements, though, reflected the spirit of the age — an age of brutality. Cock-fighting, for example, was immensely popular. Three-year, trained cocks, each fitted with steel spurs, fought a savage swirling battle, which left one of them a dead, blood-stained bundle of feathers, and the other a ragged, eyeless victor. But will you now, for a moment or so, look at the picture in the Art Section, and there study carefully not the cocks, but the expressions on the faces of the spectators. Can you tell what each man is thinking or saying? Remember, fortunes were staked on these contests.

Also, almost every town in England had not only its cock-pits, but in addition a strong post to which a bull could be tied. Half-a-dozen dogs were then let loose, each trained to seize the bull and hold on either till thrown off, or until it had torn away the piece of the bull's flesh on to which it hung so grimly. Sometimes the bull was too swift, and a belly-ripped, broken-backed hound writhed in its death agonies on the turf. Sometimes the bull, with its muzzle ripped away, and gaping gashes in its flanks, had to admit defeat. In 1747, there occurred a very rare and even bloodier spectacle still, when a full-grown tiger was baited with dogs.

From such entertainments as these — card playing, racing, cock-fighting, bull baiting — the beau duly returned home for the main meal of the day — dinner. On his return, in preference to walking, he chose a sedan chair, for the streets of those days did not encourage pedestrians — the gutter was literally knee deep in filth. Nor did the streets of those days encourage wheeled transport either. The rough cobbles were unevenly set, while gaping holes at frequent intervals smashed axles or wheels with ease. Indeed, many of those who were wise, placed their goods on sledges with iron runners.

Apart from the condition of the roads, a few dark clouds were looming in the sky, and the beau had no desire to be out in the open street when it rained. The water spouted from pipes on the roofs of the houses and fell to the streets in a series of waterfalls.

By sedan-chair, therefore, the beau reached his home. Dinner had originally been at 12 o'clock, but as the 18th century progressed it became later, till many dined at 4 p.m. It was in the late afternoon, therefore, that our hero sat down before a table laden with beautiful china and silver forks. Not that the fork was so essential an item of cutlery, for it was the knife, with its broad, rounded end which was used to convey food to the mouth. The beau now commenced the usual heavy meal. Meat and fish were eaten in plenty, vegetables and potatoes not so frequently, while the increasing overseas trade of the 18th century brought to England such fruits as oranges, lemons, bananas (usually baked in tarts) and peaches. Wine was even more plentiful than solid food, and sometimes the rich indulged in the latest beverage — tea.

As soon as he had recovered from his dinner, the beau decided that he would pay a visit to the theatre. A sedan-chair carried him comfortably over the rough cobbled streets, past the rows of solidly-built pink or yellow brick houses, each house comprising a basement and three storeys, while a large front door, with a fanlight above, was also a prominent feature of the architecture. Some of the windows, it could be noticed, had been bricked up to avoid paying the window tax which, imposed in 1696, lasted till 1851.

The finest houses of all, however, were those built by the Adam brothers, Robert and James. A visit to one of these houses the beau had never forgotten. The rooms therein were magnificent — high, vast and oval shaped, with carved marble fireplaces, ceilings decorated with graceful patterns and tinted blue, pink and green, and walls similarly enriched. Glass chandeliers sparkled and flashed as they hung from the ceiling, and were reflected in the large gilt-framed mirrors upon the walls. The furniture was light and graceful in design, for it was made by some of the most famous craftsmen of the day — Chippendale, Hepplewhite and Sheraton. From the forests of the West Indies had come a new wood, with a fine grain and a high polish — mahogany. From the opposite corner of the globe came oriental lacquered chairs, tables and cabinets. From Persia and India, too, came the beautiful carpets that covered the floors. Magnificent indeed were the homes of the wealthy in the 18th century.

The rather grim looking building at the corner of the street was a hospital — one of those noble institutions which, in the 18th century, helped people to die. Even as you entered, you had to hand over a sum of money — not for the cost of the treatment, indeed, but as a deposit for your burial fee. There were not many hospitals in existence at this time, so no records of illness could be kept owing to the pressure of work, but the number of those patients who survived was exceptionally small. The majority of doctors were little better than 'quacks', and even the most learned of them had no idea at all what caused diseases . . . or what cured them. The surgeons were human butchers; there were no anaesthetics, and no standards of cleanliness and comfort. That, in brief, was the 18th century hospital — the outpost of the cemetery.

The beau continued on his way.

Ahead of all these rich houses, with their beautiful furniture, and some distance from the hospital, lay the theatre, and having carefully adjusted his wig and his dress, the beau entered with all the dignity of a leading actor upon a stage. Indeed, it was quite obvious that he had come, not in order to see, but in order to be seen. It was equally obvious, too, that he preferred his own conversation in the box to that of the actors on the stage.

Once the play was over, the gambling fever seized him again, and he hurried away to his club to continue shuffling, dealing and staking till 2 or 3 o'clock in the morning.

As he played, fresh candles of whale oil were placed in the holders on the wall. Indeed, candles were in use both day and night — at night for illumination, and in the day so that men could light their long-stemmed clay pipes. The drawback to these candles was that the wick burnt straight, and became covered with soot at the top. Thus the flames gradually became smokier and dimmer, and someone had to go round every half-hour or so to trim off the end of the wick with a pair of scissor-like trimmers.

Down in Cornwall, however, one of the great inventors of the Industrial Revolution, William Murdock, who made a model road locomotive in 1786 (*see page* 80), turned his attention to the use of coal gas for artificial lighting. Constructing an iron cauldron for coal gas in the back garden of his home at Redruth, Cornwall, in 1792, he soon illuminated the whole of his house. After that, in 1798, he lit up the Boulton and Watt Factory at Soho, Birmingham.

But in the 18th century, there were still no street lights for the beau as he and his brotherhood returned home at two o'clock in the morning, travelling in company through the lawless streets. A link boy carrying a torch of tow and pitch, lighted their way, and on the gates of some of the houses could be noticed cone-shaped extinguishers where the boy could put out his torch.

Thus it was not until the darkness of the early hours that the beau returned at last to bed, to refresh himself for another typical day in a life that was as highly decorative as it was completely useless.

Chapter II

The Agricultural Revolution

Disadvantages of the open-field strip system

In this chapter, we are going to learn about the great changes that occurred to English farming in the 18th century — changes which have affected the lives of all of us ever since, whether we are farmers or not.

First of all, however, let us draw a brief background picture of what English farming was like before the 18th century, so that we can better understand the events which then took place.

In the Middle Ages, each village tried to produce enough food for its own needs.

In general, a village would have three large arable (ploughed) fields — the first for growing wheat or rye (for bread), the second barley (for beer) or oats (cattle food), and the third field was left fallow (empty) to regain its goodness. By an annual change-round of crops (known as the 'rotation of crops'), each field was left fallow every third year.

The richer peasants of the village each owned so many separated

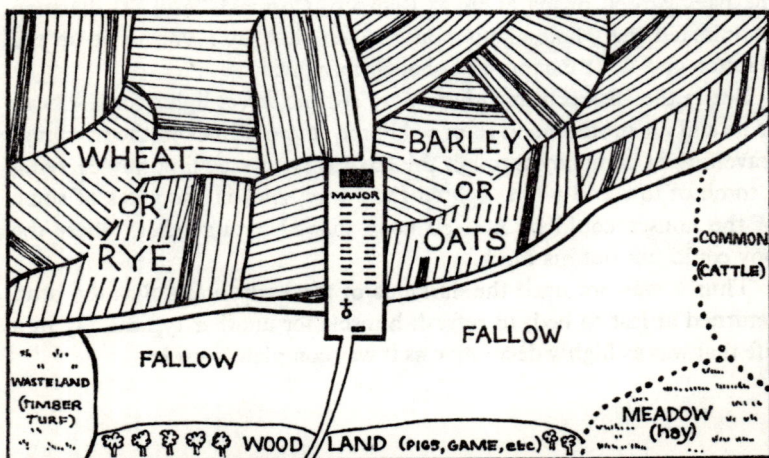

The three-field or open-field system. Each strip measured about 22 yards x 220 yards. Shaded strips indicate one villager's scattered holdings, usually to a total of thirty.

22

strips of land in each of the cropfields, the strips being scattered in order to give each man a fair share of the good land and the bad land. Usually, some 30 scattered strips were held by each villager.

All the fields were open, i.e. there were no hedges or fences round them as we have nowadays.

Cattle were pastured on the common; there was a meadow which produced hay; and the wasteland provided timber and turf.

This was the system used for half the arable land of this country, and no doubt it was quite suitable for the time of the Middle Ages. But fortunately or unfortunately, times changed, and the old system, therefore, had to change as well.

Indeed, the disadvantages of the old system were obvious. The scattered strips wasted space because they had to be separated by paths. Time was also wasted in going from strip to strip, while the narrow, rectangular shape of each strip made cross-ploughing impossible or very difficult. Equally difficult was drainage, for one man's system might be blocked by a neighbour.

There were other handicaps to farming, too. As the fields were open and hedgeless, the crops were frequently damaged by stray cattle, and also by travellers avoiding the quagmire of the road alongside the field. The weeds from a careless neighbour spread swiftly, and on the common, where all the livestock grazed together, disease spread even more rapidly.

It was not only disease that reduced the numbers of livestock. Those cattle not required for breeding had to be slaughtered every autumn, for the meadowland could not provide enough hay to feed all the animals during the winter.

Worse still, there was no possibility of improvement — the system checked any initiative or enterprise, since everyone had to plough, sow and harvest at the same time, otherwise he would interfere with his neighbour's work.

But the real cause of the breakdown of the old strip system and method of farming was the demand of the towns. The 18th century witnessed a vast increase in population. There were about $5\frac{1}{2}$ million people in England and Wales in 1700, but by 1800 there were nine million. Fewer deaths in infancy and longer life due to improved medical knowledge, earlier and illegal marriages due to declining moral standards, as well as the immigration of the Irish, all contributed to achieve this increase. These extra people needed food, and only the better farming made possible by enclosing the land, could provide it.

Then finally to end the old system, from 1793-1815, England fought the genius of the French Emperor Napoleon I. His blockade of this country checked the import of foreign corn, and English agriculture was thus required to make good the loss. Only by enclosing the land could the extra corn be provided.

Enclosure

Without doubt, therefore, some better way of farming had to be found; some better method than these open, hedgeless fields with their scattered strips, had to be devised.

Already in the 16th century, some of the land had been enclosed, i.e., men had arranged (by purchase, exchange or fraud) to have their strips all together, not scattered about, and the united holding was then fenced round. In the 16th century, the land had thus been enclosed for pasture, and now, when we come to the 18th century, we find the fields were still being enclosed, but this time for arable farming.

Indeed, enclosure in the 18th century was inevitable, because all the most powerful people wanted it. The landowners wanted it to provide more profit; the clergy desired it for more tithes (a tenth of the annual produce of land and cattle which the church claimed from the farmers); statesmen realised that there were prospects of more revenue; manufacturers desired cheap food which would mean less wages could be paid.

So the old strip system, with all its disadvantages, had to go. The procedure was simple. If the holders of three-quarters of the land in a village desired enclosure, an Act of Parliament made the enclosing legal. Commissioners were then appointed to draw up a plan to divide the land into separate fields for different owners. The common and wasteland were also included in the process.

As a result, each man no longer had a number of widely-scattered plots of land to cultivate. Instead, he possessed a united holding with a hedge or fence around.

By Acts of Parliament 1760-1800, three million acres were enclosed, and in 1801, a General Enclosure Act made the process cheaper and easier. By 1850, the enclosure movement was almost complete; only a very few strip fields remained.

Economic results of enclosure

What then, were the results of this Agricultural Revolution? What effect did it have upon the farming life of England? The answer is . . . a very great effect.

First of all, the enclosures enabled better cattle-breeding, for a man could now have all his own cattle grazing together on his own land, instead of being mixed with the poorer quality or diseased beasts of other people's herds on the common pasture.

It was in this development of cattle breeding that Robert Bakewell (1725-95) of Dishley, Leicestershire, made his name. Previously, oxen had been bred with long legs and heavy bones, since their main use was that of plough animals, but Bakewell wanted fatter, smaller-boned cattle, suitable for food, and the method by which he achieved his aims is still used today. From his herds, he selected the best animals, or those most nearly approaching his requirements, and used them for breeding. From their offspring, he then chose the ones most nearly approaching what he required, and bred these. By repeating this process of selection and mating in each succeeding generation, he finally obtained the required type.

Although Bakewell improved cattle, however, his greatest success was achieved with sheep. These had previously been bred for hides and wool, but Bakewell's New Leicester sheep (now extinct) were excellent for mutton rather than wool.

The fame of his experiments spread far and wide, as well they deserved. To the farm at Dishley came many distinguished visitors, not only from England, but also including French, German and Russian royalty. They were shown the farm buildings and the herds of cattle; they admired the famous bull, 'Twopenny', and the great ram, 'Two Pounder'; and everywhere they went they saw evidence of the latest developments in breeding. They were entertained to dinner in the great hall, and while they dined, they gazed not at famous paintings beautifully framed in gilt, or at other wondrous objects of art, but instead, at the skeletons of cattle arranged around the room, and at prize joints carefully preserved in pickle.

As a result of the efforts of Bakewell and others, sheep increased from 30-80 lbs. in weight, and bullocks from 400-800 lbs. in weight. At Ketton, Charles Colling bred the famous Durham Shorthorns. His 'Durham Ox' travelled on exhibition throughout England — a magnificent beast, weighing nearly $1\frac{3}{4}$ tons. As a later result, indeed, England was able to breed strains of livestock that became the envy of the world — breeds from which came the great herds of Argentine cattle and the vast flocks of Australian sheep. English bulls and rams have sold for thousands of pounds in the world's markets.

Enclosure of the land, however, enabled not only better cattle-breeding, but also better cultivation. One of the earliest of the new farmers who tried to improve the soil was Jethro Tull (1674-1741) at Mount Prosperous, a farm near Hungerford in Berkshire. His was the belief that crops needed air, and to effect this (i) he hoed his fields, and (ii) he invented a drill which ploughed three furrows at the same time to a proper depth, sowed a row of seeds in each furrow, and then covered over the furrow afterwards. To prove the value of his belief, he produced 13 successive crops of wheat from the same land, without manuring, and all the crops were of a standard higher than his neighbours'. For those who wanted to follow his example, his book on *Horse Hoeing Husbandry* was published in 1733.

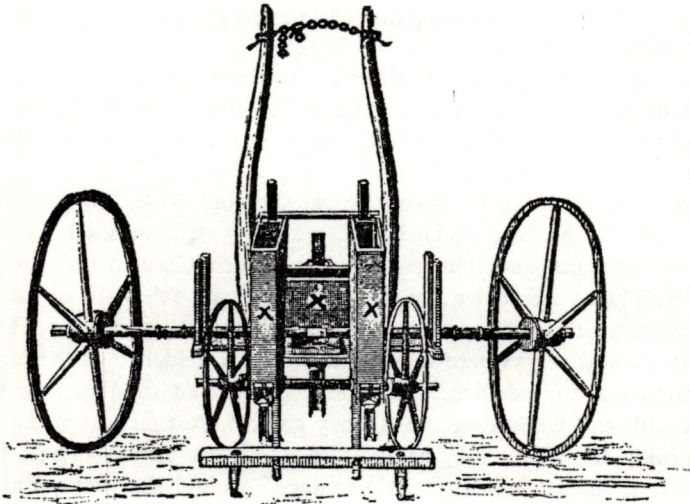

TULL'S DRILL
(From '*Horse Hoeing Husbandry*')

There were three seed boxes (X, X, X), one in front and two behind.
Seed was placed in each seed box, and fell down through the tube at the bottom. In front of each tube, a metal projection, like a small ploughshare, made a furrow into which the seeds then fell.
The action of the two rear tube projections covered the furrow made by the front tube projection. The furrows made by the rear tubes were covered over by the harrow at the back of the machine.
Thus the machine made three furrows, planted the seeds evenly in each, and then covered them over. This was better than the old method of scattering the seed in handfuls from a basket (the 'broadcast method').

Even more famous was Viscount Townshend (1674-1738). In his early career, he had been Secretary of State from 1721-30, but after a quarrel with his brother-in-law, the Chief Minister Sir Robert Walpole, he left the mire of politics for the mud of his Norfolk farm. It was indeed a poor estate which he possessed at Raynham, the chief crop being nettles. But Townshend set to work, and gradually began to improve the earth by using marl — a mixture of sand, chalk and clay soil. Then his eye fell on the fallow field. Though this, of course, was left uncultivated so that the soil might regain its goodness, it was really land wasted for a period, and Townshend wondered if he could plant some crop which would still not prevent the refreshening of the ground. Thus it was he who developed in England the answer discovered earlier by the Dutch — the planting of turnips and clover. Both of these root crops were a winter cattle food, and actually invigorated the soil instead of weakening it. Hence the crop rotation on Townshend's farm was wheat, turnips, barley and clover — (the 'Norfolk rotation' as it was called), and so enthusiastic was he about his system that he was rewarded with the title of 'Turnip Townshend'.

Not far away from Townshend's estate in Norfolk was the land owned by Thomas Coke (1752-1842) at Holkham. It was in 1776 that Coke took over the land — an extremely poor, sandy area, which struggled to produce a small amount of rye, and could scarcely support a few thin sheep and fewer still half-starved cattle. Coke of Holkham, however, was one of the hardest of workers. He used marl (a mixture of sand, chalk and clay soil), so that the three ingredients — sand, chalk and clay — were mixed in the right proportion to form an excellent soil. After that, he used a horse-drawn wheel plough instead of the old ox-plough. He manured. Then he carefully selected his seed, and sowed it by means of a drill. He grew wheat, turnips and clover, and when his crops were ready, he used reaping machines, threshing machines, chaff-cutters and turnip-slicers — the latest developments in agricultural machinery. He fed his cattle on oil cake, and in stalls. He toiled like a slave. He spent £500,000 on constructing and repairing farm buildings and cottages, and to improve the estate in other ways. It was a tremendous effort and a colossal expenditure, but it reaped its reward. His rents alone rose from £2,000 to £20,000 per year, and he died a very wealthy man.

At this time, too, a rich addition to England's agricultural land was obtained by the draining of the Fens in East Anglia. Around the Wash lay a vast marsh, intersected by islands, banks, meres and reedbeds —

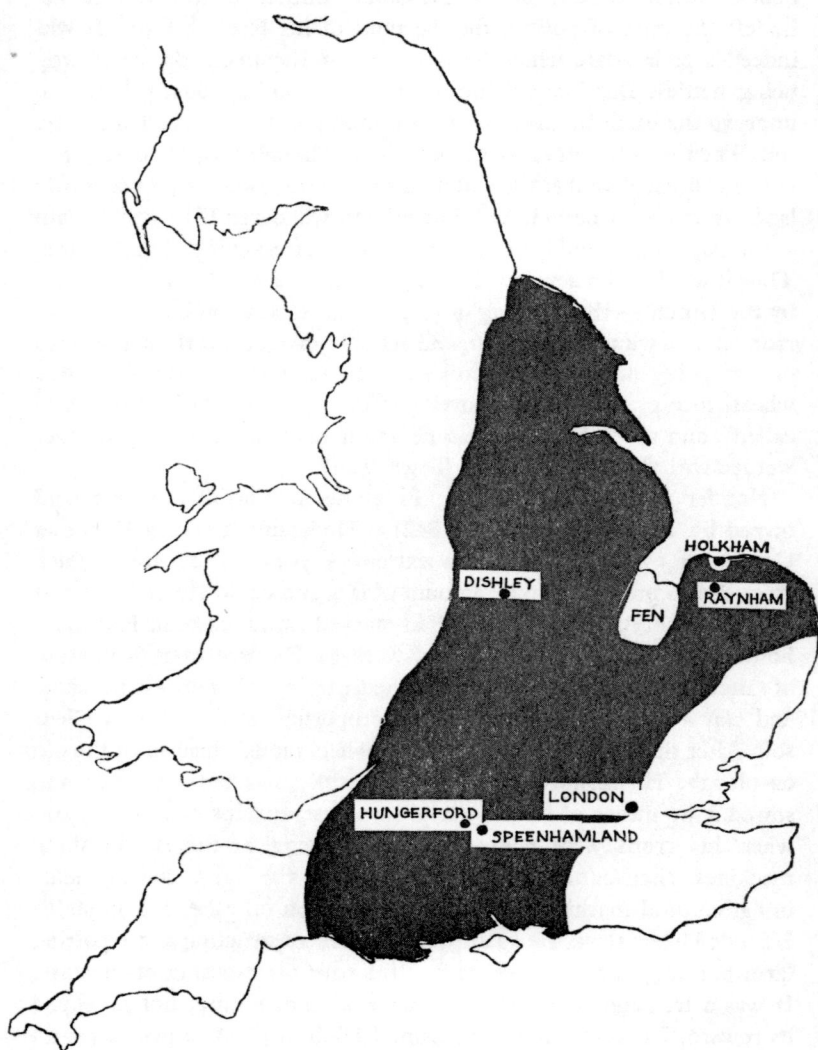

AGRICULTURAL REVOLUTION.
Shaded areas show enclosures 1700-1850.

a water-logged area of some 700,000 acres. Every day, the tide swept up the rivers, forcing the fresh water over the banks, and as the mouths of the rivers were blocked with mud, the water could not drain away. It was in 1630 that the Earl of Bedford tried to drain part of the area, but he and his followers had to face not only the difficulties of drainage, but also the hostility of the Fenmen. The Fenmen were a race of their own indeed — a wild and lawless people who lived by their skill in snaring the vast numbers of wildfowl. Great flocks of wild geese, ducks and swans, as well as cranes and bustards, were attracted by the swampy reaches of the Wash, and thus provided a good living for the trappers equipped with their nets and guns. If the area was drained, of course, the birds would settle elsewhere. So for three generations a battle raged between those who wanted land and those who wanted marsh. Success went to the Fenmen, particularly when the Civil War 1642-9 gave them the opportunity to destroy the dykes, ditches and embankments which had been constructed, so that their beloved swamps and marshes could be re-created. During the 18th century, however, reclamation began once more, and this time succeeded, until the richly fertile land of the area assumed its present-day appearance.

Then, as if to set the seal of respectability upon this Agricultural Revolution, it was patronised by Royalty. George III had a model farm at Windsor, and wrote agricultural articles in the press under the name of Ralph Robinson. So he became even more affectionately known as 'Farmer George'.

Knowledge of these developments was spread by the Board of Agriculture founded in 1793 and ending in 1822, its first Secretary being the writer and traveller, Arthur Young (1741-1820). As a farmer, Arthur Young was a complete failure. So he travelled abroad and around England, writing and teaching others how to farm, and in this he was very successful. ("Those who can, do; those who can't, teach.") For those who wish to re-live the 18th century farming life, he left an outstanding record in his *Tours* and *Annals of Agriculture*. It was Young who advocated the enclosing of fields, the creation of larger farms with long leases, and who also founded agricultural societies and shows.

But despite the richer yield of corn from enclosed land, progress was still slow. It took a long time for ideas to travel round the country, and even longer for them to penetrate the skulls of conservative farmers. In many cases, the new methods were costly, and not suited to all districts, while those who held their land on short leases were not prepared to make improvements from which only the landlord would benefit when the lease ended, and they therefore perhaps had to leave. This slow progress meant that the increased population was still short of food, so in 1773, the Corn Law Act allowed foreign corn to enter this country without paying any duty when English prices rose above £2.40 per quarter. In general, the various Corn Laws that were passed in this period tried to keep the English price within £2.30 to £2.70 per quarter.

So far, then, we have discussed the effects of the 18th century enclosures as regards cattle breeding and cultivation.

Social results of enclosure

But there is another aspect of the Agricultural Revolution which is also very important — its effect upon mankind. Here indeed, the consequences were amazingly varied.

The richer yeoman (i.e. the large freeholder, the leaseholder, who paid an agreed rent for so many years, or the copyholder*) benefited, for he could afford the cost of enclosing, hedging, ditching and manuring his land. Then he reaped his reward in the form of more produce and of increased rents from his tenant farmers. Ultimately, indeed, he became a squire — the wealthy local landowner, looked up to by the villagers, setting the standard of local society, hard riding and drinking, Justice of the Peace, a kind-hearted despot. The poorer yeoman (the small owner-farmer), who could not compete with the larger farms, as well as having to endure heavy taxes and bad harvests, declined, particularly between 1660-1790. Some became tenant farmers, while others went abroad or into industry.

But is was upon the labourer that the effects of the Agricultural Revolution were the most sad and sorrowful. At the outset, many of them had no legal right to the land they occupied. They or their ancestors had drifted into the village — no matter how or why; they had settled there in some out-of-the-way place, and had been allowed to remain because labour at the time was scarce. But they still had no legal right to the land they occupied, and on which they had built their house or hovel. So when the Agricultural Revolution came, and the land was required for enclosing, many were turned adrift, together with their wives and families. Even landowning cottagers were evicted, if they could not produce proof that they owned the land.

---

*This term arose in the Middle Ages when a villein had to undertake so much work for his lord. Often, however, the lord agreed to accept money instead of work, and the fact was recorded on the Rolls of the Manor. Usually the villein received a copy of the entry, and was henceforth called a 'copyholder'.

In some cases, it is true, the lord of the area was kind-hearted, and they were permitted to stay, but of what real value was that to the bewildered labourer? At one time, there had been a common field where he might keep his cow, chickens, a pig and a few geese, and wasteland where he might gather turf and wood for his fire. It was not much, but it had helped him to live, and to bring up a family. Above all, it had given him hope. Now, the common field and wasteland had gone, swallowed up by the enclosures, and "All I know is that I had a cow and an Act of Parliament has taken it from me," said one poor man.

There were reasons other than the Agricultural Revolution, however, which also worsened the life of the peasant. The landowner increased his rent, but where was he to earn the money since even the new enclosed farms could not absorb the population increase of labourers? Nor could he turn to local industries such as spinning and weaving, dyeing, tanning, etc., for such work was now being carried out in town factories in the Industrial Revolution (Chapter III).

Under the circumstances, he might decide to move to another village where the prospects of work seemed better. But here again he was checked — checked by the Laws of Settlement which had been passed as far back as 1662. By 1697, a worker who wished to leave his native village had to obtain from the parish a certificate accepting full responsibility for him if he became a charge on the poor rate of the place to which he was going. Unless he had such a certificate, the new area had legal power to return him, and generally did so, for obviously no parish would allow a newcomer to settle there if they risked having to pay for his upkeep. An Act of 1795 did, indeed, allow a man to stay in another parish until he actually became a charge on the poor rate, but the moment he did so become — the moment he was out of work and destitute — he was immediately sent back to his former home. So a poor man's own parish became his prison; he could not leave, for nowhere else would have him.

For the labourer, therefore, the position was hopeless, and as time passed, the utmost of misery appeared. His home became a hovel, with damp floors, and rain pouring in through the ill-thatched roof. His family were clad in rags, as well as pinched and starved. There was no meat, butter or fresh cheese. Barley bread soaked in boiling water provided breakfast; a bit of old cheese, an apple and a few green herbs had to suffice for dinner; and nothing more could he afford.

There was, indeed, only one answer to such desperation. The labourers stole. They stole the turnips from the farmer's fields, they dug up the farmer's potatoes, they stripped his fruit trees, and then they entered the game preserves. The landowners replied. Game Laws were passed in 1770 by which a first conviction was awarded three to six months in prison, and a second conviction six to twelve months together with a public whipping. But desperation was not to be checked by such relatively mild deterrents, and fiercer and more savage became the conflicts between game-owner and poacher. So the law increased in severity, until two people found in possession of a gun without due cause could be imprisoned for two years, and if any resistance was offered, the penalty was death. By 1816, just carrying a net at night, without being caught actually poaching, was punishable by seven years' transportation. Nor did the law suffer from any weakness on the part of those responsible for enforcing it, for some of the magistrates were game preservers. Thus between 1827-30, over 8,000 convictions were recorded. If any further discouragement was needed, mantraps with steel-toothed jaws were laid down — traps capable of almost completely severing the leg of the luckless poacher who stepped on them.

Thus the old rural England passed away, and its practices, customs and revels are now but memories sometimes faintly revived. The peasant had become at best a landless wage-earner, and often provided labour, not in the fields, but for the industries of the 18th and 19th centuries.

But though the labourer suffered so severely, it must be remembered that the Agricultural Revolution also had its benefits.

Without doubt, it enabled England to withstand the Napoleonic Wars (1803-15). In 1806, the Emperor Napoleon I of France passed the Decrees of Berlin and in 1807 the Decrees of Milan, forbidding the Continent to have any trade whatsoever with England. At intervals, however, he did allow wheat to be sent to this country in exchange for gold which he so desperately required, and these official imports, together with a generous amount of smuggling, assisted England's food supplies. But the main safeguard against England's starvation was the increased corn available as a result of the Agricultural Revolution, for three times as much corn could be grown on enclosed land as upon an equal area of open strip fields.

Without doubt also, the Agricultural Revolution prevented thousands of poorer people from dying of starvation. The increasing population of England and Wales (about $5\frac{1}{2}$ million in 1700, nine million by 1800) was making its home in the towns where the factories and coal mines offered employment. But these people who worked in industry did not produce any food for themselves, yet they had to be fed, and only the increased yield from the enclosed fields and better farming could supply them.

Moreover, the growing of winter crops (clover, turnips) now enabled the farmer to keep his cattle through the winter, instead of having to kill off most of them in the autumn because he had no food for them. Fresh meat, milk and butter could thus be obtained all the year round, and the health of the population benefited accordingly.

So great, indeed, were the progress and the prosperity in the Agricultural Revolution that there arose the famous figure of 'John Bull', an imaginary but typical, successful English farmer, and who has ever since been regarded as the national symbol of our country.

B

Chapter III

The Industrial Revolution

Causes of the Industrial Revolution

The word 'revolution' immediately brings to one's imagination the roar of explosions, the thunder of guns, the whine of bullets, and the fullness of destruction, massacre and misery. But in the revolution which will be related in this chapter, there were no explosions, not a cannon was fired, no massacres took place, and no great destruction occurred. Yet there was all the misery and suffering . . . and more. This was the Revolution in Industry.

By the end of the 18th century, everything was ready for a revolution of such a kind. For many reasons, trade and industry had to be, and could be, developed.

In 1688, King James II fled from this country after a rebellion had broken out, and Parliament therefore requested William of Orange (in Holland) to become the next king of England. Thus ended the century-old struggle to decide whether Crown or Parliament should be the more powerful and govern the country. Parliament had now won, for James had fled in defeat and William of Orange was king, not by right, but by Parliamentary invitation. More important, however, was that the Members of Parliament were merchants and landowners who, of course, were absolutely certain that anything which benefited them must also benefit the country. Parliament, therefore, would unhesitatingly support any trading developments which occurred.

At this time, trade followed the battle flag; after the soldier came the merchant. Thus from 1702-13, England fought the War of the Spanish Succession, and by the terms of the Treaty of Utrecht in 1713, she gained the right to sell 4,800 slaves a year to the Spanish colonies in the New World, and to send one trading ship per year to the great fair at Portobello in Panama. In those days, however, British traders were by no means slow, and the number of slaves they sold to the Spanish colonies was far more than the number officially allowed. Also, the annual trading ship to Portobello used to sneak out of the harbour at night, and reload from other British ships waiting out at sea.

Then from 1721-42, Sir Robert Walpole was the Chief Minister of

34

England, the longest period so far that any Prime Minister has remained in office. During these 21 years England followed a policy of peace which enabled her to build up her strength. Thus refreshed, she then waged, from 1756-63, the Seven Years' War with France and Spain which left her supreme in India and Canada. After that, she fought the Napoleonic Wars from 1803-15, thus gaining several West Indian islands from the French, and also Ceylon and South Africa from the Dutch. All these areas — India, Canada, the West Indies, Ceylon and South Africa — were excellent markets for English manufacturers, particularly cloth manufacturers.

Strangely enough, the chief salesmen who went out to these distant lands were the missionaries, . . . to whom, of course, the nakedness of the natives was an unchristian sin . . .

At the same time, too, the population of England was increasing. There were about $5\frac{1}{2}$ million people in England and Wales in 1700; but by 1800, there were over nine million. Hence, the home market also required English manufactures.

It was these increasing demands from the colonial and home markets which caused English manufacturers to consider a new and very important theory of trade. The idea came to them, that numerous cheap sales would be more profitable than a few dear ones. Now remember this: numerous cheap sales would be more profitable than a few dear ones. Accordingly, the manufacturers began to seek to expand their businesses and to produce more goods.

The means were all ready to be used: (i) At the outset it was not possible to continue with the method that had lasted for centuries — the method of making everything by hand. Quite obviously, the old hand-powered industry could not cope with the urgent, booming demand for more and quicker production. Hand-power, indeed, was far too slow. But what other means were available? Two alternative sources of power were wind and water, yet neither of them was reliable (for example, in periods of calm, frost or drought). It was, however, realised that water could also be employed very effectively in the form of steam, and steam required coal and water. The means, as we have said, were all ready to be used; the north of England had rich iron and coal deposits as well as flowing streams and rivers.

(ii) If cotton goods were required, England was again fortunate. The western winds from the Atlantic drove the moisture-laden clouds against the Pennine barrier to form rain. The damp climate that resulted was ideal for the cotton industry, since cotton threads break if too dry.

(iii) For the production of new types of goods, the opportunity was there, too. To England came French refugees, fleeing from the religious persecution in their own country. Between 1670-90, 80,000 of them came, bringing with them their skill and their industries, especially the silk industry which they established at Spitalfields, just outside London.

(iv) Where development required labour, this was supplied by the farm workers who, no longer required on the enclosed farms of the Agricultural Revolution, drifted to the nearby towns to earn money.

The business side of development was organised by the Puritans and the Methodists. Grim their religions undoubtedly were, but these men who denied themselves the usual pleasures of the world around them, regarded success in business as the just reward for their way of life. Their faith, indeed, exalted the virtue of hard work.

(v) Where development required money, capital could be borrowed from the Bank of England, founded in 1694. Merchants and rich landowners invested in industry, too.

(vi) Once we had produced the goods, we were in a favourable geographical position on the world trade routes to export them.

All was thus ready for the Industrial Revolution, so let us now find out what happened in the three main industries of coal, iron and textiles.

THE COAL INDUSTRY

Coal was required for steam, and already by the 18th century, steam engines had long been in use to pump water out of the coal mines. The trouble was that many of these pumping engines were highly inefficient. This was particularly true of the one invented by Thomas Newcomen in 1712, for it used a tremendous amount of coal compared to the amount of work which it did. As you can see from the diagram following this page, valve A was opened and steam entered the cylinder, while the weight of the pump rod pulled the piston up. Then valve A was closed, and valve B opened to let in cold water. This cold water caused the steam to condense, forming a vacuum, and atmospheric pressure on top of the piston pushed the piston down, so dragging up the pump rod. Valve B was then closed, and valve C opened to drain away the water. Valve C was then closed, and valve A opened to allow steam to enter again. Thus you realise that every time the beam and pump rod were moved, the cylinder had to be made as hot as possible, then as cold as possible, and then re-heated — a tremendous waste of heat.

It was James Watt (1736-1819), a young mathematical instrument maker, who, from 1769-88, improved steam-powered engines to such

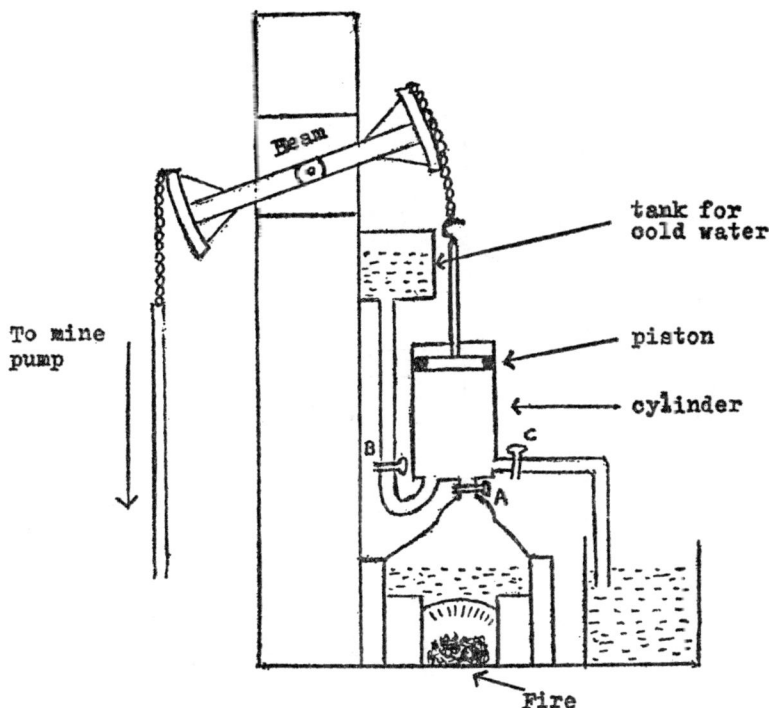

Newcomen's Engine, 1712

an extent that they could be used in industry. He first did so by using a separate condenser. As the diagram shows, valve A was opened and steam entered the cylinder while the weight of the pump rod pulled the piston up. Valve A was then closed, and valve B opened to let the steam escape to the condenser. Valve C was then opened to let cold water into the condenser to condense the steam and form a vacuum. The cylinder now had a vacuum, too, whereupon atmospheric pressure pushed the piston down, thus dragging up the pump rod. Valves B and C were then closed, valve D was opened to drain away the water, then closed, and valve A opened again. Thus there was no need to re-heat the cylinder each time.

In the course of further improvements, Watt admitted steam first to one side of the piston to push it up, and then to the other side to push it down again, whereas Newcomen's engine had depended upon the

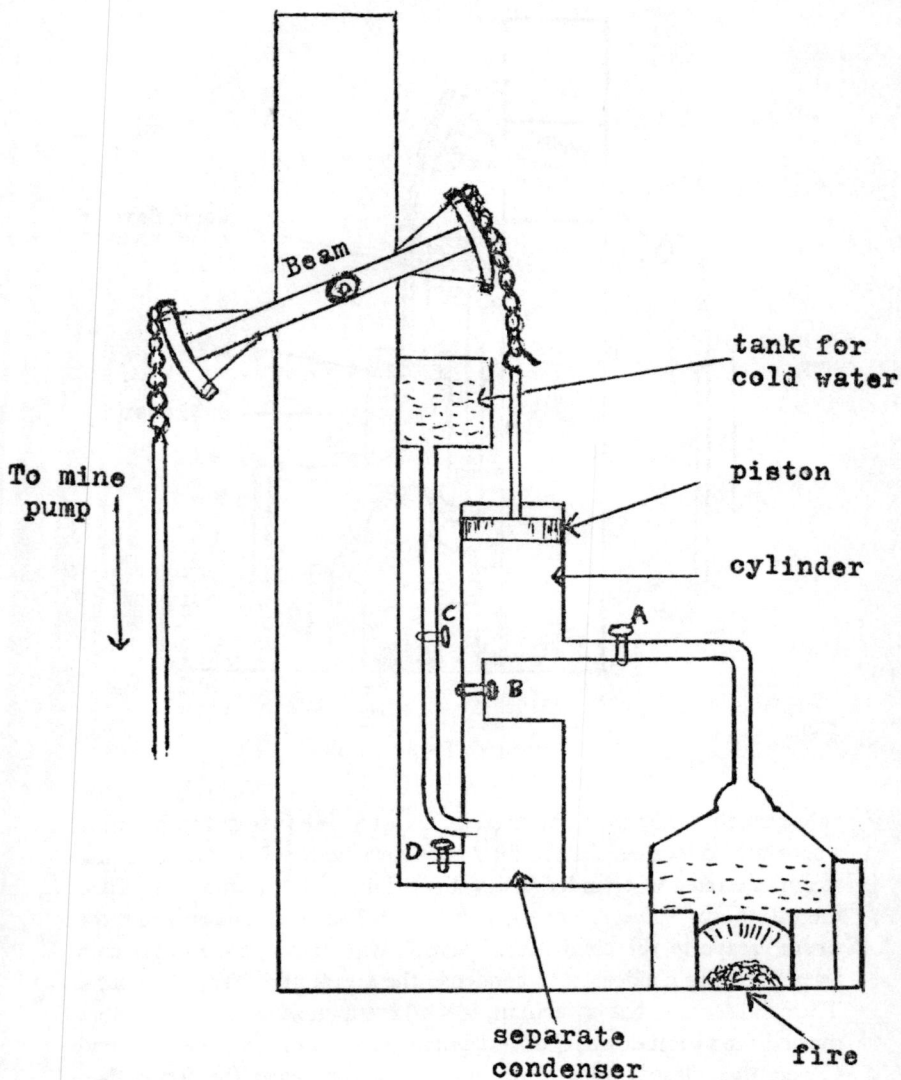

Watt's Separate Condenser.

pressure of the atmosphere to push it down. This new type of engine
was called double-acting. In 1781, Watt made an engine that had a
rotating movement instead of up-and-down, so that steam engines
could drive machinery. To achieve this rotating motion, he invented
the sun-and-planet gear — a rod from the beam had a toothed wheel
at the end; this engaged another toothed wheel on the shaft or wheel
that had to be turned. A device called a 'governor' controlled (i.e.
governed) the speed of the machine.

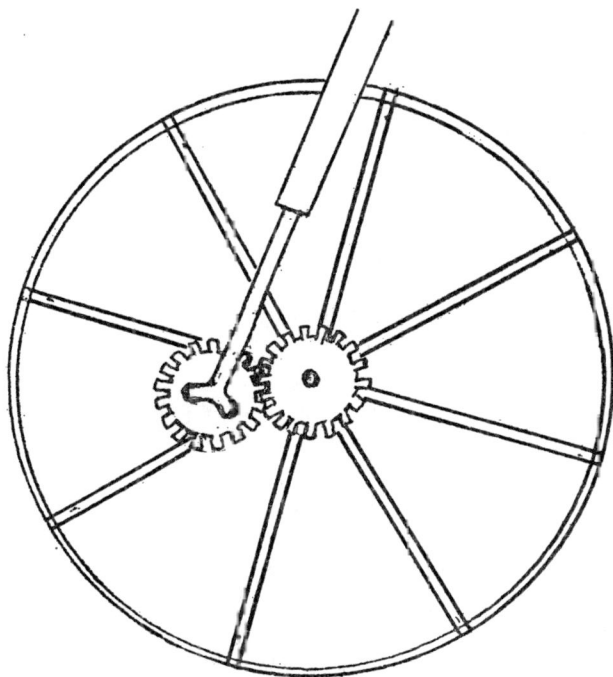

Sun and Planet Gear

The two cog wheels were called the 'sun' and 'planet'.
*As the rod moved up and down, the 'planet' (on the end of the rod) revolved round
the 'sun' (at the end of the wheel axle), thus turning the wheel.*

James Watt himself, born at Greenock in Scotland, had been a
weakly child, and suffered from agonising headaches all his life. But
his intelligence was in no way dulled. In London, he completed a

seven-year apprenticeship in one year, and returned to his native country as an instrument maker at Glasgow University. It was while here that he was asked to repair a model of Newcomen's engine, and in consequence invented his own. To produce his machine, he entered into partnership with the ironmaster John Roebuck of the Carron iron works, but the inaccuracy of the workmanship there made the new engine useless amid clouds of escaping steam.

After Roebuck went bankrupt, Watt was fortunate enough to enter into partnership with Matthew Boulton (1728-1809), a man who provided capital, skilled labour and a brilliant business mind. These assets, together with the mechanical genius of James Watt, resulted in a perfect partnership, and from their Soho works near Birmingham, more and more steam engines were produced.

And it was these steam engines which created the Industrial Revolution, as the following results very clearly show.

By experiment, Watt discovered that a powerful cart-horse could lift 33,000 lb. one foot in an hour, and on this basis he originated the term 'horse-power', so that a mine owner would know how many fewer horses he would need for pumping if he used a steam engine instead. Be it also noted that a machine which develops 1,000 horse-power can achieve the work of 20,000 men.

Not only in the coal mine, however, were James Watt's inventions required; they were soon in use in all branches of industry — textiles, pottery-making, breweries, flour mills, and to work the bellows, steam hammers and rollers in iron foundries. One of his steam engines was even installed at the Birmingham Mint, where, in 1797, it produced the largest British coin ever made — the famous 'Cartwheel' two-pence — $1\frac{1}{2}$ inches in diameter, and two ounces in weight.

Still later, and more important developments of his work were, of course, the locomotive and the steamship.

New trades arose, too — engineer, tool-maker, fitter, turner.

Since these steam-powered machines could work better, longer and more reliably than any powered by wind, water or men, the Industrial Revolution really developed, with its mass production at cheap cost.

Naturally, these new steam engines created a demand for more coal. At one time, wood charcoal and timber had been used for fuel, so England's coal-mining activities had been limited to on or near the surface (open-cast mining). In the case of mines, only primitive techniques were used. Passages (or 'adits') were constructed to drain away water to lower levels, while ventilation was caused by a down draught through one shaft, and an up draught through another. Ventilating doors directed the fresh air along the passages to prevent it taking short cuts and leaving pockets of foul atmosphere.

We must realise that these pits were very small; a colliery could employ as few as ten men, and rarely more than fifty. Under these circumstances, the total amount of coal excavated in England in 1750 was only about five million tons, and chiefly from Newcastle, the Midlands and South Wales. After the middle of the 18th century, however, the demand for coal began to increase, and deeper digging, which reached 1,000 feet, had to be attempted. So by 1830, the amount of coal produced was 23 million tons.

Indeed, there is no doubt that during the century 1750-1850, working conditions in the coal mines developed considerably. As the miner hacked his way along the seam, timber pit props replaced the pillars of coal to support the roof. Pit ponies (1720) then hauled the coal trucks along cast-iron rails (1767) to the shaft. Here, wire cables invented in 1839, and operated by steam engines for hauling, replaced the ladders up which the coal had had to be carried on human backs.

Ventilation was improved by the exhaust fan, 1790, while the steam engines of Thomas Newcomen or James Watt pumped up the water to prevent flooding. Finally, in 1815, George Stephenson, of 'Rocket' fame (*see page* 82) invented a safety lamp — a small oil lamp with a wire gauze chimney that conducted away the heat so quickly that the gas outside did not become hot enough to catch fire and cause an explosion. If there was too much bad gas, and therefore a danger to the miner, the lamp flame turned blue. Though Stephenson invented the lamp, the name 'Davy Lamp' has been given to it because Sir Humphrey Davy, a great British scientist, made a similar invention on his own a short while later.

THE IRON INDUSTRY

The thud and clatter of the new steam machinery now became more and more common, but unfortunately the wooden constructions could not withstand the vibrations of steam power, and were often shattered to pieces. Steam-powered machines, therefore, had to be built of iron, and so the story of the iron industry must now claim our attention.

To make iron, the ore had to be heated by charcoal, and since the charcoal came from wood, the iron industry was originally established near forests, e.g. the Weald in Sussex, the Forest of Dean, the West Midlands and North Lancashire. Unfortunately, by the mid-18th century, England's forests had become very seriously reduced in size, and the iron industry was coming to a standstill. It must be remembered that six to eight tons of charcoal were needed to heat one ton of iron out of the iron ore.

The thick layers of charcoal, iron ore and limestone were poured into 25 foot high furnaces (nowadays 40-100 feet high), whose hand- or water-powered bellows sent blasts of air into the fires to make them burn more fiercely. The iron was thus melted out of the iron ore, fell to the bottom of the furnace, and was known as 'pig iron'. The unwanted matter, being lighter, floated on top like a scum, and was called

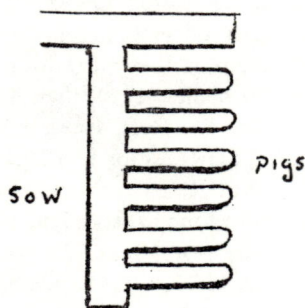

Iron: Sow and Pigs

The white hot metal was poured from the furnace into these troughs (which resembled a sow and a litter suckling) and allowed to cool.

'slag'. This slag was drained off, cooled, and piled in heaps. In the course of years, these heaps from coal mine and furnace, became man-made mountain ranges, towering hideous and ugly over the countryside — an eyesore and a danger.

Each furnace in the early 18th century produced about 15 cwt. of pig-iron at a time (now they produce about 80 tons each). From this pig-iron:

(i) Cast iron could be made by heating and running into a mould. Cast iron contains from two to five per cent carbon, melts easily for casting, and is very hard but brittle;

(ii) or wrought iron was made by reheating the pig-iron, hammering it to remove impurities, and then beating it into shape. Wrought iron has about 0.3 per cent carbon, is soft, not brittle, can be welded and can be drawn out into wires;

(iii) or steel could be made by heating wrought iron and charcoal. Steel can be hammered and welded, then hardened (by heating and sudden cooling), and tempered (re-heating to a moderate temperature and cooling).

Four great improvements in the iron industry must now be noted:

1. In 1709, Abraham Darby the First, at Coalbrookdale in Shropshire, discovered a way to use coke instead of wood charcoal to make cast iron, so that the shortage of English timber was overcome. The iron industry, therefore, moved to the coal areas of South Wales, the Midlands, South Yorkshire and the Clyde. This was not until the later 18th century, though, for the Darby family kept the secret some 50 years, and for a long time could only produce coke iron of rather poor quality.

2. About 1740, Benjamin Huntsman of Sheffield produced a very high grade steel by using small clay pots, each capable of holding 34 lb. of metal. They were filled with bars of wrought iron, charcoal and ground glass, then heated to a very high temperature in a coke furnace till the metal melted. This method produced a very hard steel suitable for razor blades and watch springs. As it was made in clay pots (or crucibles) it was called crucible steel.

3. In 1760, John Smeaton made a compressed air pump, driven by water power, which improved the blast, and in 1828, James Neilson, manager of the Glasgow Gas Works, designed a hot-air blast, which, to the surprise of the ironmasters who had tried to keep the blast as cold as possible, enabled iron to be smelted with a third less fuel.

4. Then, in 1784, Henry Cort, at Fontley, near Portsmouth, made wrought iron by 'puddling', i.e. using a furnace where the heated pig-iron was stirred, or 'puddled', in a trough. There was a fire at one end of the trough, but out of contact with the metal, the heat from the fire being reflected from the roof of the furnace down on to the metal to smelt it. (This type of furnace is called a reverbatory furnace.) In this way, carbon was removed from the pig-iron, and wrought iron was left. As wrought iron contains very little carbon, it is malleable, and the same year Cort then passed the metal through a series of rollers to remove any remaining impurities. From these sheets of iron, boilers, rails, bars, etc., could be made in mass production — and mass production it certainly was. The old tilt hammer, raised by a water-wheel and falling under its own weight, hammered the impurities out of the

pig-iron to produce one ton of wrought iron in 12 hours. Cort's rollers produced 15 tons in that same time.

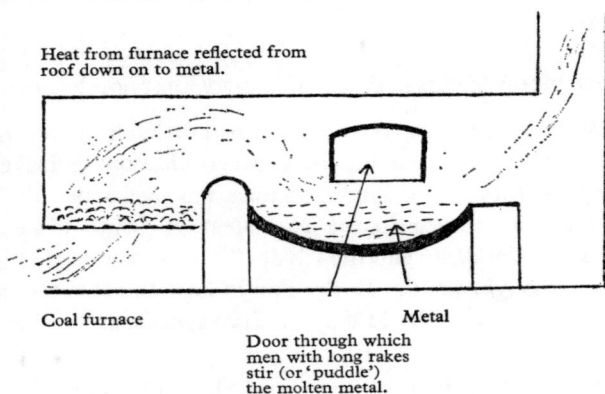

Heat from furnace reflected from
roof down on to metal.

Coal furnace   Metal

Door through which
men with long rakes
stir (or 'puddle')
the molten metal.

Puddling Furnace (reverbatory).

Iron had yet other uses, of course. In 1767, the first iron rails were laid down in a mine at Coalbrookdale in Shropshire, and the first iron bridge crossed the River Severn at Coalbrookdale in 1779. At a place called Carron, near Falkirk in Scotland, the ironmaster John Roebuck made the deadly naval guns called 'carronades', from 1779 onwards.

But the greatest of all the ironmasters was John Wilkinson (1728-1808). He was, in truth, 'iron mad'. From the roaring flames and jarring noise of his great Broseley, Bradley or Bersham works, he produced iron cylinders of such extreme accuracy for those days that no steam was wasted, and steam power could thus become more efficient. *Until his time, be it noted, anything up to one-eighth of an inch out of true was considered to be first-class workmanship.* Among those particularly grateful to him, was James Watt whose steam engines were thus made efficient.

In 1787, Wilkinson built the first iron boat in the world — 70 ft. long and 7 ft. wide, for use on canals. A year later, he made cast-iron water-pipes for the city of Paris. He used iron rollers to grind wheat. He built a Wesleyan chapel of iron, complete with iron pulpit; his own home had window frames and window sills of iron, and it is not surprising, therefore, that when he died in 1808, he was buried in an iron coffin . . . beneath an iron tombstone.

These developments in the iron industry which we have just related had many important consequences.

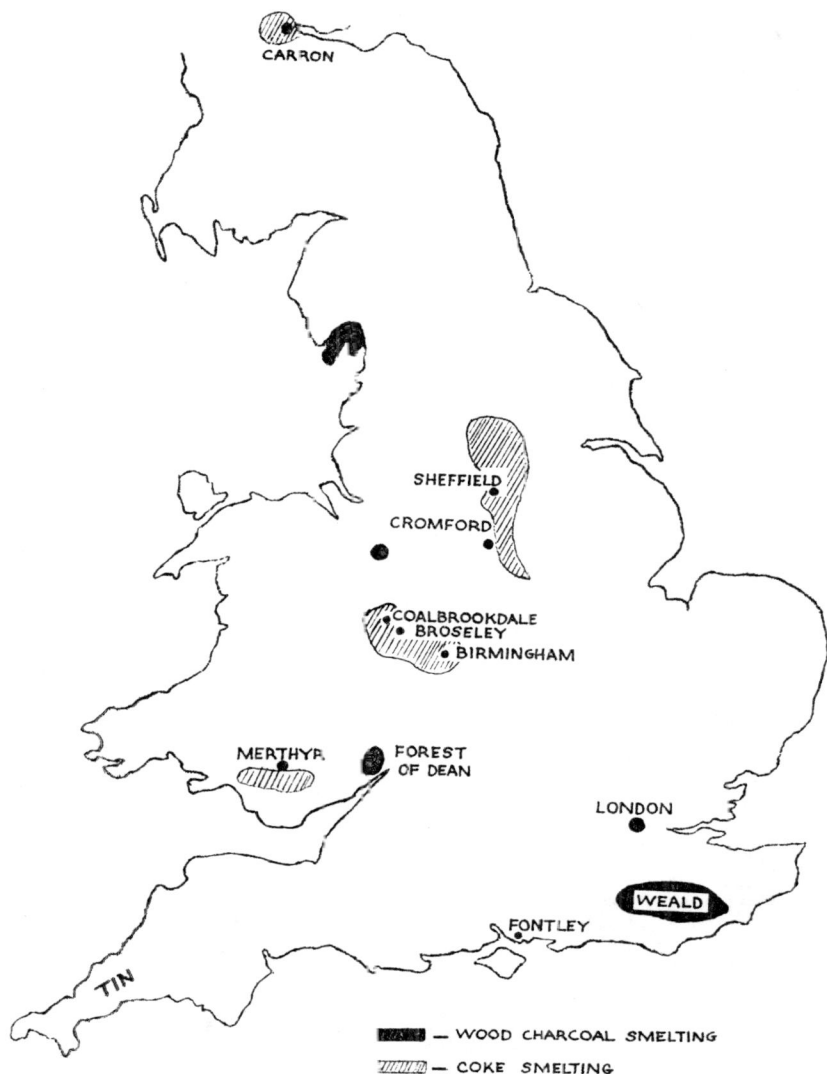

CARRON

SHEFFIELD

CROMFORD

COALBROOKDALE
BROSELEY
BIRMINGHAM

MERTHYR.
FOREST
OF DEAN

LONDON

WEALD

FONTLEY

TIN

▪▪▪▪ — WOOD CHARCOAL SMELTING

▨▨▨ — COKE SMELTING

IRON AND STEEL INDUSTRY.

After Abraham Darby used coal instead of wood charcoal for smelting, the industry moved to the coalfields of South Wales, West Midlands, South Yorkshire and Clyde, and in these areas huge businesses developed covering the whole process from mining to manufacture. One of these huge businesses was that of the ironmaster Richard Crawshay in South Wales, who, from 1785, transformed the little village of Merthyr Tydfil into a vast industrial centre.

A large amount of cheap iron was now being produced, for heavy iron was used for guns, bridges, engines, railways, and also for ships whose iron hulls were stronger, thinner, lighter and more fire-proof than wood. Light iron was used for machinery, machine tools and farm implements, and even for such household purposes as ceilings, furniture and ornaments.

The manufactures in iron meant new skills and industries developed, such as machine tool-maker, turner and fitter.

So England led the world in the manufacture of iron, and had a vast export trade therein.

THE STEEL INDUSTRY

After the middle of the 19th century, the age of iron passed into the age of steel.

It was Henry Bessemer (1813-98) who discovered, in 1856, that

Bessemer Converter.

A — air blast. When the converter is upright so that A is at the base, air is blasted through pipes (tuyeres) into the molten metal.
The converter is then tilted over for pouring.

steel could be made from pig-iron by using a pear-shaped container
called a converter. In this converter, a strong blast of air was driven
through a six cwt. mass of molten iron, thus burning most of the carbon
and impurities out of the iron. These impurities became either gases
or slag. A controlled amount of carbon could be added to the soft-iron
to make steel. The converter was then tilted over, and the metal poured
out. As a result of this invention, the production of steel in England
increased tremendously, and it replaced iron for most purposes.

Unfortunately, Bessemer had lined his converter with acid material,
and this would not remove any phosphorus which happened to be in
the iron ore. Consequently, only iron ore which did not contain phosphorus could be used until, in 1878, an amateur chemist, Sidney
Gilchrist Thomas, and his cousin, Percy Gilchrist, solved the problem.
They lined the converter with dolomite and clay, which extracted the
phosphorus. As dolomite is a basic substance, the process was called
the 'basic process', and the steel produced was called 'basic steel'. Then,
if ferro-manganese was added to the iron, Bessemer steel was produced
— more reliable, stronger and cheaper than wrought iron. So steel
works were now set up beside areas of phosphorus iron ore, especially
in Cumberland and at Corby (Northants.) and Scunthorpe (Lincs).

Another means to make steel was by William Siemens' Open Hearth
method, 1866. Molten iron was placed on an open hearth, and burning

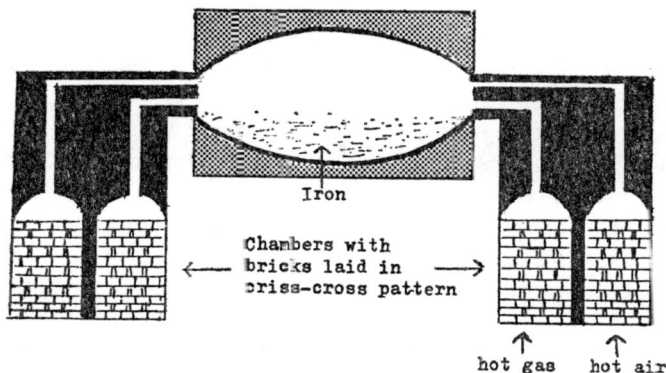

Open Hearth Furnace

*Hot air and gas passed through the right hand chambers, over the iron in the
furnace, and as they went out through the left hand chambers, the heat was absorbed
by the bricks.*

*Every half hour or so the flow was reversed. Hot air and gas now passed through
the left hand chambers and were further heated by the bricks, thus increasing the
temperature in the furnace. Then as the hot air and gas went out through the right
hand chambers, they heated the bricks there.*

gas together with a blast of hot air produced enough heat to convert the pig-iron to steel. This was a far better device, for the Bessemer process worked in a sealed container, so that if anything went wrong, no-one knew until the completion of the job. The Open Hearth method, however, could be supervised the whole time, and any defects that arose in the process could be remedied as they occurred. Indeed, so efficient was Siemens' method that by 1956 it had replaced Bessemer's converter, and some 90 per cent of the pig-iron now produced is made into steel. Even greater heat could be obtained by Siemens' electric furnace, 1878, which attained a temperature of 3,500°C.

Then, in 1913, Harry Brearley of Sheffield added some chromium to a piece of steel during one of his experiments, and thus invented stainless steel.

Steel was later improved by the addition of other substances: manganese, vanadium or nickel gave it strength and hardness; tungsten rendered it exceptionally hard; while silicon gave it magnetic properties.

NEW METALS. By the time of the 20th century, not only steel, but new metals altogether were in use: titanium withstood heat and stress so well that it was used in jet engines; zirconium was proof against heat and corrosion and was therefore used in nuclear plants; lithium, the lightest of all metals, and magnesium and aluminium, among the next lightest of metals, also had their uses.

MACHINE TOOLS. But though coal gave the power for machines, and metals provided the materials to construct the machines, it was still necessary to make the machines efficient. Thus came the demand for machine tools.

The first of the great machine-tool makers was Joseph Bramah (1748-1814) who went to London to make his fortune. At this time, water closets were coming into fashion, and while installing them, Bramah added and patented a water cock. With the profits, he opened a shop and there designed locks, a hydraulic press, a planing machine and the pull-over tap used to draw beer in public houses.

One of Bramah's assistants was Henry Maudsley (1771-1831). He invented not only a screw-cutting lathe to make screws of exactly the same size, but also, and more important, he invented a slide rest. Previously, the worker had used and guided his lathe by sheer physical strength. If he was not sufficiently strong, or if he became tired towards the end of a large piece of metal, his work was inaccurate. By using the slide rest, however, very little physical effort was required, only enough to turn the screw to hold the cutter against the face of the metal.

Living at the same time as these other two was Joseph Whitworth (1803-87), who adopted standard sizes of screw-threads and machine parts, and these standards are still used today. At the Great Exhibition of 1851, he was the chief machine-tool maker in the country, as well as showing a measuring machine accurate to one-millionth of an inch.

There also lived James Nasmyth (1808-90) who, in 1839, produced his steam hammer — a machine possessed of a tremendous force, moving at a great speed, yet which could be controlled so as to crack an egg-shell.

THE TEXTILE INDUSTRY

Now we must turn to the textile industry, to see what effect the Industrial Revolution had there.

At the beginning of the 18th century, Norwich was the centre of worsted manufacture, with the most important woollen centres being in the West Country (Gloucestershire, Wiltshire, Somerset and Devon), and cheaper cloths being produced in the West Riding of Yorkshire.

In East Anglia and the West Country, the organisation of the woollen industry was an extremely slow process — a long drawn-out story. First, the farmer sheared his sheep, and then cleaned and carded the wool. (Carding involved combing it with a wire brush to separate the fibres.) The wool was then sold to the most important person in the business — the clothier. The clothier carefully checked the quality offered, removed any horse hair in the lower part of the sacks, and purchased the wool he required. Then in the summer, he set out on a horseback tour of the countryside to distribute (or 'put out', as it was called) the wool to the homes of the local spinners.

When the spinning was completed, he collected the thread, and distributed it to the homes of the weavers. The organisation was thus unsatisfactory, for both spinners and weavers received low pay, irregular work, and toiled for long hours in dim light. So in return, they produced poor work, and stole some of the thread or cloth.

(At this point, we must note that since the workers spun and wove in their own homes, the organisation was known as the Domestic System.)

The clothier collected the cloth from the weavers, and arranged for it to be fulled (i.e. beaten in water containing fuller's earth to clean and thicken it), bleached (a process which could take as long as six months), patterned and finished off. Then he arranged to sell it, usually at the great cloth markets at Bakewell Hall in London.

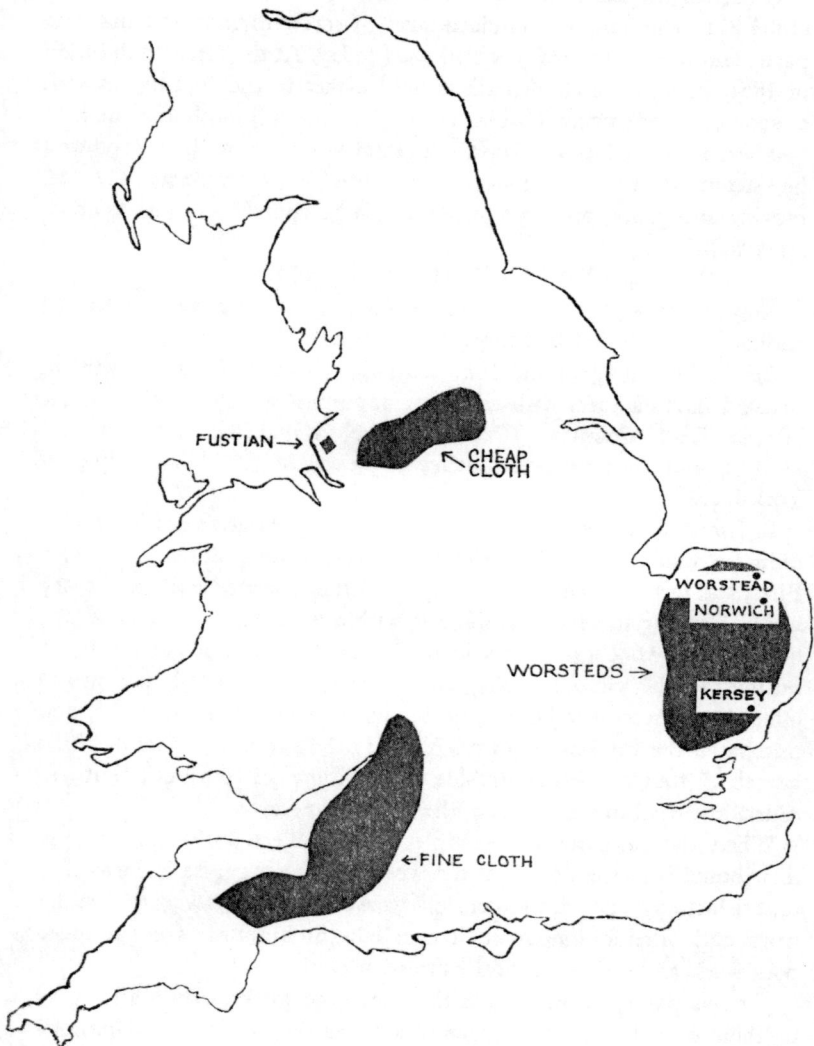

FUSTIAN →

← CHEAP
   CLOTH

WORSTEAD
NORWICH

WORSTEDS →

KERSEY

←FINE CLOTH

WOOLLEN INDUSTRY ABOUT 1700.

Shaded areas indicate main centres.

The whole procedure from sheep to cloth market thus took many months.

In Yorkshire, the organisation was different. The worker bought his own material, used his own equipment at home with family labour, and sold the manufactured goods in the cloth markets at Halifax, Wakefield or Leeds. Nevertheless, it was a part-time occupation, combined with farming, so the output was slow and limited.

Not only the organisation of the woollen industry, however, but also the actual methods of production were slow.

In the old-fashioned method of weaving, the long threads (called the 'warp') were all stretched out from a bar in a row. The other ends of these threads were attached alternately to two rods, so that the even-numbered threads were attached to one rod, and the odd-numbered threads to the other rod. The first rod was then lifted, so that the even-numbered threads were raised. The triangular space between the two sets of threads was called the 'shed'. A length of thread (called the 'weft') was fastened to a shuttle and passed through the shed from hand to hand by the weaver. The even-numbered threads were then lowered, the odd ones raised, and the shuttle passed back through the shed.

But these old hand-looms were in due course to belong to the past. The process was too slow, and the Industrial Revolution required more goods more quickly. Thus in 1733, John Kay of Bury produced a Flying Shuttle — an arrangement by which the shuttle ran on wheels through the shed, being struck to and fro by hammers placed one on each side of the loom. To control the hammers, they were connected by strings to a stick which the weaver jerked towards him. Once the hammer had struck the shuttle, the former was checked by a bridge at the end of its guiding rod, and was then returned to its original position by a spring-pivoted arm attached to it. With this new device, the weaver could work ten times faster than by passing the shuttle from side to side by hand, and as one man could now do the work of ten, it also meant that many weavers would lose their jobs. Kay was indeed unfortunate. Manufacturers used his invention without paying him; mobs of angry weavers, fearing unemployment, wrecked his house. In the end, he sought refuge in France, and died there in poverty.

Some years later, about 1765, James Hargreaves of Blackburn invented a Spinning Jenny. Though he was only an illiterate weaver, he devised a wheel and a moving carriage which worked not one, but eight spindles, and later the number was increased to 100 spindles. A fine, but not a strong thread was produced.

Four years later, Richard Arkwright of Preston (1732-92) made a Water Frame in which a thread was drawn through four pairs of rollers, the second pair revolving a little faster than the first, and driven originally by horse power, later water power. This 'frame' (or 'machine') made a harder, stronger yarn which could be used for the warp (the long threads). Thus the real cotton industry began, because previously the warp had had to be linen which was stronger. But Arkwright's machine resulted in two other developments that were landmarks in the textile industry. It marked the beginning of the Factory System, for the machine was unsuitable for use in the worker's home. Then, even more important in those days of cheap labour, the Water Frame could be operated by children, so the sorry story of child slavery commenced. Arkwright, too, was a hard worker in his factory at Cromford, in Derbyshire. He worked hard with his mind, with his body and with his tongue — the greatest of these being the last. So he rose from a humble barber to become a knight of the realm, and today most of the world's cotton is spun on rollers similar to his.

In 1779, Samuel Crompton of Bolton combined the moving carriage of the Spinning Jenny with the rollers of the Water Frame, and naturally called the resulting machine a Mule (a mule is a cross-bred animal from a mare and a male ass; in the same way, Crompton's invention also came from two different sources). It spun a very fine but a strong yarn, and so enabled muslin to be made in England. The Mule, originally worked by hand power, was adapted to water power in 1790, and with subsequent improvements is still one of the chief machines in the cotton industry today.

But these last three inventions — Hargreaves' 'Spinning Jenny', Arkwright's 'Water Frame', and Crompton's 'Mule' — all benefited the spinning. An over-abundance of cheaper, better quality yarn from the factories reached the weavers, whose work was still with hand-looms at home. And the weavers made the most of their opportunity. They strutted along the streets of the industrial cities with five-pound notes stuck in the bands of their hats, for they had more work than they could cope. It was not until the Rev. Edmund Cartwright invented a 'Power Loom' in 1785, later driven by steam, that the speed of spinning was equalled by the weaving. For in Cartwright's Loom, the warp threads were raised and lowered by power, the shuttle was thrown across by power, and the cloth was unwound by power.

Then, as soon as the cloth was ready, it had to be bleached. The old method was to soak it in sour milk, and then to lay it on the grass in the sunlight, a process which took as long as six months. In 1785, however, a French chemist discovered that chlorine could be used, and the time was reduced to a week.

At this time, another invention was recorded. Previously the pattern was put on a cloth by using a wooden block bearing the design, and stamping it all over the cloth by hand. Then a new invention called cylinder printing was patented by Thomas Bell in 1783, the cloth passing over inked rollers.

So we come to the end of the main developments in the textile industry — Kay's 'Flying Shuttle', Hargreaves' Spinning Jenny', Arkwright's 'Water Frame', Crompton's 'Mule', Cartwright's 'Power Loom', chlorine bleaching and cylinder printing. Now, after studying these carefully, we must face the inevitable question: what were the results of these new machines and these new discoveries?

The effect of the seven inventions we have just noted could be gathered from the increase in England's raw material imports. Look at the following table:

	1730	1830
Imports of wool	about 1 million lb.	32 million lb.
Imports of cotton	about $1\frac{1}{2}$ million lb.	260 million lb.

What a tremendous progress in the course of a hundred years this represents!

But at the same time, you may also ask why the imports of cotton increased more outstandingly than the imports of wool. The answer is that there was now a plentiful supply of cheap cotton from the southern United States and Egypt, and secondly all the new inventions were first applied to the cotton industry which benefited accordingly. On the contrary, the wool industry had to rely on the limited home supplies of raw material (since only a little came from abroad) while, more important still, the old-established woollen firms resented any change to newer machinery and methods. As, they argued, we have become so wealthy under the old methods, why change to the new and untried? It was not until after 1830 that the sheep runs of Australia and New Zealand increased England's supplies of wool, and the woollen firms began to realise the value of the new machinery. The woollen industry then settled in Yorkshire, where water, coal and iron were available for machinery.

Nevertheless, you can easily see that the factories were devouring both wool and cotton to an amazing extent, and soon an abundance of manufactured goods had been produced, including 500 million yards of woven cloth for export alone. Once the goods were ready, they had then to be sent away from the factories, and that, of course, involved the problem of transport, which we must consider in the next chapters.

In your reading about the textile industry, an explanation of the following words may help:

Fustian	— Linen warp (long threads), cotton weft (short threads).
Worsted	— Long wool, dyed before woven. Named from a village near Norwich.
Woollen	— Short wool, fulled after weaving.
Serges	— Long wool warp, short wool weft.
Broadcloth	— Best short wool, heavily fulled. To weave this double width required two men at the loom before the Flying Shuttle was invented.
Baizes and Kerseys	— Short wool, rough loose fabrics. Named from Kersey, near Sudbury, Suffolk.
New draperies	— Light fabrics of worsted type developed in East Anglia by Flemish and Dutch immigrants in 16th century.
Eli Whitney's Gin	— This American machine, 1793, had a revolving cylinder with metal spikes. These spikes pulled away the cotton from the cotton boll, leaving the seeds behind.

Results of Industrial Development

With coal, metals, machines and machine tools, together with railways and a shipping fleet to distribute the goods, while our colonies provided raw materials and markets, it is not surprising that from 1850-75, England was 'the Workshop of the World'. By 1875, indeed, we produced over half the world's coal and pig iron, and nearly half the world's cotton cloth and steel.

One of the greatest public proofs of our ability and enterprise was the Great Exhibition of 1851 in London, when six million visitors from all over the world walked within a gigantic palace of glass designed by Joseph Paxton (the Crystal Palace — destroyed by fire in 1936), and marvelled at the manufactures that England could produce.

It was almost unbelievable. . . . They gazed upon railway engines, marine engines, fire engines, a hydraulic press, printing presses, threshing and hay-making machines, and a loom with 1,200 spindles.

In the manufacturing section, there was everything from pins to anchors, from pans to heavy artillery. Also in the Exhibition, there was an iceberg, a crystal fountain, the great Koh-i-noor (a 14th century Indian diamond weighing 186 carats) in a golden cage, a natural elm tree fully grown, a huge organ of 4,474 pipes, a swarm of 200,000 bees in a hive, an alarm bed which at a pre-set hour revolved to tilt out the sleeper, an alarm clock which not only rang a bell but also fired a pistol, a papiermâché piano, papiermâché armchairs, a three cwt. lump of gold from Chile, a five ton block of coal, chimney stacks designed to carry smoke into drains, a model of a railway bridge from England to France, a knife with 300 blades, and thousands of other equally interesting objects. The whole exhibition, indeed, was a world-showing display of what our country could do.

Magnificent though it was, however, such a state of superiority could not last for ever. Towards the end of the 19th century, this industrial power of England was challenged, and the challenge came from America and Germany. America became united when the Civil War ended in 1865, and Germany was created a nation in 1871 by the joining together of several smaller states. In both these countries, railways linked widely separated areas and so brought coal and iron ore together for smelting. As a result both nations produced more pig-iron than England, while in particular, American manufactures between 1860-90 increased six-fold. Another reason for the amazing industrial development of these two countries was that they learnt from Britain's earlier mistakes, and thus equipped themselves with new and better machinery than we possessed. Foreign governments, too, helped their manufacturers; the English government did not.

At the same time, another overpowering challenge came from the cheap labour of Japan, which enabled extremely cheap costs of production. As England had recently become a free trade country in 1854, that is, we had abolished all customs duties, there was now nothing to prevent a flood of better and cheaper imports which would ruin our own manufacturers.

These threats to England's industrial power were thus becoming serious . . . and ahead loomed the First World War.

Chapter IV

Roads and Canals

Difficulties of early road transport

The roads of the 18th century were a disgrace and a danger. This was not surprising, for they were more or less the same roads which the Romans had constructed and used about 1,500 years before, or routes of the Middle Ages, to which very few repairs had been done in the meantime. Just pause for a moment to consider that, . . . used for about 1,500 years . . . very few repairs.

The results of such neglect were appalling, and almost unbelievable nowadays. Narrow, single track lanes, . . . huge boulders amid the quagmire, . . . and gaping potholes of formidable depth, . . . these were all a *commonplace* occurrence to encourage the venturesome traveller. On some journeys, indeed, the traveller would find that the coach had to be drawn by oxen, for these were more powerful than horses, a very important consideration when you realised that the Preston to Wigan route, for example, was hampered by ruts four feet deep. On the great London-Holyhead journey, however, even oxen were powerless. The coaches had to be dismantled at Conway, and the pieces taken by packhorse to the Menai Straits for re-assembly there — so utterly impassable were the roads.

We know, of course, that in 1555, a law had been passed whereby each parish had to provide compulsory unpaid labour for six consecutive days every year to repair its roads, a task under the direction of a surveyor (also unpaid). In practice, therefore, this meant that the surveyor, whose knowledge of road repairing could be as limited as his salary, watched while the villagers tipped a few cartloads of stones into the larger craters, and then declared the rest of the time a public holiday. So, although the law lasted till 1835, its existence of nearly 300 years was not of great value. In winter, the road traffic was embedded in quagmires; and in summer, it disappeared in dust.

Equally valueless was the Broad Wheels Act, which, in 1753, ordered that the wheel rims of heavy vehicles should be at least nine inches broad. This was due to the mistaken belief that such would cause less damage to the roads. In actual fact, they only made the ruts wider.

Now you are acquiring some idea of the consequences of 1,500 years' neglect, and many other examples could easily be mentioned — more than enough to fill a book. But grim and incredible as all this may seem, it is still not the complete story of travel.

So far, we have quoted instances only where there was at least some indication of an actual road. But for those brave persons who wanted to travel the full length or breadth of this country, it must be understood that many of the routes did not possess a road at all. Instead, the journey lay across vast heaths, or over wild moors and marshes, places so desolate that lighthouses were established on land to guide the wanderers through the wilderness. The Weald of Sussex had nothing better than posts set up in the mud to mark the way. As a result, a whole coach load of travellers might be marooned for hours or even days in mire or snowdrift, blizzard or gale, until search parties from the neighbouring villages could find them.

And as if all these dangers and difficulties were not enough, we must add yet another. To complete the risks of travel, there were the highwaymen.

Of all the classes, creeds and occupations of society that England has known, none has been more over-romanticized and legendized than the highwaymen. A wondrous light of glory shines about them, gay, laughing adventurers, crossing quick-wittedly and courageously with the law, gallant and courteous, men with the pleasanterie of Claude du Val, who insisted that the ladies of the coach should dance with him, the echoing moonlight cry "Stand and deliver", the thud of horses' hooves through the night, the splendour of heroes who robbed the rich and helped the poor. Such were the highwaymen that most of us imagine.

Yet no description or belief could be more utterly false. However regretfully we must let the image leave our mind, it must be frankly realised that the highwaymen of reality had little courage except that of desperation, and even less of glamour. Their numbers were of cut-throats, murderers and petty thieves, no more and no greater. They were not the 'Gentlemen of the Road'; they were the scum of the gutter.

The greatest idol among them is, of course, Dick Turpin, but the true story of his life removes all possibility of hero-worship. He was born in 1705 in Hampstead, Essex, at the Rose and Crown Inn (which is still standing), and was taught by a schoolmaster named Smith.

His career in crime was not caused by a gallant desire for adventure and fame. His career in crime was caused by debts which he could not pay, so he turned to cattle stealing, deer stealing, and house breaking. When the law began to press him too hard, he turned highwayman, and established himself in Epping Forest. Here, in a cave, he lived on the food brought by his wife and friends. Not entirely without cunning, he shod his horse with circular shoes, so that it was not possible to tell from the tracks whether he was coming or going. Only a Forest Keeper ever managed to trail him to his lair, and promptly paid for his skill and folly with his life.

For nine years, Turpin continued as a highwayman. His end was no valiant duel with the forces of the law, no brave suicide to cheat the gallows. He was arrested, not for some heroic death fight against the local militia, but merely for shooting a cockerel in the street in York. The owner of the bird had him arrested, and while waiting in York Castle for trial, Turpin, whose real identity was not known, wrote to his brother in London to give him a character reference. The letter was never delivered to the brother, and was returned to the Post Office, where by the strangest of chance it was seen by the schoolmaster, Smith, who recognised the handwriting. Turpin was hanged at York in 1739.

His story would have ended there — unknown, unhonoured and unsung, as in the case of countless other highwaymen. But the novelist, Harrison Ainsworth, took his name, and created an entirely imaginary hero who earned glory from the gallantry of his purely imaginary deeds. So let us face historical fact. There was nothing gallant about the real Dick Turpin. There was not even a horse named Black Bess; there was certainly no famous ride made by Turpin from London to York.

As we have said, the highwayman at best was but a petty thief; at worst, a killer.

Is it to be wondered, therefore, that a prudent man of this period of time, first insured himself, and then made his will, before setting out on a long journey?

Even if the traveller did avoid all the dangers of the road and arrived safely, the rate of his progress was still exceptionally slow. The journey from London to York endured for seven days; from London to Edinburgh, it took a fortnight. Indeed, you could cross the Atlantic quicker than you could travel from London to Liverpool, . . . and travellers said you were just as likely to be drowned in the waves of the ocean as in the potholes of the Great North Road from London to Edinburgh!

To add further difficulty and delay to progress, the shortest route between two places was not necessarily the swiftest. Thus, for example, the swiftest way from Horsham, in Surrey, to London, was via Canterbury. The swiftest trade route from Cheshire to London was to Burton-on-Trent, downriver to Hull, and then by sea to the capital. Trace out these on a map, and you will soon realise the difference in mileage caused by the round-about passage.

In actual fact, it was sometimes quicker to walk. John Metcalfe the road builder, once refused a 200-mile coach ride from London to Harrogate, because, he said, he could arrive there sooner on foot. What is more, he did so . . . and John Metcalfe was blind.

Without doubt, the swiftest and surest method of transport in those days was the packhorse, making its way at a steady three miles per hour along the roughest of roads. Trains of some 30 or 40 of these animals, moving in single file, and wearing bells to give warning of their approach were a familiar sight in the 18th century. Also you can still see in England today, the narrow, high-arched packhorse bridges with low walls so that the huge panniers on the horse's back could swing clear. Wool, cloth, metal-ware, pottery, even coal and fish, were carried in this manner, each pannier bearing about 140 lb.

But not only commerce was concerned with the difficulties of the roads. In 1745, one of the most gallant figures in Scottish history, whose personality can never be forgotten — the Young Pretender, 'Bonnie Prince Charlie' — rallied the clansmen in his attempt to gain the English throne. He routed the English at Prestonpans; he crossed the border and captured Carlisle. Thence he marched south to Manchester, and by December he was at Derby. By this time, too, London was in a panic. Richer citizens were packing their goods, crowds gathered outside the Bank of England to withdraw their money, and a ship stood by to convey George II back to Hanover. Contributing in no small measure to this panic was the fact that the British troops were finding it difficult even to reach the Young Prince's army owing to the appalling state of the English roads. Fortunately, at Derby, the Prince turned back.

Such then was the account of transport and travel in the early years of the 18th century.

But the Industrial Revolution was not prepared to tolerate conditions such as these. Manufacturers first of all required raw materials to be delivered to the factories, then, once the goods had been made, they had to be distributed — and all had to be done as swiftly as possible.

Improvement of roads

The first sign, therefore, of any attempted improvement came in the form of the turnpike trusts, the first of which was created by Parliament in 1706*. Individuals, or groups of individuals, called trusts, obtained permission from Parliament to take over a stretch of road, keep it in good repair, and in return charge a 'toll' (or fee) on all traffic using it. To prevent people using the road without paying, a tollgate or turnpike (a wooden barrier with spikes on top, turning on a pivot post in the road) was placed across the way.

These turnpike trusts, however, only looked after the most frequently used roads, were often inefficient, dishonest or charged high rates, and were therefore very unpopular with those who had to pay. For example, indeed, travellers journeying southward from London found no fewer that 87 tollgates within a four-mile radius of Charing Cross. But on the London to Falmouth road, there was not a single turnpike for over 200 miles. Around Bristol, the system was so hated that gangs of villagers destroyed both gates and tollhouses in 1749, and it required the regular cavalry to quell the riots. On the other hand, some of the larger trusts employed qualified road-builders, and the roads were well maintained.

Generally speaking, the trusts did enable some improvement to take place, and which otherwise would not have occurred.

It was due to them, moreover, that three men in the 18th century achieved greatness.

The first of these, John Metcalfe (1717-1810), 'Blind Jack of Knaresborough', did not let the fact that he was blind prevent him from building 180 miles of roads and bridges in Yorkshire, Lancashire and Cheshire.

The second great name was that of Thomas Telford (1757-1834), who emphasized the need for a good *foundation* of the road, a base of close-set stone. Apart from over 1,300 miles of road, including the London-Holyhead route, he built 1,200 bridges, among them the graceful suspension bridge shafting high across the Menai Straits, and the beautiful bridge that lies in front of Conway Castle. (He also constructed the Caledonian Canal in Scotland; and the Ellesmere Canal from Chester to Shrewsbury, in 1805, to link the Severn to the Dee and Mersey.)

---

*Earlier trusts from 1663 had been the responsibility of the Justices of the Peace

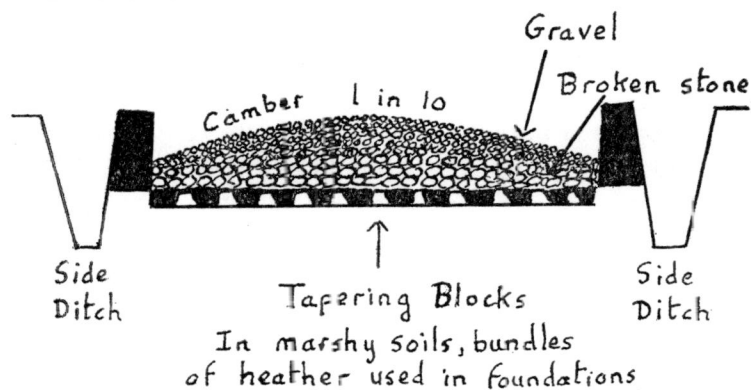

Gravel

Broken stone

Camber 1 in 10

Side Ditch

Side Ditch

Tapering Blocks
In marshy soils, bundles
of heather used in foundations

METCALFE

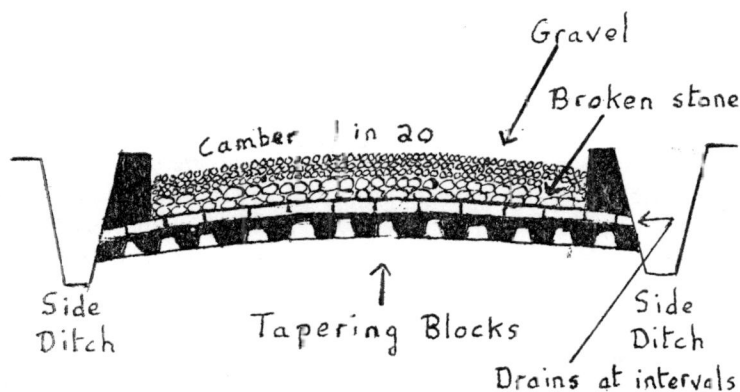

Gravel

Broken stone

Camber 1 in 20

Side Ditch

Side Ditch

Tapering Blocks

Drains at intervals

TELFORD

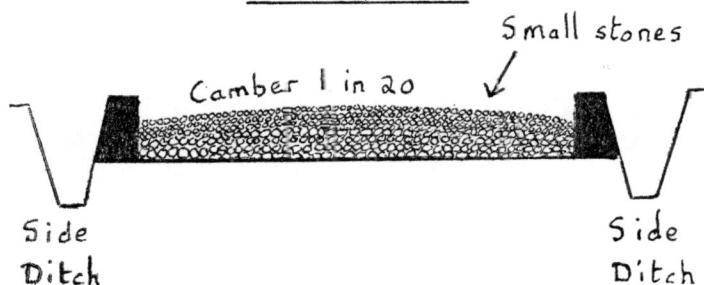

Small stones

Camber 1 in 20

Side Ditch

Side Ditch

McADAM

Road construction.

Most famous of the road-builders, however, was the Scotsman, John Macadam (1756-1836), who emphasized the need for a good *surface* on the road — a covering of small hard chippings, which the traffic ground and pressed into a kind of concrete. His roads were cheaper than Telford's, and such was his insistence that we have the term 'macadam road' and 'tar macadam' or 'tarmac' to this day (though the use of tar, be it noted, occurred after Macadam's death). In 1827, he was appointed Surveyor General of England's roads, and was himself responsible for over 1,000 miles of construction. On his advice, too, a much better scheme of road maintenance was introduced in 1835, when each parish had to maintain its own roads, and pay for this from the rates instead of using compulsory unpaid labour.

Results of road improvements

The work of these three men was of the greatest importance, as we can now learn.

Over the new and better roads thus constructed and maintained, travelled the stage coaches, drawn by four to six horses. On the new hard surfaces, on the new firm foundations, the carriage wheels rumbled with ever-increasing speed. The average rate of progress doubled from four to eight miles-per-hour. From London to Exeter, a distance of 170 miles, took 36 hours in 1730; a hundred years later, only 17 hours. By 1830, London to Brighton took $5\frac{1}{2}$ hours, London to Holyhead $1\frac{1}{4}$ days. Also, the number of coaches increased. From one London inn alone, 80 coaches a day sped to the north; from another, 53 a day set out for the west.

Thus the great age of coaching existed from 1820-37, and it produced a pageant that could never be forgotten. . . .

As the first rays of the dawn shafted through the clouds and lit up the ivy-covered inn, there came the shrill, strident, triumphant notes of a bugle. This challenge to the morning was followed by the heavy rumble of wheels over the cobbled courtyard, and then through the wide-flung gateway, came the carriage. What a resplendent sight it was! The harness glittered and glistened in the light, the horses shone with careful grooming, the coach was brightly painted, while even the very name emblazoned on the panels gave a thrill of excitement — the Shrewsbury 'Wonder', the Manchester 'Telegraph', the York 'Highflyer'.

On his high perch sat the coachman, buried in a heavy overcoat, beneath a broad-rimmed hat and neckerchief. A bright nosegay decorated his buttonhole. With a skill born of long practice, he handled the reins, guiding the way out of the inn, through the town and out into the open country where the coach then travelled along at a steady nine miles-per-hour. Night and day, it travelled, over plain and across the mountains, and at each village the triumphant notes of the coachman's bugle heralded the great arrival. So punctual, indeed, were these coaches, that the hamlets set their time-pieces by them, and one coach-owner refunded the passengers' fares if the coach was late. Not a moment was ever wasted. As they approached the changing post for the horses, the guard's horn rang out some half mile distant, so that by the time the coach reached the inn, the fresh horses were harnessed and ready. Many of these coaching inns, indeed, stabled 600 or more horses. The old horses were led out of the shafts, sweating, foaming and almost exhausted. It was a killing business, which limited the life of a horse to about four years.

But this emphasis upon timing had its disadvantages not only for the horses, but also for the passengers. There were two classes of passengers, the inside and the outside. As the coach rattled along, those inside, wedged closely together — men, women, children, bags, boxes and bundles — swayed and jolted on a weary, boring journey. Those on the outside, either in the luggage basket slung between the rear wheels, or perched perilously on the roof, were exposed to wind, rain and cold till they became numb and unconscious. They ran the risk, indeed, of falling off unnoticed, and dying of exposure by the wayside.

Also, the insistence upon punctuality meant a rigid time-table which allowed but ten minutes for breakfast and twenty minutes for dinner. Should, therefore, any delay occur in the serving of the meals at the inn, there was time for only a few mouthfuls before having to remount the coach. Some unscrupulous innkeepers, indeed, made a deliberate delay, or bribed the coachman to depart early, until the art was so perfected that none of the passengers had time for a meal, and the same joint served three or four different coach arrivals.

When mail coaches (which also carried passengers) commenced in 1784, the discomfort increased with the speed — and the mail coaches most certainly wasted no time. They paid no tolls, and indeed it was an offence in law not to have the tollgates open for the mail to career unchecked upon its way.

A far better — and far more expensive — means of travel was by the privately owned or hired post-chaise (pronounced 'poshays'). This was a light, four-wheeled vehicle usually drawn by two horses, with a rider (called a 'postillion') on the nearside horse. At intervals of every ten miles or so, fresh horses and riders were available at inns called 'posting houses', and it was thus possible to cover up to 40 or 50 miles in the course of a day.

But in any event, these fast coaches, whether public or private, were only for the rich; speed was determined by wealth. The poorer people had to travel by the heavy, covered stage waggon, which lumbered carefully along at a rate of twelve miles per day. This huge vehicle, with wheel rims each fifteen inches broad to prevent sinking into soft ground, and drawn by six to eight horses, required nearly a month to jolt from London to Edinburgh.

So above all, these were undoubtedly the greatest days of English coaching, days which have gone for ever, yet are still brought to mind by the sight of old prints and modern Christmas cards.

Nevertheless, though passenger and mail coaches developed, though local markets developed, the Industrial Revolution did not gain so great an advantage from the improvements in road transport. Before the benefits could be realised, the railways overwhelmed the roads.

Now, for a moment, let us turn to a somewhat different scene of England's transport system in the 18th century.

CANALS

The rivers of England had long been the highways of the nation. By the 18th century, great convoys of craft including some ships each capable of carrying 50 tons of cargo, made their way along such navigable rivers as the Thames, Severn, Dee, Mersey, Trent, Ouse, Humber and East Anglian rivers, so that the towns beside such waterways prospered accordingly.

But even the best of these navigable rivers were liable to seasonal variations in the water level (floods in winter, drought in summer), became silted (particularly the River Dee), followed winding time-wasting routes, and in any event failed to serve most of Wales, Lancashire and the Midlands.

To the Industrial Revolution, therefore, whose success depended upon the swift delivery and despatch of goods, these disadvantages were intolerable.

So it was that a new aspect in England's 18th century transport system appeared. The heavily laden barges now travelled slowly along a canal. Beside them were the green fields; ahead lay the factory chimneys. James Brindley (1716-72) was the great canal builder — some 360

Cock Fighting

This picture was drawn by the famous 18th century artist, William Hogarth (1697-1764), who accurately and mockingly portrayed the life of his time. Do you notice the man having his pocket picked?

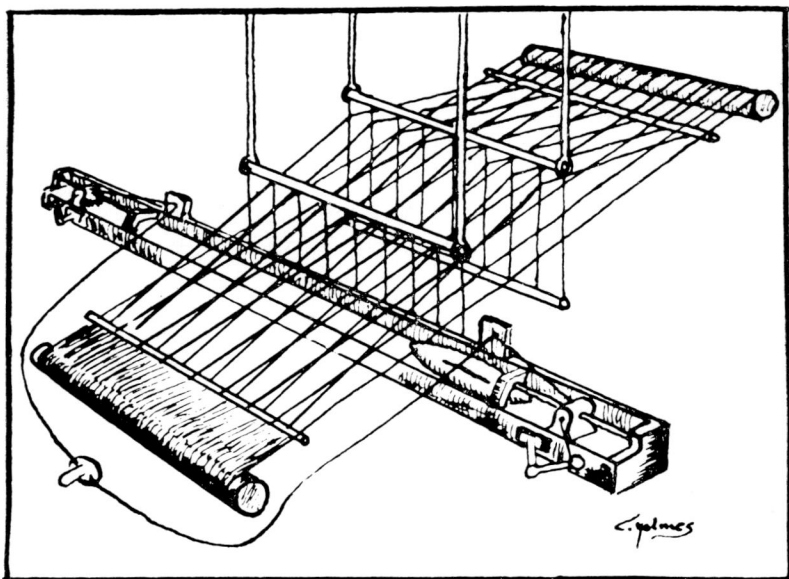

Kay's Flying Shuttle

Hargreaves' Spinning Jenny
(Replica)

miles in all. His most famous constructions, often completed after his death, were:

(i) The first canal he built, the Bridgewater Canal from Worsley to Manchester, seven miles in length, 1759-61. This canal was ordered by the Duke of Bridgewater for the carrying of coal, and at one point, to everyone's amazement, was carried across the River Irwell by an aqueduct 200 yards long, 12 yards wide and 40 foot high.

(ii) The Manchester to Liverpool Canal, 1761-67 — an extension of the Bridgewater Canal, reaching the Mersey at Runcorn. In consequence, Liverpool became the greatest Atlantic port, for the wool and cotton goods of Manchester now passed through there instead of Bristol.

(iii) The Liverpool to Leeds Canal, 1770-1816, from which a navigable river led to Hull (the port for the Baltic), so that Liverpool and Hull were linked.

(iv) The Grand Trunk Canal, 1766-77, which linked Liverpool to the Trent, and possessed 75 locks, five tunnels, over 160 aqueducts, and more than 100 road bridges. It was this canal which opened up not only the salt mines of Cheshire, but also the potteries of Staffordshire.

Here in the Potteries, at Etruria, near Stoke-on-Trent, the great Josiah Wedgwood (1730-95), could thus obtain Cornish clay to make his fine china. Previously, the clay had been sent by sea from Cornwall, via Land's End and the west Wales coast, round Anglesey and then to Liverpool. From Liverpool, it had to be conveyed to the Potteries by packhorse. But now, both to bring his clay, and then to carry away the finished pottery, Josiah Wedgwood could use the Grand Trunk Canal — a means of transport causing far less breakage than the jolting panniers. Indeed, Wedgwood's pottery was far too valuable to be broken. So high was his standard that, as he walked through his works, he smashed all imperfect pieces with his stick. True was his boast that twelve dozen of his plates could be stacked on top of each other without fear of falling, so even and accurate was each piece.

To achieve success, Wedgwood insisted on the 'division of labour' — one man to one job only. So instead of an article being made from clay to finished product by one man on his own, each separate stage — mixing the clay, fashioning it on a wheel, firing, glazing, decorating — was undertaken by a separate worker who thus became perfect in a

c

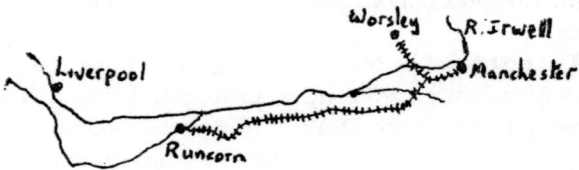

Bridgewater and Bridgewater Extension Canals.

1. Bridgewater Extension C.
2. Liverpool-Leeds C.
3. Grand Trunk C.
4. Staffordshire-Worcestershire C.
   (Grand Trunk to Severn)
5. Oxford C.
   (Grand Trunk to Thames)
6. Worcester-Birmingham C.
7. Grand Junction C.
8. Thames-Severn C.
9. Kennet-Avon C.

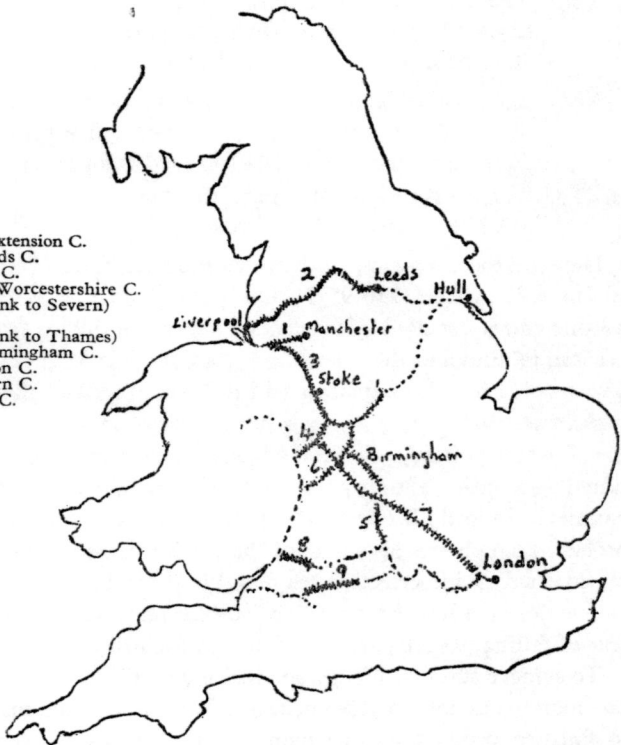

Main Canals about 1820.

single job. In this way, Wedgwood increased both quality and quantity of output.

Together with this high standard of manufacture, Wedgwood also insisted on an equal beauty of design. Thus he obtained his peak of success in the production of the Russian dinner service specially ordered by the Empress Catherine II. There were no fewer than 952 pieces in the full set, and each piece had painted on it some famous building of England. But Josiah's most famous ware — *perfected only after he had made nearly 10,000 trial pieces* — was a type called Jasper ware, with its white figures set in relief against a background of blue or other colours.

At the same time, however, Josiah Wedgwood was alive to the new commercial policy of his age — namely, that numerous cheaper sales were more profitable than a few dear ones. So apart from the costly, but limited, manufactures that he produced for the nobility, he also made large quantities of good quality but cheaper goods for the popular market, including the famous 'willow pattern' ware.

This pottery was in great demand, for the tastes of society were changing. In the 18th century, tea, coffee and chocolate had come into favour, and to drink these beverages, pewter ware was not very common, porcelain cups were too frail, and silver ware was too costly, so pottery had a ready sale.

As a salesman, too, he was supreme — organising, advertising, and offering the first 'satisfaction-or-money-back guarantee' in the history of commerce. So he died a very rich man, and the art, the beauty and the popularity of Wedgwood ware have remained to this day.

The Grand Trunk Canal was joined in 1772 to the Severn River (whence ships could reach Bristol), and to the Thames via Coventry and Oxford 1768-91 (whence ships could travel to London). Thus one of the most important results of this great age of canal building was to link Liverpool to Hull, Bristol and London.

In days when there was no power-driven machinery, the actual labour of excavating these canals was undertaken by gangs of workmen. They were strong, muscular men, indeed, hard working but hard living and drinking, the terror of the neighbourhood where they encamped. As the canals were called 'inland navigations', these men were nicknamed 'navigators'. This was later shortened to 'navvies', and the word has passed into the English language.

But the navvies did their work well. By the end of the 18th century, there were 3,000 miles of canal in England to supply the demands of industry, and by 1830, 4,000 miles.

The reasons for this development were clear, for these artificial waterways could carry heavy merchandise (iron, bricks, timber), food (corn, meat, groceries), fragile goods (pottery), and human labour to the towns at one-third of the cost of the cheapest form of road transport. A packhorse could carry two cwt., a horse pulling a wagon could move a ton; the same horse could pull a railway truck carrying 10 tons; but the same horse again could pull a canal boat carrying 70 tons. Also, unlike rivers, canals were direct, and enabled such areas as South Wales, Lancashire and Birmingham to develop.

In 1894, the Manchester Ship Canal was built. Ships from the ocean could now travel 30 miles inland, and Manchester became a prosperous inland port.

There were, however, disadvantages. The heavily-laden barges travelled *slowly* along the canal. Thus the farmer producing butter and milk found that the canal service, though cheaper, was not swift enough for his perishable foodstuffs. Any attempt to increase the speed by the use of steam-driven vessels would cause the canal banks to collapse under the pressure of the wash. Even more unsatisfactory was progress in times of drought or frost, or along canals that were too shallow, too narrow, or hampered by numerous locks each of which could involve as long as a 12-hour delay. Another difficulty was caused by the different ownership of canals, so that to travel from Birmingham to Hull, for example, involved the use of ten separate canals, and the payment, therefore, of ten separate dues.

But the real death-knell of the canals was sounded by coastal shipping and by the railways. The railways in particular provided not only a transport free from the disadvantages of the canals, i.e. faster, cheaper and more reliable, but also bought up many canals either to prevent competition or to use the routes for railway lines.

So it is to the development of sea and rail transport that we must now turn.

Chapter V

Shipping

The story of shipping

Shipping in the 18th and 19th centuries meant speed, especially for the China tea trade and for the cargoes of Australian wool.

During the greater part of this period, the ocean highways were white with sails. Full-rigged vessels carried their wind-driven cargoes from port to port, and the most famous of these vessels were the Clipper ships. They had over twenty sails, and could travel from the Far East to London in about 100 days. Not only were they fast, but also they were beautiful. There was little to equal the glory of the sun-flashing white canvas outlined against the blue sky, and the skilled craftsmanship of wood and metal cleaving cleanly through the waters, as a Clipper ship glided swiftly over the sea.

It was indeed a pity that such a scene could not continue, for it was really worthy of preserving. But already in the early 19th century, there came the dark shadow of a rival to sail — steam power. There was nothing beautiful about steam power. It was ugly and dirty. It was also faster and more reliable, being independent of winds and calms. Thus in 1788, William Symington's steam-driven boat travelled on a Scottish lake at five m.p h., and by 30 years later, this new form of power had been extended to cover the Holyhead to Ireland passage, then to the cross-Channel route, and then to cross the Atlantic.

Unfortunately, however, the vibration and burden caused by the new, more powerful machinery was too great for the wooden-built ships of the time. So in 1829, Laird of Birkenhead launched one of the first sea-going steam vessels made of iron. These newly-constructed ships were not only stronger, more fire-proof than the older ones, but, strangely enough, lighter, for thin iron weighs less than thick wood — one inch thickness of iron equals 12 inches thickness of wood in weight — and there was more cargo space since the iron was thinner. In the 1880s, when steel replaced iron, we could build even larger, lighter and longer-lasting vessels.

In all these ships, the machinery was used to drive paddle-wheels —

a method of propulsion which had its disadvantages. The projecting
wheels increased the resistance of wind and waves, and as the vessel
heeled over in a gale, one wheel might be lifted right out of the water,
and waste its energy thrashing the air. Worse still, if the huge rollers
of the Atlantic smashed a wheel, the engine thereupon became useless,
since the efforts of the remaining paddle would only drive the ship
round in circles. Such disadvantages, however, were overcome by the
invention of the first practical screw propeller in 1836.

Then in 1858, all stages of previous history were combined to form
the most famous ship of its time — the 'Great Eastern', designed by
Isambard Kingdom Brunel. This great vessel, indeed, was built of
both wood and iron, and it was propelled by all the three forms of
power we have just mentioned. There were 6,500 square yards of sail,
borne by six masts; five funnels belched forth smoke from the engines
that had to be sufficiently powerful to drive two paddle-wheels each
56 foot in diameter and weighing over 90 tons; and at the rear of the
ship was a screw propeller.

The 'Great Eastern' was certainly a masterpiece of engineering, conceived on a truly gigantic scale for those days. It was nearly 27,500 tons;
it was 680 feet long (and remained for 40 years the largest ship in the
world), so it is not surprising that it held 15,000 tons of coal, and could
carry 6,000 tons of cargo and 4,000 passengers. That is why it failed.
It cost too much to run, and in the 19th century such a vast quantity
of cargo and so large a number of passengers were not likely to travel
on one voyage. The ship did indeed achieve some success in laying a
telegraph cable across the Atlantic in 1865-6, but in 1890 it had to be
broken up as a commercial failure.

The development of power, however, continued. In 1854, the
compound engine was invented by John Elder. Previously, in the
usual type of engine, steam passed into a cylinder, pushed a piston,
and was then expelled. But it was realised that this expelled steam still
had some power left, so in the compound engine the steam entered a
small cylinder, pushed a piston, and was then expelled, not to waste,
but into a second and larger cylinder where it worked another piston.
It might even pass thence to a third cylinder, or to a fourth or a fifth.
Thus the same amount of steam now did much more work, and the
engines were known as triple, quadruple or quintuple expansion
engines.

Then in 1883-4, Charles Parsons invented the reaction turbine. (*See
the illustration.*) This was a series of wheels revolving on a common

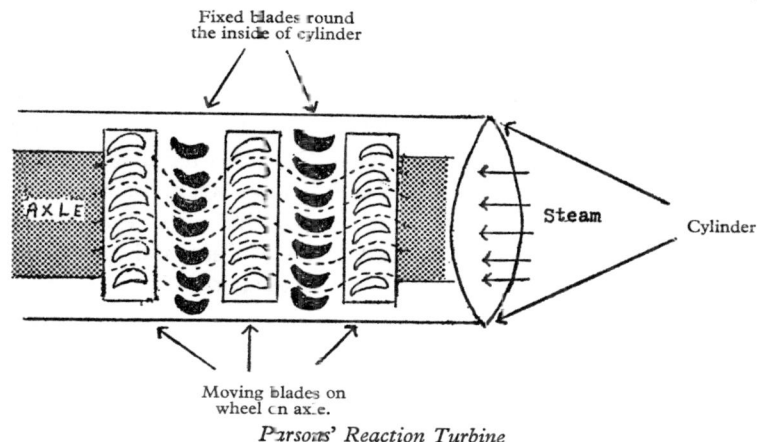

Fixed blades round
the inside of cylinder

AXLE

Steam

Cylinder

Moving blades on
wheel on axle.

Parsons' Reaction Turbine

axle, each wheel having a number of blades on its rim. The wheels and axle were enclosed in a cylinder around the inside surface of which was fitted a series of fixed blades in such a way that each ring of fixed blades was between two of the wheels with moving blades. Steam was directed on to the wheel blades, causing the wheel to revolve. The steam naturally altered course towards the inner surface of the cylinder, but there it met the fixed blades which turned it back to its original direction. Hence it passed to the next ring of movable blades, and so on alternately from movable to fixed blades until it was exhausted. Perhaps we should mention that the older form of turbine, the impulse turbine, was worked by a series of impulses, or jets, of steam against the blades. The reaction turbine worked by the continuous pressure of the steam through the blades.

Determined to influence authority with his invention, Parsons decided to join the great naval review at Spithead, in 1897. There, amid the awe-inspiring assembly of battleships, cruisers and destroyers — the mightiest navy in the world, assembled in honour of Queen Victoria's Diamond Jubilee — his 44-ton vessel, *Turbinia*, wandered at will, gaily and successfully mocking the fastest vessels in Her Majesty's Fleet to catch it. It was a lesson not lost upon the high-ranking audience. Warships, as well as ocean liners, were subsequently fitted with steam turbines.

The effect of replacing wood by steel, and sail by turbine, may be summed up by saying that in 1816 it took 33 days to cross the Atlantic, in 1856 only 10 days, and by 1896 the time had been further reduced to five days.

Two other developments also shortened travelling time. The first was the opening of the Suez Canal in 1869, after ten years' labour and £16 million cost. Before that, travellers had had to journey by camel across the desert from Cairo to Suez — over 3,000 camels being required for the shiploads of passengers. Now, this inconvenience, or that of travelling round the Cape of Good Hope, was to be remedied. The distance from London to Bombay, via Suez, was lessened by 4,500 miles out of 10,719. Then what the Suez Canal did for the old Egyptian desert or Cape of Good Hope route, the Panama Canal, opened in 1914, did for the old Cape Horn route. The distance from Southampton to Wellington in New Zealand, via the Panama Canal, was lessened by about 800 miles out of 12,000 miles.

So more powerful, faster ships travelled by shorter routes, and as they journeyed, the flags at their mastheads showed to what company they belonged. For business men were quick to see that these advantages of swifter travel could be used to make profits, and so they formed companies for the purpose. In 1824 the General Steam Navigation Line was founded; in 1837, the Peninsular and Orient Line. In 1839, Samuel Cunard founded his line with four wooden steamers of just over 1,000 tons each, and was soon followed by the Pacific Steam Navigation Company. In 1870, the White Star Line was born.

These ships and shipping companies certainly opened up a tremendous trade for England. Thanks to them, it was possible to colonise Australia, New Zealand, America and Africa — all of which became valuable markets for our goods. To these areas, we were able to export our manufactures (iron, steel, cotton and wool) and our coal, as well as many other goods, for almost any item could be carried by sea. Similarly, England's import trade also benefited, for we received a plentiful supply of raw materials, and ship-loads of more varied, cheaper food (particularly when refrigeration enabled food to be kept for long voyages — e.g. New Zealand mutton).

Altogether, shipping was a very profitable business, until the last quarter of the 19th century when trade declined so much that there were more ships than cargo. At the same time, there developed a serious competition from Germany, whose shipping was helped by the State. So British shipping companies joined together, and made agreements about the prices they should charge for carrying goods.

Two World Wars

Then came the first World War, 1914-18, and English sea-faring had to face Germany's blunt announcement in 1917 that every merchant ship either leaving or approaching the shores of Britain would be torpedoed without warning. This was no idle threat. From February to March, England lost an average of four ships per day; in April, 196 ships, totalling 600,000 tons, were lost, while one ship out of every four leaving the British Isles never returned. By the end of 1917, no fewer than 1,271 ships — over $3\frac{1}{2}$ million tons — had been sunk. This was a disastrous situation, and only desperate remedies, such as the convoy system, Q-ships (armed vessels disguised as innocent merchantmen), depth charges, hydrophones and strict food rationing, enabled Britain to stave off defeat, and gradually to recover.

With the termination of the War in 1918, however, a far worse crisis arose. Originally, our shipping had borne most of the world's trade, but now there was much less carrying to be done. Our once vast export trade — coal, iron, steel, shipbuilding, engineering, cotton and woollen goods — declined because other countries were too poor to pay, or had begun to make their own requirements. Thus when India and Japan produced their own cotton goods, Lancashire was ruined. When other countries began to use oil or hydro-electric power, they did not want British coal.

The Second World War (1939-45) also saw heavy shipping losses, but when the hostilities ended, these losses were made good by confiscating 46 per cent of Germany's merchant ships, and by vigorously building more of our own, so vigorously, indeed, that by 1946 Britain undertook 50 per cent of the world's shipbuilding. The chief centres of the industry were the broad banks of the River Clyde, Newcastle-upon-Tyne, the well-known firm of Cammell-Laird at Birkenhead, and the yards at London, Portsmouth, Southampton and Plymouth.

In all these areas, there seemed no end to the size and speed of the ships which were made. Gigantic liners of 80,000 tons, such as *Queen Elizabeth* (83,673 tons), which could cross the Atlantic in three days, were launched, while even tramp steamers attained a size of 8,000 tons and could travel at 10 knots. Many of these new ships were driven by oil, a much better means of power than coal. Coal has to be hauled, heaved and stacked; oil flows easily and freely, and gives more power for the same weight. Also, oil-driven ships do not need a stokehold, and therefore have less labour.

Marine Insurance

Even in peace-time, however, ships were sunk by storms or collisions, and such losses had to be covered by marine insurance.

This was not a new idea, for as long ago as the 15th century, merchants had been able to insure against the loss of their ships, and by the 17th century these insurers, or underwriters as they were called (since they wrote their signatures under the terms of the insurance policy), used to meet at Lloyd's Coffee House in London. Edward Lloyd, however, was not only interested in running a coffee house, but in 1696 he also published a newspaper giving commercial news. So in 1707 when a number of underwriters decided to form a club, they naturally took the name of Lloyd's, and in 1734 the first Lloyd's List, giving shipping news, was published. Though in 1774 the marine insurers moved to the Royal Exchange, the old name was kept, and remains so to this day. It is also interesting to know that in assessing a ship, the quality of the hull is indicated by a letter, and the quality of the equipment by a figure. Hence 'A.1' indicates a ship whose hull and equipment are both in excellent condition, and the term has passed into common use.

The seamen

So we have thus learned how the demands for speed were satisfied first by sail, then by steam. We have learned how speed was enabled by better hulls (wood, iron, steel), better propulsion (paddle wheels, screw propeller), and better engines (compound, triple, quadruple, quintuple expansion, reaction turbine, oil-driven); by shorter sea routes (Suez, Panama); by the organisation of shipping companies (General Steam Navigation Line, P. and O., Cunard, Pacific Steam Navigation Company, White Star Line), and by marine insurance (Lloyd's).

But in this demand for speed, one thing has been overlooked. What about the men . . . the men who sailed in those ships along those sea routes in the service of those shipping companies? What about them? For, after all, it is the seamen who are most important, as in their absence the other factors could not exist. What then, was the life of a sailor in the 18th and 19th centuries?

It was grim.

Those who wished to go to sea, usually commenced at the age of ten. At that age, they were expected to sweep the decks, coil the ropes, and to climb the spars and rigging either to reef and unfurl the sails, or to move them in order to catch the wind. They were taught to splice ropes, mend canvas and to steer. There was no doubt that it was a very rough life, every day filled to the full with hard and often dangerous work. At night, the crew slept either in the steerage at the rear of the ship, or in the fo'c'sle at the front. The cabin they occupied would sometimes be only four to five foot high, and its only light and air came from an opening on the deck which had to be closed in heavy seas. In that low, narrow, ill-ventilated cabin, were crowded cables, ropes, casks, chests, canvas, men and rats. Nor were any better standards found at meal times, for the food on board ship was usually pork, salted beef and maggoty biscuits.

It was, as we have said, not only a rough, but a dangerous life. Many a seaman was swept overboard, or fell from the mast to his death, even in only light gales, but when the real storm came, there was terror indeed. As the pitiless savagery of the heaving seas drove the ship towards the rocks, it must be remembered that by 1849 there were only about 20 life-boats *round the entire coast of Britain.* Moreover, if a ship was wrecked on shore, it was more than likely to be plundered by the waiting villagers, and the exhausted sailors murdered to prevent their giving evidence against the looters.

But to these normal perils of the sea, there was then added a danger far more sinister and callous. As a result of the system of insurance, a ship and its cargo could be made more profitable to the shipowner if they sunk than if they floated. This may seem strange to understand, but it is true . . .

An owner would insure his ship for such a large sum of money, that if it sank, he would obtain more money in compensation than the ship and its cargo were worth. Then he did his best to make sure the ship sank. In some cases, the vessel was so neglected that even in a slight storm it would easily be sent to the bottom. Of course, the crew would drown as well, but that was an inevitable and minor matter to the ship-owner as long as he made a profit from the insurance money he received. Some ship-owners not only neglected their ships till they became unseaworthy, but deliberately hastened the process. Vessels were sent out to sea so overloaded that they were flush with the water level amidships. It was obviously a suicide voyage, but what could the poor seaman do? If he refused to sail, he could be imprisoned for breaking his contract, unless he could prove that the ship was unseaworthy. Such proof might seem easy, but when he was brought before the magistrates, he was only allowed to complain, and not allowed to give any evidence. How then could he prove his case? Moreover, if he lost the case, as he was almost certain to do, he had to pay the costs. Thus the seaman was compelled to go on board a ship which he knew would become his coffin.

It was really murder, and something had to be done. In 1854 and in 1894, the Government passed Merchant Shipping Acts to examine mates and masters, to state the conditions of work for seamen, and for the Board of Trade to inquire into wrecks.

Improvements to sea-faring

Even more helpful was the work of Samuel Plimsoll (1824-98), Member of Parliament for Derby, and 'the Sailors' Friend'. In 1876, his efforts to make the seaman's life safer were rewarded, for thenceforth deck cargoes were to be limited, and all ships had to have a loading line — the Plimsoll Mark. If you look at this mark, you will notice two sets of lines, one for Fresh Water (F) and the other for Salt Water (i.e. Summer, which continues the line L.R. across the circle). There is a reason for this. A floating body displaces the same weight of water as its own weight. Salt water, however, is obviously more dense and heavy than fresh, so a ship will displace less water (and therefore float higher) when out in the salty ocean. Thus a vessel in a freshwater river may be loaded to the freshwater mark, and then, when it goes to sea, it will rise till the water level reaches the L.R. line.

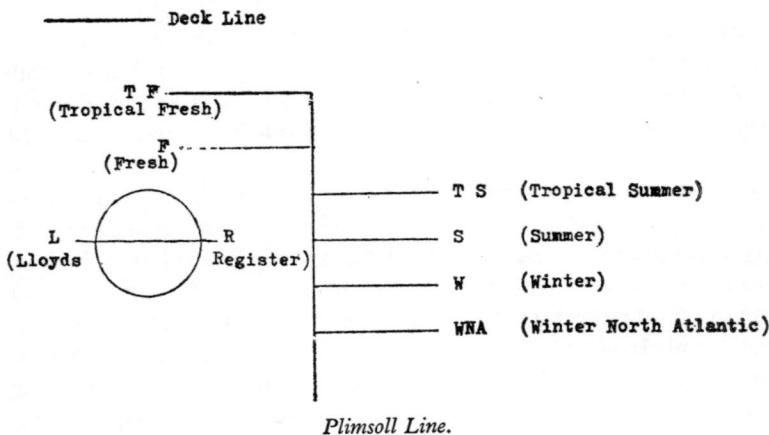

Plimsoll Line.

In 1894, all ships had to carry life-belts and life-boats.

The voyages of the merchant ships were also made safer by the work of John Smeaton (1724-92), who built the third Eddystone Lighthouse off Plymouth in 1756-59. The first had been destroyed by storm, the second by fire, so to ensure the permanence of the third, Smeaton had the natural rock hollowed out, and constructed his lighthouse of hand-hewn dovetailed stones. It was a work well done. For 122 years, until 1881, it remained, and had then to be taken down only because the sea had undermined the natural rock on which it was built. As a tribute to the builder, it was re-erected on the land at Plymouth Hoe by public subscription. The present lighthouse, the fourth, was constructed in 1882.

There were other aids to navigation also. A ship's position at sea is determined by finding the latitude (the position north or south of the Equator), and then the longitude (the position east or west of the meridian). It had been known even in ancient times that to find latitude you must measure the angle between the sun and the horizon, but the various types of notched sticks used for this purpose gave only very poor results. Not until 1731 did John Hadley invent his sextant, whereby the position could be found more easily and accurately.

After that, the next step was to find longitude, and for this both a sextant and a chronometer were needed — a chronometer being a clock which will keep accurate for a long time. Thereupon the difficulty arose, for neither the ancients nor the middle ages nor even the 15th to early 18th centuries possessed a timepiece with the necessary capabilities. For centuries, therefore, the finding of a ship's position based on longitude was really only a matter of guesswork, and, for example, many a mariner found himself coasting off the Azores when his calculations indicated the shores of Spain — an error of some 800 miles . . .

So difficult and so important was it to find longitude, that in 1714 the British Government offered a reward of £20,000 for an instrument which would give the ship's position correct to within 60 miles. So John Harrison (1693-1776), a clock-maker, set to work. His first attempt in 1735 earned him £500 from the Government to continue his experiments, but it was not until 1759 that he completed an instrument which was certainly the most accurate chronometer then known. After five months at sea, it was still less than 15 seconds slow. So navigators were now able to find both the latitude and the longitude in which they were travelling, and thus know their position exactly.

The next great aid to navigation was not until the development of radar by Sir Robert Watson-Watt in 1934. Rays of light were sent out, were reflected back from any object ahead, and the results shown on a radar screen. Thus, particularly in foggy weather, the reflected rays would give warning of an invisible object ahead.

So the Merchant Shipping Acts of 1854 and 1894, the efforts of Samuel Plimsoll, and such navigational aids as lighthouses, sextants, chronometers, and radar, have all rendered sea-going a far safer occupation nowadays. Moreover, for those who are contemplating entry into the Merchant Navy at the present time, it may be mentioned that rules were drawn up in 1947 regarding pay, hours of work, leave, comfort and food on board ship, so that a great improvement in the conditions of a seaman's life has now taken place.

Chapter VI

Railways

(This chapter has been divided into six sections: early history of railways; difficulties of early railways; improvements to railways; State control; results of railway development; trams.)

Early history of railways

1. In the 1st century A.D., Hero of Alexandria invented a machine where steam turned a sphere.

2. In 1602, flat wooden planks with sleepers were used by trucks at Newcastle for the transport of coal — (they may have been inspired by those used in Germany from the 15th century onwards). By this means, one horse could pull ten to fifteen tons, and so popular became the idea that within a century no fewer than 20,000 horses were employed in the northern coalfields.

These early rails, however, were only flat wooden planks, and the smooth truck wheels were as likely to run off them as on them. So in 1766, John Curr, a colliery agent of Sheffield, made a rail with a flange on the inside (called a 'plateway'), and the next development was by William Jessop who, in 1788, fitted a flange to the wheel instead of to the rail.

Flanged rails

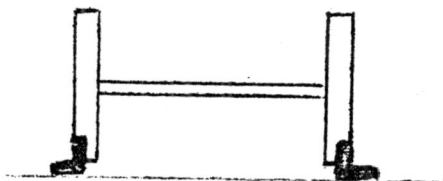

Flanged wheels

But the wooden rails still warped and wore away, and though some were later covered with iron plates, it was a real improvement when, at Coalbrookdale in 1767, the first entirely cast-iron rails were laid down.

Now, put Nos. 1 and 2 together, and you have the beginning of modern rail travel.

To a Frenchman, Nicolas Cugnot, goes the honour of being the first person to make a steam-driven vehicle, which he constructed in Paris in 1769.

It was some years before an Englishman took up the challenge, and then William Murdock (1754-1839), an assistant of Boulton and Watt, made a model road locomotive in 1786 — a strange three-wheeled affair, steered by a kind of tiller, and worked by a piston rod which forced up and down a beam attached to the crankshaft.

Naturally, he desired to experiment with his invention to see how it would travel. So one evening, he took it out along a quiet country road near the village of Redruth in Cornwall where he lived. With the boiler working at full pressure, and uttering smoke and steam, the little road locomotive commenced its journey.

It was a calm and beautiful evening, soothed by the wonderful peace of the countryside, the quietness of still places. It was most unfortunate, indeed, that on that same evening, the local vicar had decided to take a walk for the benefit of the fresh air. He was thus strolling quietly along, amid the peace and the calm, gently meditating upon his sermon for the following Sunday when, gradually, there dawned upon his consciousness a rather strange noise which did not suggest any of the usual countryside sounds. Then, as he continued his walk, the noise became louder and louder, until suddenly, along the winding road, between the high hedges, there came a strange and terrible creation of sparks and steam.

The vicar was a brave man — at any rate, for a moment. Boldly he stood his ground, and recited a prayer. But this did not prevent the machine from advancing, and as it rumbled nearer, both courage and prayer alike were forfeited. Clasping his Bible firmly beneath his arm, the gallant clergyman fled for his life, shouting for more worldly assistance, and finally seeking sanctuary in a ditch. It is understood that the sermon that he preached on the following Sunday caused considerable comment among the congregation. Never before, indeed, had the preacher been known to speak with such amazing energy and sincerity. The text, incidentally, referred to 'The Devil and his works'.

It was also in Cornwall that the next development occurred. Richard Trevithick (1771-1833), a mining engineer and a real inventive genius, designed a much better, high pressure engine, and having fitted it to a wheeled framework in 1801, he thus made the first passenger-carrying steam car in England — the 'Puffing Devil'. Stoking up the fire with a pair of bellows, the inventor took seven or eight passengers a distance of about two miles at a speed of five to six miles per hour. Unfortunately, after a later journey, they all then entered an inn to celebrate, leaving the fire still burning, the water evaporated, and the red-hot engine burst into flames.

But progress was now turning from roads to railways, and in 1803 the first public railway was opened — the Surrey Iron Railway, where horse-drawn wagons took goods traffic along the $9\frac{1}{2}$ miles from Croydon to Wandsworth at a steady two m.p.h. With his interest thus aroused, Trevithick, in the following year, made the first steam railway engine in the world. It was an ungainly, bulky machine with a colossal fly-wheel, and was used to haul iron on the nine mile Penydarren railway near Merthyr Tydfil, South Wales.

Then in 1808, this same pioneer Cornishman made the first public steam railway engine in the world to carry passengers — the 'Catch-me-who-can' — which ran at 12-13 m.p.h., on a circular track in London near the site of the present Euston station.

So the next time you go to London, Euston, remember this.

These inventions of the Cornish genius have not been excelled in the history of railways. When the last steam locomotive for use in this country was completed for 1960, there were alterations, additions and amendments most certainly, but it bore no major change from that first amazing design some 160 years before.

It was even more tragic, therefore, that all Trevithick's schemes failed — the rails were not strong enough for his engines, the public was not interested in his projects, and his genius began to fade. Inevitably he fell into debt, and in the end only the generosity of his fellow workmen saved him from a pauper's funeral. Even though there was a window to his memory in Westminster Abbey, the exact whereabouts of his grave in Dartford's humble churchyard is still unknown.

Such, alas, is the tragedy of genius. How many people, even today, have heard of, or know anything about, Richard Trevithick of Cornwall, the pioneer of England's railways, the pioneer of the railways of the world? The answer is — very few.

The greatest and best-known name in railway history, indeed, was to be that of George Stephenson (1781-1848). He was born at Wylam, Northumberland, in a home consisting of one room in a cottage. In this single room, a place of unplastered walls, bare rafters and a floor of clay, there lived a family of six children and their parents. The father, Robert Stephenson, was an engineer at a local colliery where he worked twelve hours a day for the same number of shillings a week. Under such circumstances, the children had no schooling; they had not even shoes.

At the age of eight, indeed, young George began to earn his living — 1p. a day, watching the cows on a neighbouring farm to prevent them straying on to the railway line that ran near the cottage. The young lad watched the line even more attentively than he minded the cows, and it was his keen eye and powers of observation which enabled him to study the engines at the colliery where he was subsequently employed. Thus he became a skilled engineer before he could even read, and knew far more about engines than the engineers who had studied science and machines. Gradually he acquired a local fame as 'the engine doctor'; whenever an engine failed to function, Stephenson was summoned to repair it.

The big spur-wheel engaged the teeth on the rail

Blenkinsop's Rack-and-Pinion Railway

At this time, however, it was still doubted whether the smooth wheels of a locomotive would be able to grip the smooth rails satisfactorily. So in 1811, John Blenkinsop built his rack-and-pinion railway — a locomotive with a toothed wheel which engaged with a toothed rail. From Middleton colliery to Leeds, the engine could haul 94 tons of coal along the $3\frac{1}{2}$ mile journey — and did so for 20 years.

However, the toothed wheel and rail were really unnecessary. In 1813, the engineer at Wylam colliery, William Hedley, produced his 'Puffing Billy', another famous railway engine, whose smooth wheels ran on the smooth track beside Stephenson's cottage.

Thus inspired, in 1314, Stephenson constructed the first locomotive of his own — the 'Blucher' (named after a Prussian general who later fought at the Battle of Waterloo). It could haul a load of 30 tons up a gradient of 1 in 450 at four m.p.h. — an admitted achievement, but still too costly to represent a decisive advantage over horses.

In 1825, however, he had his first really great opportunity when he built the Stockton to Darlington railway, and then constructed a railway engine, the 'Locomotion', to run on it. This single locomotive, be it noted, did the work of 40 teams of horses. The railway itself was originally intended to carry goods only, until first one horse-drawn carriage was provided for passengers as an experiment — the coach itself being so named — then another carriage was added, and finally there were seven. This was Britain's, and the world's, first practical steam railway for goods and (later) passengers.

But is was the Liverpool to Manchester railway of 1830 that placed Stephenson in a security of fame. The growth of the Lancashire cotton industry had greatly increased the trade between Liverpool and Manchester and the route of this trade was along the Duke of Bridgewater's canal — a canal utterly unable to cope with the heavier volume of traffic.

A railway was the solution, so the preliminary plans were made. These included the surveying of the land against the wishes of the landowners who had no desire to have a railway anywhere in the neighbourhood. So a regular tactical campaign was fought. When the landowners mustered their array of gamekeepers and farmers, Stephenson advanced with his army of 'surveyors'. Flanking sorties were made to distract attention, while the main assault overran the desired area, armed with compasses and measuring devices. Two prize-fighters guarded the standard of the theodolite. Where force proved of no avail, craft won the day. While the rich landlords were dining in style at home, the surveyors infiltrated their land; while the farmers slept, Stephenson worked. The lands of hostile vicars were surveyed during the Sunday sermon.

Once these difficulties had been overcome, and the necessary Act of Parliament passed at the second attempt, Stephenson commenced to create the Liverpool to Manchester railway.

The track alone was a masterpiece of construction, for it had to conquer three major obstacles. The first was Olive Mount, where a cutting two miles long and 100 feet deep had to be made through the solid sandstone rock. Further ahead was the Sankey Valley, across which a brick and stone viaduct 70 feet above the water, with nine 50 foot spans, was built. The third obstacle was the most difficult — Chat Moss. This treacherous area occupied some 12 square miles, and was a moss-covered marsh varying from 10-30 feet in depth. It seemed a sheer impossibility to cross this with a rail track, but the courage and determination of Stephenson were not daunted. First of all, he had hurdles interwoven with heather and pressed into the marsh to form a firm foundation in layers; on top of these came a layer of gravel, and finally the sleepers and the rails. Thus the railroad crossed Chat Moss.

But Stephenson's greatest fame was yet to come. At the opening of the railway in 1830, one train was powered by his engine, the 'Rocket', which had defeated all its rivals in speed and reliability, at the trials at Rainhill, 1829. It also, incidentally, caused the first fatal accident in railway history when Mr. Huskisson, a former President of the Board of Trade, was knocked down, and died later from his injuries.

But the 'Rocket' was certainly a magnificent engine, painted yellow except for a white chimney, and the black cylinders, wheel rims and fire box. It weighed four tons, and could draw a load of 20 tons at 30 m.p.h. The boiler, which was lagged with wood, contained 25 copper tubes each three inches in diameter. The driving wheels were at the front, and the cylinders were originally at a steep angle, but as this caused the train to rock rather badly, they were later lowered to a more horizontal position.

Difficulties of early railways

So, thanks to Trevithick and Stephenson, the railways developed.

And you should have heard the objections . . .

The coach owners, horse-keepers, innkeepers and canal owners, naturally opposed the railways with all their power, for they feared and faced ruin. The great country gentlemen also joined the opposition for fear that their fine houses would be burnt by sparks or crushed by falling embankments. The local squires feared lest the fumes from the engines should cause unhealthy foxes and spoil hunting. The farmers were no less concerned, for the sparks could burn down crops, hay-stacks, farmsteads and all, while the nervous effect upon the livestock, of course, would be immeasurable — hens wouldn't lay, cows would give sour milk, horses would have nervous breakdowns, and gamebirds would be poisoned by the fumes.

The doctors, too, opposed the railways, for it was quite definite to any good medical man of those days that if you attempted to travel through the atmosphere at faster than 60 m.p.h., the sheer speed could have fatal effects on the heart, liver and lungs. Even the breakneck rate of 10 m.p.h., might cause the passengers to lose their reason. Tunnels, too, were guaranteed to cause colds, catarrh, consumption and suffocation. To be fair to the medical profession, however, it should be stated that some doctors did feel that the jolting of a railway journey could be an advantage in helping to digest a heavy meal. The clergy, of course, opposed the railways — you had only to gaze upon one of these infernal machines, thundering along amid flames and smoke, to appreciate that it could not possibly be other than the work of the Devil.

Apart from such opposition, the railways had other difficulties to face. Profiteers were not slow to seize any advantage. They bought up the land on which it was intended to build a track, and then charged the railway company as much as £8,000 a mile to purchase it. The cost of obtaining an Act of Parliament to build a railway would vary from £500 to £5,000 a mile, and then there was the actual building to pay for. So the total cost to construct a track was on average a colossal £56,000 per mile.

When the railway had been built, the passengers, too, had their difficulties. Originally there were three classes of travel — first, second, and third. The first-class carriages had cushioned seats, sides, doors, windows and a roof. Despite such comfort, however, the jolting motion of the train caused many cases of sea-sickness, and it was not unusual to see several heads out of the windows like ocean-going travellers' through the portholes. Outside was a guard, sitting on a high perch — a dangerous position wherein the man might be killed by the striking of his head against a low bridge.

The second class passengers jolted along in a compartment equipped with bare boards for seating, no windows, and sometimes no doors. The third class travelled in a compartment without seats, doors, windows or roof — mere open trucks. The wealthier class, if they wished, could arrange for their horse-drawn road carriages to be run on to a flat truck and lashed down with ropes, so that they could continue their journey without alighting, and by what was certainly the most comfortable method of rail travel. There was, however, always

the possibility of sparks from the engine setting alight to the carriage . . .
or the ropes might slip. Never a dull moment!

Meanwhile, the advice given to early travellers could well be re-
printed here:

Rule 1.   Never attempt to get into or out of the railway carriage
          when it is moving.

Rule 2.   Never sit in any unusual place or posture. On some lines
          of railway, seats are provided on the roofs of the carriages.
          These are to be avoided . . . If a second class carriage, as
          sometimes happens, has no door, (Passengers) should take
          care not to put out their leg.

Rule 9.   Beware of yielding to the sudden impulse to spring from
          the carriage to recover your hat which has blown off, or
          a parcel dropped.

The railway engines as well as the carriages had their imperfections,
too. Steam power had by no means reached its most powerful stage of
development, and in consequence some trains carried a horse which
would be let out of its truck when necessary to help the carriages up
steep gradients. Or fixed winding engines were provided at the top of
steep hills, ready to haul up the locomotives by means of cables. Nor
were the early trains very punctual, especially if there was a head wind,
and it is a significant fact that the first *Bradshaw* — or *Railway Guide*,
so-named from its originator, George Bradshaw, and issued in 1839 —
though it gave the departure times of trains, did not print the times
of arrival. Sometimes, indeed, the trains arrived early, but this was
most frequently due to unsuitable drivers — "You should see 'im go
when 'e's 'ad a drop to drink."

On a train journey of any distance, frequent changes were necessary
as a result of different companies owning different stretches of line.
Some of these stretches covered only a few miles, and by 1851, indeed,
there were only two companies with over 100 miles of rail track. So
on the way from London to Carlisle, for example, it was necessary to
make five changes. The different companies also had different gauges
— the Great Western Railway, built by I. K. Brunel, had a seven foot
gauge, and passengers from Bristol to Birmingham, had to change from
this broad gauge to a narrow gauge at Gloucester.

There was also an unnecessary duplication of lines. From London
to Manchester, three different railway companies each provided its
own line and services. Manchester and Liverpool were similarly linked
by three separate railway lines of three separate rail companies.

Improvements to railways

But all this opposition and all these difficulties could not halt the progress of the railways. Remember, it was cheaper to lay rails than to build a road or a canal. So in 1830, there were 70 miles of track; but in 1870 there were 13,500 miles, including the results of the Railway Mania of 1846 when no fewer than 272 schemes were approved by Parliament, some of them so full of smoke and hot air that the investors lost their money. One person involved in this 'railway mania' was the Yorkshireman, George Hudson, (1800-71) — the 'Railway King', as he was called. At the height of his fame, he controlled one-third of the nation's railways, including the Midland Railway. Until his dishonest dealings were discovered, many new lines were built and others amalgamated for better organisation.

Natural difficulties were also overcome. Across the Tyne a bridge was built in 1849, the Menai Railway Bridge was constructed by Robert Stephenson the following year, and in 1890 a masterpiece of engineering, the Forth Bridge, crossed the Scottish Firth near Edinburgh — to quote but three examples. Where it was not possible to go over, the railways went under, and the Severn Tunnel was thus completed in 1886.

Other developments were made so that the unpleasantness of rail travel was reduced. Gradually the carriages were improved. In 1833, they were fitted with springs, then followed gas lighting (1850), sleeping cars (1873), dining cars (1879), electric light from a dynamo on the engine (1884), and corridor cars (1892). Next, to avoid unnecessary changes, the different railway companies began to unite, or arrange to carry passengers at a single charge over more than one line. In 1846, a standard gauge of 4ft. 8½ins. was determined — though the Great Western kept their gauge until 1892.

The railway engines soon began to increase their speed, particularly when longer boilers for more power were constructed. This, however, involved dangers. As the engine became longer, it began to rock rather dangerously when travelling at full speed, so a pair of trailing wheels (i.e. not driven by the engine) were fixed at the back. Another danger was the breaking of the crank axles as the train rounded a bend — a catastrophe which might cause the engine to be de-railed. So the front part of the engine was placed on a bogie — a four- or six-wheeled truck not driven by the engine, and fixed to the underside of the boiler by a swivel. The bogie was introduced in 1848 after trial efforts some years before.

About the same time, it was found that outside-rod-coupled driving wheels, which had first been designed on Stephenson's 'Locomotion' for the Stockton to Darlington Railway in 1825, gave a better grip of the rails when starting.

Then, in 1860, the water scoop was invented, being first laid down on a length of North Wales track on the Holyhead line. A trough of water between the rails extended for some distance, and a scoop lowered from the engine tender gathered up the water as the train travelled. An express could thus refill with 2,500 gallons of water in 15 seconds, and long-distance runs could be made non-stop.

The increased speed of trains also involved the need for greater safety, and one of the most important devices in this respect was the Westinghouse automatic pressure brakes, introduced in 1872. From 1885, continuous brakes had to be fitted — brakes which the driver can apply through the whole length of the train.

But the demand for swifter travel still urged on the railways, and the great locomotive engineer of the 20th century was Sir Nigel Gresley. At this time, designers of aircraft were working out plans to overcome the air-resistance encountered at high speeds. So the idea of stream-lining began, and it was Sir Nigel who realised that the same principle could be applied to railway engines. Accordingly, in 1935, on the London, North-Eastern Railway, there appeared the shimmering beauty of the Silver Jubilee Train, with its low funnel and streamlined casing based on the shape of an aircraft wing. Even on the trial run, all previous records for speed were broken, and as the metalled unit flashed across the landscape, for the first time in locomotive history there was a real beauty added to usefulness. Three years later, the streamlined locomotive, the 'Mallard', reached a record of 126 miles per hour — a record for steam power that will be difficult to exceed.

Signalling, too, had to be improved. The first signal in railway history was a lighted candle, which the station-master on the Stockton to Darlington railway placed in the window of his office when he wanted the train to stop. Another early method in 1830 was by men in top-hats and swallow-tail coats standing at intervals along the line. Each of them carried flags in the day-time — a red flag for danger and a white one for all clear — and red and blue lamps at night. When it was foggy, they had to get within shouting distance of each other.

Then in 1837, a ball (or, at night, a lamp) was slung to a pole, and lowered to the ground for danger, or hoisted to the top for all clear. By 1841, the Great Western Railway had a cross-bar and red light for danger, and a round disc for all clear.

A great improvement was made in 1846 when the signals were connected by wires to a frame in the signal box, and, later on, from that method, electric signalling was installed. This latter was of very great benefit. At large stations and busy junctions, a tremendous amount of hard physical labour pulling full-size levers could be replaced by one or two finger-tip flicks of switches. At the same time, there came another important safety device — the Block System, made compulsory in 1889; the line was divided into sections (or 'blocks'), and only one train was allowed in each section at a time. A considerable amount of modern signalling in these sections is automatic, whereby each train in passing operates an electric contact to set a signal at danger, and when a good distance away operates another electric contact to return that signal to the all clear.

Meanwhile, the electric telegraph, devised by William Cooke and Charles Wheatstone, and first used for railways 1838-9, enabled officials to know whereabouts the trains were, and thus lessen the number of accidents. It was also useful to bring criminals to justice, as, for examples, by warning the next stations that an escaping murderer was on the train, or that a person with a second class ticket was sitting in a first class compartment.

Electricity, indeed, was not slow to enter railway history. Apart from electric signalling and the electric telegraph, two other important events were the first electric train service, in 1842, when Davidson's electric locomotive ran from Edinburgh to Glasgow, and the construction of the Liverpool Overhead Railway in 1893. This Liverpool Railway was a $6\frac{1}{2}$ mile dockside track, raised 16 foot above ground by steel columns — the first overhead electric railway in the world. It was dismantled in 1956.

The advantages of electric trains are obvious. There are no fumes especially in tunnels, the cleaner labour of driving is more attractive, stopping and starting are swifter, and electric-powered engines can also exceed the record for steam locomotives of 126 m.p.h. set by the 'Mallard' in 1938. Moreover, the electric engine uses power only when actually moving; the steam engine wastes fuel during the warming up, while halted at stations and termini, and again while cooling down. All these advantages far outweigh the drawbacks of a possible power failure, or of snowfall or frost forming ice on the conductor rails.

So the electric locomotive drawing current from overhead cables, or the diesel electric locomotive in which diesel engines drive generators to produce its own current, is now entering modern times.

Not only above, but also below ground, the rail tracks continued to extend. The first underground steam train ran from Farringdon Street to Paddington in 1863, and in 1870 the first Tube railway in the world was opened — from Tower Bridge to the other side of the Thames, and using cable-drawn cars. The next, and tremendous, stage of progress, came in 1890, when the three miles of electrified rail from the Monument to Stockwell marked the construction of the first Electric Tube Railway.

State control of railways

Such progress as this could certainly not be ignored by the State, and the 19th century saw a gradual increase of State control.

From 1840, the Board of Trade inspected new lines, and had the power to hold enquiries into accidents. Also the Board could fix carriage rates so as to prevent the railway companies from favouring one employer, class of goods or district, and ruining another. Travel was made much easier when, in 1842, the Railway Clearing House was set up to arrange for railway companies to share their lines so that through bookings could be made, and time-tables co-ordinated. Then, by Act of Parliament in 1844, it was laid down for each company that at least one train per day in each direction should provide passenger transport at the cheap rate of 1d. per mile — 'the Parliamentary train'.

From 1914-20, rail transport came under State control for war reasons, and the directors of the various different railway companies thus realised the advantages of a central controlling authority. So after the war, in 1923, 123 different companies were joined together to form four main companies — the London, Midland and Scottish Railway (L.M.S.), the London and North-Eastern Railway (L.N.E.R.), the Great Western Railway (G.W.R.), and the Southern Railway (S.R.).

At the same time, a Railway Rates Tribunal was established by the Government to fix standard rates and fares which would provide the new companies with sufficient money to enable them to operate. Furthermore, it did not seem right that these four powerful companies should be able to charge what they liked (thus fleecing the public) and also be able by favouring one employer, class of goods or district, to develop one and ruin another. But though the Railway Rates Tribunal was set up to prevent such occurrences, it need not have worried unduly. The railways could not afford to increase rates and fares, or to have favouritism in their dealings, for they had to face a very successful competition from the roads. It is obviously more pleasant to travel by road to enjoy the scenery, it is certainly much cheaper, and for the business man it is more convenient to have delivery from door to door instead of having to carry to and from a railway station. So the railways, indeed, began to decline, and had to receive Government help.

When the Second World War occurred, 1939-45, naturally the State took control once more, paying the railway companies £43 million per annum in return for all receipts.

During the war, the railways deteriorated, and by 1945, the lines, engines and rolling stock needed repair. Only the Government could afford the cost, and also stop wasteful competition among the four great railway companies. Another consideration was that even if the railways could not be run at a profit (and thus attract private companies to organise them), they were nevertheless vital to the nation. So the Government took over the railways (i.e. 'nationalised' them) in 1947, and a new Transport Tribunal controlled rates and fares.

Nevertheless, largely due to road competition, by 1960 British Railways was running at a very serious loss. So Dr. Reginald Beeching, a director of one of England's largest companies (Imperial Chemical Industries), an extremely capable organiser and business man, was appointed to try to make the railways more profitable. This he proposed to do by modernising all the equipment, improving the organisation, and reducing costs by closing down lines that did not pay.

His heroic efforts failed to stop the losses, and by the 1968 Transport Act, the Government had to cancel most of British Rail's debts.

Results of railway development

The results of railway development were, of course, outstandingly important. True, the canals and the coaches declined and decayed, but other aspects of social and economic life received a tremendous benefit.

The iron and coal industries developed considerably, for the railways themselves required the products of both, and also carried these products all over the country for sale.

The farmer, the fishmonger and the manufacturer, too, had a home market far wider than ever before, especially as livestock or items likely to perish or deteriorate could be taken swiftly to their destination. Moreover, since goods could be taken right to the docks, a great 19th century export trade resulted as well. Trade, indeed, now became a matter of large-scale organisation as vast quantities of goods were moved from place to place; the day of the local fair and the wandering pedlar began to fade, and their services were taken over by a retail shop.

Areas of England not previously used were opened up by the railways. Inland towns were created — Crewe, Rugby, Swindon — for sufficient supplies of food could now be brought to them. Factories were set up away from overcrowded regions, as they could now obtain delivery and despatch of goods very easily.

Suburban areas in which to live, developed outside existing towns, for people could now travel easily backwards and forwards to work.

Perhaps one of the most pleasant results of the development of railways was that all classes of society could benefit. The rich invested their money to make further profit. The middle class gained wealth from an expanding, better organised trade. The workers found that prices were cheaper as a result of quick, easy transport, and in addition to employment on the railways, they could travel further afield to find work. It was even possible to go for a holiday to Blackpool or Brighton.

The different classes of society became more aware of each other as they met on railway platforms, or as the rich in their first class carriages travelled past the rail-side slums.

The railways also influenced the Government of the country, by bringing Members of Parliament within closer reach of their constituencies; and the swifter, more widespread delivery of post and newspapers unified the nation.

An interesting minor consequence of railway development was the establishment of a uniform time throughout the country — the London (Greenwich Mean) Time. Before 1840, there were different times in different areas, so that the time in Reading was four minutes later than London time, while still further west at Cirencester, the time was 17 minutes ahead of London. Railway time-tables, however, could not cope with such local oddities, so London Time gradually extended over the whole nation.

Trams

Before we finish this chapter, however, let us spare a moment and a paragraph to consider the neglected offspring of the railways — the tramways. In 1860, Birkenhead had the first tramway in the United Kingdom, and as other towns followed the example, this form of transport improved from horse-drawn to steam to electric power.

Admittedly, the tramways lessened the possibility of accident due to human misjudgment, for the driver did not have to steer, but as the roads became more crowded, the trams, unable to manoeuvre freely in and out of the traffic, became so great a nuisance that they were gradually abolished.

Chapter VII

Road Transport

Carriages, bicycles and buses

It seemed that the railways killed the roads. The coaches were left to rust and crumble, the inns closed down, and on the deserted highways the grass grew, and the ruts and the potholes appeared.

Local transport, of course, was not affected. In the towns, people travelled in sedan chairs, or in a vast variety of four-wheeled carriages including the popular brougham (pronounced 'broom'), designed by the Lord Chancellor of that name in 1838. As you will notice from the illustration on this page, the brougham had a guard-board fixed behind the body to prevent the pole of a following carriage from penetrating the back. There were also many two-wheeled vehicles, such as gigs,

Brougham

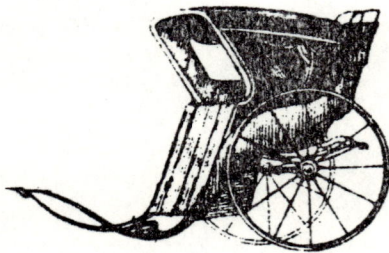

Hansom Cab

94

two-horse curricles, cabriolets (hence 'cabs'), dog-carts, and the hansom (a very well-known cab, with the driver at the rear in a position from which he could just see the horse's ears and from which, moreover, he had to speak to his passenger through a trap-door in the roof).

Then, in 1791, a Frenchman invented what was later called a 'Hobby horse'. It was a bicycle, whose rider sat on the saddle, and pushed against the ground with each foot alternately. Unfortunately, it was a rigid construction, so that it was necessary to dismount and lift it round a corner. In 1818, however, an Austrian, Baron Drais, devised an improved version with swivel handlebars, and this was introduced into England the same year.

Hobby Horse.

Penny Farthing

From such origins there developed the more familiar pedal-driven bicycles, including the famous 'Boneshakers' — with iron tyres! — and, above all, the 'penny farthing'. This latter monstrosity was indeed the star of its time. It had a front wheel some five foot in diameter, above which were the saddle and handlebars, while the rear wheel was only one foot in diameter. So in order to mount, the rider had to lean the bicycle against a wall, and climb up to the saddle like a mountaineer. Or he had to hold the machine upright, straddle the rear wheel with his legs, and vault skywards into the saddle like a trapeze artist doing a balancing act. Once on board the vehicle, he sat perched five foot in the air, pedalling furiously along the road in a cloud of blinding dust. Each turn of the pedals, which were fixed to the hub of the front wheel, drove the bicycle some five or six yards. Should the front wheel, however, strike a large stone or other obstacle in its path, disaster was almost certain to follow. The rear wheel at once rose up high above the saddle, while at the same time the rider dived gracefully forward to bury his nose in the road. Even to dismount in a more normal fashion involved either another trapeze act, or some form of five foot crash-landing.

Later, in 1885, J. K. Starley devised a 'safety bicycle' of similar-sized wheels, driven by pedal and chain as they are now, and even greater comfort was afforded when John Boyd Dunlop re-invented the pneumatic (i.e. air-filled) rubber tyre in 1888. (R. W. Thompson had made one in 1845, but there had been no further development due to the cost of rubber and the scarcity of cycles). Then, in 1899, three-speed gears were introduced.

For those who were not sufficiently wealthy to possess their own carriage or bicycle, public transport was provided; and in London in 1829, Shillibeer's omnibus, brightly painted in green, with yellow wheels and red curtains, and with accommodation for 22 passengers, travelled from the City to Edgware Road.

After this beginning, the public transport of London developed rapidly, and horse-buses became a familiar sight. These Victorian horse-buses were painted in different colours to indicate the different routes along which they travelled. And the competition among them, became grim — very grim. Rival buses raced at break-neck speed through the streets in a desperate attempt to reach the passenger halts first. The conductors then leapt to the ground, each seizing hold of as many passengers as possible, in a frenzied effort to bundle them into his bus before his rivals could get them into theirs. Indeed, frequent delays occurred at these halts whilst determined conductors fought it out between themselves, the winner taking the passengers.

As the population of London increased, so did the work of the horse-buses, and in the year of the Great Exhibition, 1851, there were so many visitors to the capital that seats — long back-to-back forms — were put on top of the buses to cope with the extra numbers of passengers.

So the horse-buses continued to prosper. For a short while indeed, there was a threat from steam carriages, but the high road tolls charged

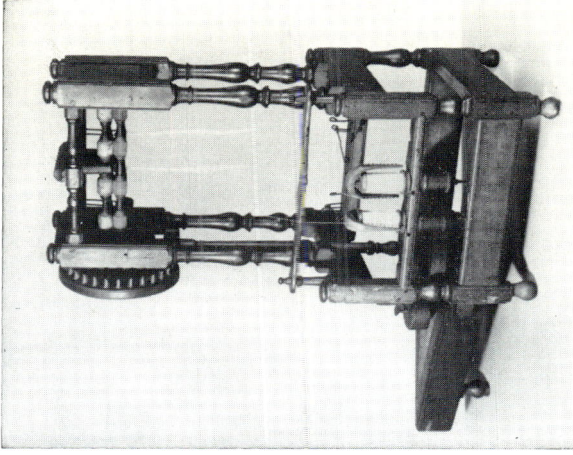

Above: The original spinning machine made by Sir Richard Arkwright in 1769.

And left: A replica of Crompton's Mule, both in the Science Museum, London.

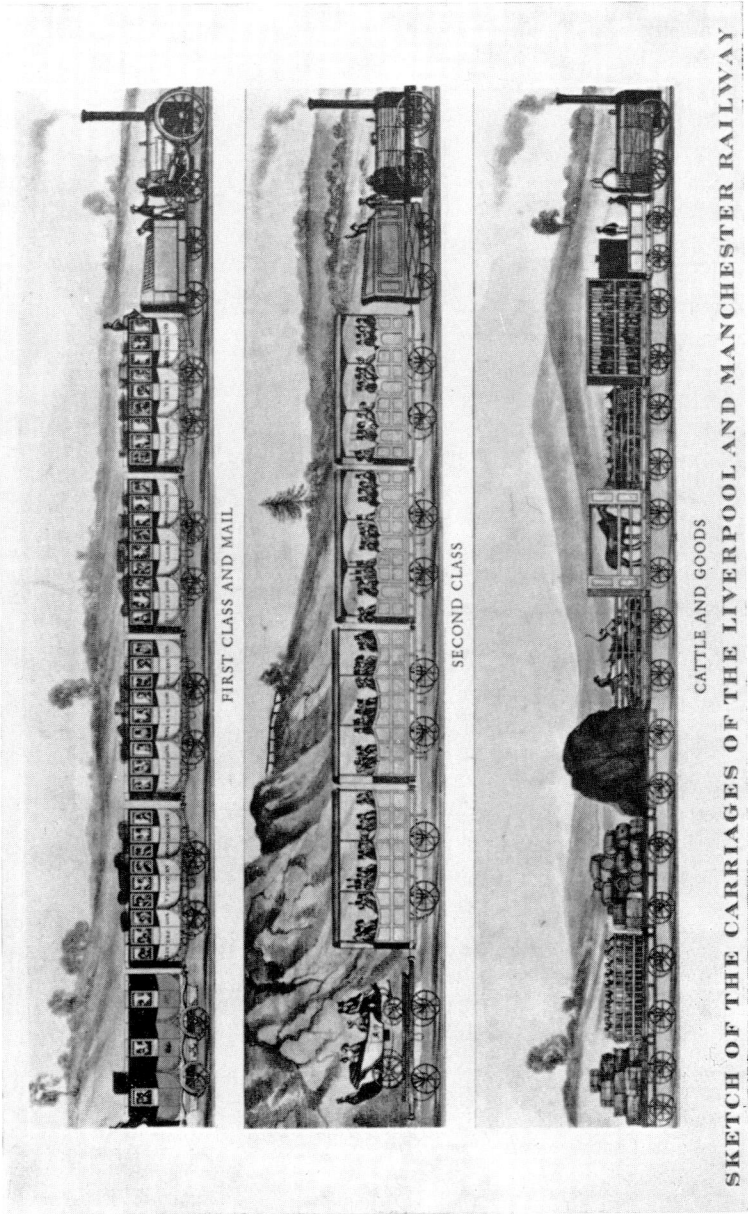

FIRST CLASS AND MAIL

SECOND CLASS

CATTLE AND GOODS

SKETCH OF THE CARRIAGES OF THE LIVERPOOL AND MANCHESTER RAILWAY

prevented their development, and they were then crippled by the Red Flag Act of 1865, which ordered that, for the safety of the public, no mechanically propelled road vehicle was to travel at more than four m.p.h. (two m.p.h. in towns), and must have a man with a red flag 60 yards in front to warn other road users. In any event, the heavy boiler took a long time to heat up, and even then was often too hot for the passengers' comfort. There was also a threat of competition from electric cars, but the difficulties over the batteries in those days seriously hampered progress by this motive power.

Motor cars

But though horse-drawn transport was safe from competition in England, a very serious threat indeed was developing on the Continent.

It was in 1860 that Etienne Lenoir, a Frenchman, produced the first really successful internal combustion engine, which worked by the explosion of coal gas and air in a cylinder.

Development followed steadily. Nikolaus Otto of Germany made a four-stroke engine in 1876. Nine years later, in 1885, Karl Benz of Germany used an electric spark to ignite the petrol vapour in his three-wheeled car. The modern road vehicle had arrived.

Further developments, however, were still confined to the Continent, where Karl Benz and Gottlieb Daimler of Germany became famous for their cars. In England, as we have said, the Red Flag Act of 1865 ordered that, for the safety of the public, no mechanically-propelled road vehicle was to travel at more than four m.p.h. (two m.p.h. in towns), and must have a man with a red flag 60 yards in front to warn other road users. Such regulations did not encourage the manufacture of British cars, so for some years any Englishman who wished to own a car, despite the speed restrictions, had to buy a Continental vehicle made by Benz or Daimler of Germany, by Panhard and Levassor, or de Dion and Bouton, or Bollée or Peugeot, all of France.

But protests against such a ridiculous law gradually increased, until it had to be withdrawn in 1896. Vehicles under three tons were then allowed to travel at a maximum speed of 12 m.p.h., and no red flag was required. This was a really great occasion, and the rejoicing of the motor-car owners spread throughout the country. To celebrate the event in particular, some 40 of the latest car models set off on a London to Brighton run to demonstrate how safe and reliable these vehicles were. It was unfortunate that most of them broke down on the journey.

All honour, however, to these brave pioneers of Motor Car History.

They broke down once a mile; they might have set out under their own power, but they usually had to be pushed or towed home. As their vehicles jolted and jarred along, there was the constant clatter of odd nuts and bolts falling on the road, or the piercing hiss from a punctured tyre, while the slightest hill roused clouds of steam from the radiator.

Even when the engine was going well, the driver jolted along swathed in clouds of dust, and wondering what lay around the next sharp bend. There was always the likelihood of an encounter with stray farm animals or pets, with fatal consequences to the latter. And the claims for compensation were likely to cause bankruptcy. The skinniest fowl, once it had been run over, became a prize breeding specimen; the mangiest, filthiest mongrel, once it had been run over could immediately trace its pedigree in the register at Cruft's. The attitude of the general public, indeed, was usually hostile. The poor car driver was even stoned or attacked by the crowds, and when he broke down, he had to endure the jeering advice of passing horse-drivers, "Use a whip, mister", "Give 'im a nosebag".

The hostility of the police was another adventure in motoring, for the speed limit was strictly enforced. Constables, disguised in plain clothes and hidden in the hedgerows, checked their stop-watches against passing vehicles, and prosecutions were fast and frequent. Thus was the Automobile Association created in 1905, to organise regular patrols on the main roads, and to warn motorists of the police traps ahead. The warning signal was a red disc, or a salute, and motorists thus had ample time in which to slow down before covering the measured distance. The police, however, were not to be cheated of their prey so easily, and the constables therefore moved their traps so that the A.A. patrols would be signalling actually inside the marked area. Thereupon the unfortunate patrolman would be summoned, and fined for obstructing the police in the performance of their duty.

But the A.A. was not to be outwitted so easily, either. Swiftly it advised its members, 'When a patrolman does not salute, stop and ask the reason'. Thus every motorist realised that the patrolman who failed to salute indicated the existence of a speed trap, while of course no court could convict a man who stood at the roadside doing nothing at all.

Motor car engineers
Further to help the motorist came the productions of six great engineers. One was an American, and five were British.

The life of the American, Henry Ford, is not of real concern in a History of England, but his influence upon the story of English motoring is of the greatest importance.

It was in 1908 that Ford produced his Model T car, affectionately to be known ever after as the 'Tin Lizzie', and undoubtedly the most successful of his models. No one ever suggested there was anything beautiful about the Ford Model T, but it was absurdly cheap — cheap to buy, cheap to run, and to the joy of the unskilful driver, cheap to repair . . . At the same time it was most reliable, its high grade steel body and 20 h.p. engine could carry four people, possibly five, and could go almost anywhere. To add to these qualities, its owners were delighted to find how easily it was to drive, and how simple to maintain. Naturally its success was phenomenal. In 1911, the English Ford company was founded in Trafford Park, Manchester and by fourteen years later, some 250,000 vehicles had been built in England alone. Indeed, of all the cars that History has so far known the Ford Model T is among the famous few, and it was this tremendous challenge from Henry Ford that British car engineers had to meet.

It was Dr. Fredrick William Lanchester (1868-1946) who designed and made the first petrol driven car built in England. He was not only an engineer, however, but a scientist as well, and the more he studied existing models the less he liked them. So in 1895, he produced the first Lanchester car, with a single cylinder, air-cooled engine in the centre of the vehicle, and steered by a tiller. But he believed in progress — each new design was intended to remain only until a better one had been found. Thus later improvements saw Lanchester cars with more cylinders, the first pedal accelerator, the first magneto ignition, and with wheel steering, while as early as 1901, the designer introduced a pre-selector gear mechanism, and in 1903 a form of disc brake.

Later in the same year as Dr. Lanchester's first car, Herbert Austin (1866-1941) entered the lists. In 1895, he designed the first of the Wolseley cars, a three-wheeler made of steel tubing, and with a two h.p. engine whose silencers were packed with coke. It had its disadvantages — among them, no reverse gear. The following year, 1896, the second Wolseley car appeared — another three-wheeler but improved to the extent of two cylinders and a three h.p. engine. Not until 1899, was the first four-wheeler produced.

But Austin was a man of wonderful determination, who could not tolerate the lack of enterprise shown by the Wolseley Company, so in 1906, he parted from them and launched his own company at

Longbridge, near Birmingham. From this factory came the first of his famous line of cars — a 25 m.p.h., 30 h.p. model with four speeds, but made somewhat difficult to drive by the fact that the gear lever and the brake were both by the driver's right hand.

It was in 1922, however, that Austin reached his greatest triumph — the Austin Seven, the first small English car. It was cheap, it was easy to maintain and could survive the most appalling neglect. The strong sturdy frame could be relied on to carry four adults at 50 m.p.h., practically anywhere in England. Thus the English public honoured it accordingly. For 15 years the Austin Seven remained in production, with a total output of 300,000 vehicles. The great engineer continued his efforts, however, and by 1946, five years after his death, the millionth Austin car left the works.

Just as determined was William Richard Morris (1877-1963) later Lord Nuffield. He began as a cycle repairer before turning his attention to motor cars. It was a time when the famous American Ford cars were triumphing over all British firms, and the fact that he was a self-taught man did not deter Morris from entering the fight against them. To succeed, he had to make a car cheaper and more reliable than any other of that time, and his first effort was the Morris Oxford of 1912 with four cylinders, 10 h.p., capable of 50 m.p.h. and 50 m.p.g., but its best known feature, perhaps, was the 'Bull-nose' radiator.

By 1914 there were only 132,000 cars of all makes in use in Britain, but the war taught many people to drive military vehicles, so that when the hostilities were over, a real demand for mechanical transport had been created. William Morris saw no reason why the American Fords should be allowed to meet this demand, and in 1919, the Morris Cowley came into production. To make a cheap car, Morris bought individual parts from different car part manufacturers, and by thus using other companies' works did not have to build his own factories to make the items required. All he needed to do was to assemble the various pieces at his Cowley works.

As a result, by 1921, more Morris cars were produced than by any other British firm, but the dynamic English engineer had no intention of resting on his laurels. In 1923, the first M.G. (from the initials of the Morris Garages, Holywell Street, Oxford) was produced — the first cheap sporting car, and capable of 55 m.p.h. Then in 1925, mass production started, rising to a pitch of 53,000 cars a year, and by this time Morris made his own parts, and was selling more cars in England even than Ford. There was no question of the popularity of these familiar 'bull-nose' vehicles; they could all withstand the roughest treatment from incapable drivers.

It is indeed a tremendous change which we now have to face when we consider the next car which England produced. It was in 1904, that J. H. Royce (1863-1933) met the Hon. C. S. Rolls (1887-1910) to enter into a partnership that made history by producing a car that has never been surpassed. The first Rolls Royce was made in 1904, but three years later, in 1907, the classic of motor car glory was reached — the Silver Ghost. It stood there, its great aluminium body beautifully polished till it shone like silver; the great 50 h.p., six cylinder engine drove the car at 53 m.p.h.; but even so, it still moved as silently as a ghost.

There have always been two outstanding qualifications of the Rolls Royce. Firstly, it was expensive — you could buy six of the mass-produced cars for the price of one Silver Ghost. Secondly it was excellent. The design of the Silver Ghost was first class — the product of the most painstaking care and matchless technique. Every part had to be as perfectly made as humanly possible from the most perfect quality of materials available, and neither time, cost, human frailty nor anything else was to prevent the attainment of that ideal. In proof, the first model Ghost was run day and night for 15,000 miles, and an exhaustive independent test immediately afterwards found no undue wear and no fault at all. It was these factors of expense and excellence that have marked the firm ever since. There has never been any doubt that Rolls Royce made the best car in the world.

The Silver Ghost continued in production until 1924 with only minor alterations. So magnificent was its triumph that one firm produced this model only. Then from 1929-1936, the last car that Royce himself designed was produced — the Phantom II. A six-cylinder engine drove the classic craftsmanship of the bodywork at over 80 m.p.h., and even then there was no trace of vibration . . . and an almost complete silence.

Such were the efforts of Ford, Lanchester, Austin, Morris and Rolls Royce, and thanks to them in particular, the English motor car industry developed as the 20th century progressed. But as the 20th century progressed, rising costs and competition had to be faced, and in many cases the answer was to unite rather than to compete. Thus the two great firms of Austin and Morris united as the British Motor Corporation and made Austin, Metropolitan, Morris, M.G., Wolseley, Riley and Princess cars. Another organisation, the Rootes Group, now produces the former individual firm cars of Humber, Hillman, Sunbeam and Singer. Ford, however, have continued to drive along, alone; Ford make only Fords.

Progress in motoring history was still maintained, particularly when, in 1950, the Rover company invented the world's first gas turbine car. This amazing car was driven on the same jet principles as an aircraft. There was no gearbox, so the driver could accelerate without effort from a standing start to a maximum of 152 m.p.h. The vehicle could be driven on petrol or cheap kerosene, or even candle grease, but the rate of consumption would make it too costly to run. Furthermore, the jet engine was too hot for most metals, so the expense of costly alloys was also involved. Nevertheless, a beginning had been made.

The power of cars has increased amazingly. Faster and faster they can travel, with England setting the pace. It is worth while to remember that the first man to travel on land at over 200 m.p.h. was the Englishman, Major H. O. Segrave, in 1927 (203.79 m.p.h.); the first man to travel at over 300 m.p.h. was another Englishman, Sir Malcolm Campbell, in 1935 (301.12 m.p.h.); while yet another Englishman was the first to travel at over 400 m.p.h. — Sir John Cobb, in 1947 (403.13 m.p.h. — though not an official record).

So the petrol-driven vehicles continued to increase in number and variety both for public and for private transport, until millions of them, of every sort, shape and size, packed the roads. In 1959, indeed, four million motor cars, 1½ million motor cycles and one million lorries and goods vehicles controlled the highways.

And as the never-ceasing flow of faster traffic continues, every year over 5,000 people are killed and 300,000 injured by road accidents — thus making a casualty list far greater than in any war in History. Despite this tragic toll, however, no one seems to worry unduly. Many people just shrug their shoulders and remark, 'Oh, well; it won't happen to *me*'. Zebra crossings and underground passages for pedestrians to cross the roads; driving tests, speed limits, signs and traffic lights for drivers; cycle tracks for cyclists; by-pass roads to avoid busy towns, and the first motorway in England — the M.1 from London to Birmingham with double three-lane high-speed traffic, built by 1959 — all have been tried. But the casualties and the 'it won't happen to *me* attitude' still continue.

For the effects of road transport on the lives of the people and on the economy of the country, we must read pages 293 to 295.

Chapter VIII

Air Transport

It was two Americans, the Wright brothers, who were the first to achieve a powered, sustained and controlled flight — for 12 seconds, 120 feet along the ground, to a height of 12 feet and at 10 m.p.h., in 1903. It was a Frenchman, Louis Blériot, who was the first to cross the Channel by air, in 1909. But to two Englishmen, John William Alcock and Arthur Whitten Brown, came the honour of being the first to fly across the Atlantic.

They set off from St. John's in Newfoundland on June 14th, 1919 amid the cheering of a large crowd. Nearly all the first day, they had to fight the sea gales; at night, came thick cloud and mist. When they dived low to avoid the mist, they almost collided with the Atlantic waves; when they climbed high above, they found hail and snow, and Brown had to climb out on the wings to chip ice off the plane. Throughout the whole flight, they did not see a ship, and only towards the end of the journey did the weather improve. They reached the Irish coast at 9.15 a.m., the following day, and landed in an Irish bog which they mistook for a meadow — fortunately without injury. The flight lasted 16¼ hours.

From that time onwards, Britain strove to keep her lead in the air. And well she realised that speed, and still greater speed, was the key to success. So when the international air race for the Schneider Trophy was introduced, British determination put forward its best efforts. In 1927, the Trophy was won at a speed of 281 m.p.h. In 1929, came victory at 328 m.p.h., and when the Trophy was won outright by the third victory in 1931, the speed was 349 m.p.h.

The designer of these Schneider Trophy aircraft was Reginald Joseph Mitchell (1895-1937), who also designed the greatest fighter aircraft of the Second World War—the Spitfire, which roared across the sky at 400 m.p.h. This was an excellent progress for piston-driven aircraft which had to withstand vibration and weight, but the overwhelming demands for speed were still not satisfied. Somehow, a yet greater power had to be discovered to drive aeroplanes faster and still faster across the heavens.

Once again, the answer to these demands came from an Englishman.

It was in 1941, and a fine clear day, when a pilot of a patrolling fighter plane on duty over southern England, suddenly observed a strange aircraft in the sky. This was, of course, during the Second World War, so he altered altitude and approached cautiously. The small monoplane ahead flew serenely on, the yellow underside and the green and brown fuselage glinting in the light. The R.A.F. markings, too, were conspicuous on the wings. But there was a strange sinister appearance about the aircraft, and not least the eerie whine which it uttered. The fighter pilot circled slowly and uneasily, his hand on the machine gun control. Then the reason for the strangeness of the other plane dawned upon him — that aircraft had no propeller! Even as the realisation came, the other pilot waved cheerfully, suddenly increased speed, and disappeared into the distance.

Thus it was in 1941, eleven years after he had made the designs, that Frank Whittle produced in an aircraft the first successful gas turbine (or turbo-jet) engine — one of the greatest inventions in the history of flight. Indeed, one of its drawbacks was that it worked best only at high speeds. However, if a lower speed was required, the turbo-jet engine could be fitted with a propeller (and was thus known as a turbo-prop).

After all this, it was only fitting that the first jet airliner in the world, the 'Comet', which was produced in 1949, should be British, and the world's first turbo-prop airliner, the Vickers Viscount, built in 1948, was also British.

Having thus improved the engine, British engineers tried to improve the construction of aircraft. It was J. W. Dunne who, as early as 1906, designed the swept-back wings and no-tail aeroplane which later enabled British pilots to pierce the sound barrier — that is to say, to reach a speed faster than sound — about 760 m.p.h. From then onwards, the progress continued till in 1956 the Englishman, Peter Twiss, in a Fairey Delta II, established a new world air speed record of 1,132 m.p.h. — a speed faster than the sun moves round the Equator. (Far faster records have subsequently been achieved by the Americans.)

Progress has indeed moved swiftly since Wilbur and Orville Wright rose for a few seconds at Kitty Hawk in America in 1903. Now, every 20 seconds of the day, a plane begins its journey over the waters of the Atlantic Ocean — vast metal monsters of 200 tons, rising steadily above the clouds. Distance is no object to them, nor is time. From the great airports of today, no place in the world is over 24 hours' travelling time away. Even from London to Australia, it is but some 20 hours.

To assist this development of air transport, the air services of the nation were taken over by the Government (i.e. 'nationalised') in 1946, and divided into three organisations — B.O.A.C. (British Overseas Airways Corporation), B.E.A. (British European Airways) and British South American Airways.

The development of passenger comfort has kept pace with other progress. In the 1920's, when air travel began to be organised, the brave passenger collected his heavy leather jacket, his flying helmet, goggles and boots at the airport, and then staggered determinedly through the mud to the aircraft. The pilot, having wetted his finger and held it in the air to determine the direction of the wind, also climbed aboard. The plane jolted along the runway, and lurched into the air. Steadily it crossed the great city of London, blowing the grime from the dome of St. Paul's with the draught from the propellers, and then turning towards the country beyond.

The early part of the flight consisted of watching the road traffic beneath, and of then descending for up to a score of forced landings in local fields. The journey from London to Paris thus required from a few hours to three days, and the passenger arrived covered in sickness and bruises.

Now, reclining comfortably in padded seats, in an air conditioned, air pressurized cabin, dining on a four-course meal, with a bar and toilets available, the air traveller from London to Paris covers the 250 miles in an hour and a half.

But speed and distance were only two aspects of modern flight. Another line of development was the helicopter, which compensated for its lack of speed by its manoeuvrability. For take-off or landing, the latest models require a platform only 40 feet square, and like a dragonfly, can move upwards, downwards, backwards, forwards and sideways.

The designers, however, were still not satisfied. Vertical take-off had to be made swifter and still more efficient. Thus one morning in 1954, there rose from the testing ground of the Rolls Royce Aircraft Company, a curious machine of struts and wires and wheels, which could not possibly be given any other name but the 'Flying Bedstead'. It was only an experimental machine, but it rose straight up into the air by means of two downward thrusting jets, and by that method future aircraft could operate. With the advantage of vertical take-off and descent, large airliners could be used without the need for long runways.

The next stage of progress was to combine the two previous inventions — the helicopter and the turbo-prop. The result was the Fairey Rotodyne, the first of its type, and made in England in 1957. Helicopter blades enabled the machine to take off vertically, and it could then move forward by two turbo-prop engines at a speed of 200 m.p.h. It was thus ideal for short journeys such as between cities, and where there was only a small area available for landing.

Yet another development, and which again England was the first to produce, was the Hovercraft. Invented in 1959 by Christopher Sydney Cockerell, this four ton craft was lifted by means of air sucked in through the funnel, and passed out with tremendous force through narrow jets at the base of the machine. Side jets drove the hovercraft backwards or forwards, and it could achieve a speed of 25 knots.

Chapter IX

Communications

There were other means of communication, and which were cheaper and even swifter, than sea, rail, road or even air transport. So let us now consider (a) the post, (b) the telegraph, telephone and wireless, and (c) television.

THE POST

By the 18th century, the postal system was certainly in drastic need of reform. As far back as the 16th century, two posts had been established — the 'Packet Post' for Government despatches, and the 'Through Post' for private letters. In the case of the private mail, this was taken only along certain routes, and letters addressed to anywhere else had to be collected from the nearest town on those routes. Nor were there any local posts, except in London. Thus here was the first need for improvement, and between 1720-64, Ralph Allen, the person in charge of the Post, developed a series of cross-posts, i.e. direct from town to town instead of via London, until nearly all the country was thus covered.

But the post-boys still dawdled along on their journeys. The speed at which they travelled, indeed, about three to four m.p.h., had not increased for a period of 200 years or more. Sometimes their speed was even slower, as they paused to search through the mailbags to see if there was anything worth stealing. Sometimes they would be held up by the highwaymen, and robbed of all the valuables they were carrying, generally by a mutual arrangement in which they each took a share of the profits.

Clearly, therefore, improvement had to be made not only in the area covered by the posts, but also in the method of postal delivery. So in 1784, the first of the Royal Mail coaches, drawn by four swift horses, sped away with its despatches — and the person responsible for this new development was the theatre proprietor, John Palmer. For years he had fought against the old-fashioned attitude and the slow unsatisfactory methods of the Post Office, and with equal determination the Postmaster General and his officials fought back against the introduction of anything new. Fortunately, however, Palmer found an ally — the Prime Minister, William Pitt — and to the angry horror of the Post Office authorities, his scheme to deliver mail by coach was put into effect.

It was a sight worth seeing. From Bristol to London, the brilliantly-hued maroon and black coach swayed over the roads at an average speed of eight to nine m.p.h. — twice as fast as the post-boys. The guard wore a scarlet uniform with blue lapels, and further adorned with white ruffles in 1793. But he was a man, not only of dress, however, but also of character, for it was his duty to deliver the mail. If the coach stuck, he unhitched the horses and rode; if it was impossible to drive or ride, he took the mail on foot. If halted by highwaymen, he fought it out with the firearms he carried, and many a bag of mail arrived bespattered with the blood of the guard who had died to defend its delivery.

The third defect of the postal system in the 18th and 19th centuries was the organisation, for here, indeed, we had a system as full of unnecessary labour and abuse as it could possibly be. To prove this, let us trace the travel history of a single typical letter.

First of all, the letter was taken to a Post Office. Here it was very carefully examined by the clerk. If there was a single sheet, the clerk noted it, and put the charge on the letter (a charge varying from 1p. for eight miles to 5p. for 300 miles, and which was paid by the receiver, not the sender). If there were two sheets, the clerk noted it, and put double the charge on the letter. If there were three sheets the clerk noted it, and put treble the charge on the letter. If there was anything valuable in the letter, the clerk noted it, took it out, and put the letter on the fire. All the letters were then sorted and a letter bill made out for each town, recording each letter addressed there. The mail was then sent to the Head Office, where it was unbundled and checked. Other letters for the same town were added, and the mail bags were then placed in the coach.

When the mail coach arrived at its destination, the postmaster there checked the letters and the amounts which he had to collect. He then distributed the letters to the mail carriers, who also checked them and the amounts they had to collect. The letters were delivered — sometimes after several attempts because the receiver was not at home — the money collected from the receiver, and taken to the Postmaster, who checked the various amounts and sent the total back to Head-quarters.

This was all a very complicated procedure, but we have still not learnt the full pantomime of the 19th century postal system. By a special privilege, Members of Parliament were allowed to have a free postal delivery if they signed their names on the envelope or cover; this was called 'Franking'. Naturally such an opportunity was too good to be neglected, and thus, on one October day alone in the year 1794, a thousand franked letters passed through a Post Office. There was one M.P. who was also director of a firm, and he, therefore, franked all the firm's correspondence. Not only were letters franked, but also other articles which it was desired to send, including at various times, such items as fifteen pairs of hounds, two maid servants, a cow, and a cab-load of Blue Books (Government publications).

Those who were unable to have their letters franked, avoided paying the high postage charges by arranging for private delivery. Thus four-fifths of the letters which left Manchester never went through the Post Office. Alternatively, a coded message was put on the outside of the envelope, so that the receiver had only to say 'Are you sure this letter's for me? Can I see the address?' The Postman would hand it over, whereupon the receiver cast a quick glance at the code hidden in the address, interpreted it, and handed back the letter with a sigh, 'Ah, well, I cannot afford to pay all this postage. You'll have to take the letter back, that's all. Good day.'

Is it any wonder that for twenty years the income of the Post Office did not increase?

To the rescue came Rowland Hill (1795-1879), a schoolmaster, and later to become Secretary to the Post Office. Already in 1830, the Liverpool to Manchester railway had begun to carry mail, and in 1838, Hill invented the first Travelling Post Office — a converted horse box for use on the Grand Junction Line from Warrington to Birmingham, so that letters could be sorted while the train travelled.

But Rowland Hill's peak of fame was to occur in 1840, when on January 10th he successfully introduced the penny post for all half-ounce letters no matter to where the letters were sent. At the same time, franking was abolished.

Then, on May 1st the same year, he had issued the first adhesive postage stamp in the world — the famous Penny Black — designed by the artist William Wyon, and printed by Messrs. Perkins, Bacon and Petch. It has been considered that the classic beauty of this stamp has never been surpassed. There were no perforations, so the stamps had to be separated by cutting. Not until 1848 did Henry Archer invent

Penny Black

a perforating machine. From then onwards, more and different stamps were printed — the 2d. blue in 1840, the 1d. red in 1841, the ½d. lake rose in 1870 when the Post Office issued the first postcards (*free*) — and the process continued until in the year 1885, 114 tons of stamps were issued.

The work of the Post Office was further increased when the Parcel Post was introduced in 1883. On the financial side, the Post Office Savings Bank was established in 1861, and in 1881 the first postal orders were issued.

Nowadays, the Post Office has become a vast and important organisation which not only issues stamps, but also issues postal orders and money orders, despatches letters, parcels and telegrams, pays pensions and family allowances, has its own Savings Bank, and issues licences (gun, dog, car, radio and television).

THE TELEGRAPH, TELEPHONE AND WIRELESS

Now let us consider the swiftest means of communication — the electric telegraph, the telephone and the wireless.

In 1729, the Englishman, Stephen Gray, discovered that an electric current could be sent along a wire. Then, over a century later, in 1837, William Cooke and Charles Wheatstone sent electric currents along five wires so that they moved five needles over a disc at the far end. The different positions of the five needles as they moved pointed to letters of the alphabet painted on the disc, so that words and messages could thus be sent.

A better method, however, was devised in 1838. The American, Samuel Morse, invented a system whereby an electric current caused a pencil at the receiving end to mark dots and dashes on a sheet of paper on a revolving drum. These dots and dashes represented letters, e.g. three dots the letter 'S', three dashes — 'O', two dots and a dash — 'U'. From then onwards, the success of the telegraph was assured, and in 1870 the Government bought out all private telegraph companies, and placed the whole system under the control of the Post Office.

The telephone system, invented by Graham Bell in America in 1876, was likewise taken over by the Post Office, except in Hull.

But if the electric telegraph could work over land, why should it not be able to cross the sea as well? In 1851, a cable was finally laid from Dover to Calais, and fifteen years later another cable crossed the Atlantic. Once the technical difficulties of laying these deep-sea cables had been overcome, England was rapidly linked to the rest of the world. In 1870, there was a cable from London to Bombay, and four years later, South America was similarly united to Europe. By 1880 indeed, it was possible to communicate with most areas of the globe, save such isolated places as the islands of the Pacific, some parts of the Dutch East Indies and the interior of China.

But the telegraphic apparatus — the cables and the wires — was costly, and also very slow. A long message took a very long time indeed to be transmitted from one end of the line to the other. Each letter had to be well on its way before the next one could be sent out. In 1866, when the first trans-Atlantic cable was laid, Queen Victoria was invited to send the first telegram. The cable company, however, received a real shock when it was discovered that the Queen's ninety-nine words of greeting required 16¼ hours to send. So we must now turn to a cheaper, swifter, and even more important invention which brought still closer the wide-scattered world settlements of mankind. This was wireless.

The winter gale raged savagely across the bleak and inhospitable coasts of Newfoundland. Rugged rocks, storm-lashed seas and thunderous heavens completed a landscape which had once been referred to as 'the land that God gave Cain'. High on the exposed cliffs near the town of St. John's, three men were trying desperately to fly a kite. To anyone who might have been watching, a more ridiculous and senseless activity could hardly have been imagined. But the three men struggled on to fly the kite, struggling desperately and determinedly, desperately and determinedly . . . making History.

Their leader was an Italian who had come to live in England, and whose name was Guglielmo Marconi (1874-1937). Passionately interested in sending messages through space, he had already transmitted signals from Salisbury to Bath in 1897, then across the Bristol Channel the same year, and across the English Channel in 1899 — the first international wireless message.

Now, however, he was attempting a feat to dwarf all these — the spanning of the Atlantic by wireless. A transmitting station had been established at Poldhu in Cornwall, and Marconi then sailed to Newfoundland, to the exposed cliffs, the bitter cold, and the gales. Here he and his two companions struggled on. After two days they managed to anchor a kite so that it flew steadily. Four hundred foot of wire attached the kite to a mast, and from the mast another wire led to a rough shack with a receiving set. At 11.30 a.m. on December 12th, 1901, a faint, but understandable buzz, came through the receiver — three sounds — the letter 'S' in Morse, repeated over and over again. It was the agreed signal sent out from Cornwall in England, 2,170 miles away.

Marconi's efforts, however, were to be helped by another invention.

Had you lived in Portland Street in London in the year 1878, you might have seen, in the hours of darkness, a stealthy figure creeping from doorway to doorway. A crook? A burglar? An escaped criminal? No. It was just Professor David Edward Hughes (1831-1900) receiving wireless signals a few hundred yards from his home. To do so he used his new invention — the microphone — a sensitive instrument packed with charcoal behind a thin diaphragm. When the sound-waves reached the diaphragm, it vibrated, and these vibrations were then increased in volume by the charcoal so that the sound-waves could be heard more clearly. Hughes showed his device to his friends, and even to the President of the Royal Society, but his effort was received with laughter. So he ended his experiments, and turned his attention elsewhere. Thus it was not until 1892 that Sir William Crookes, a great scientist who had once joined in the laughter, then realised the truth, and at once paid to David Edward Hughes the honour that he had earned. For now the power of radio telegraph messages could be increased.

From radio-telegraphy came the next stage — radio-telephony.

In 1904, Professor Ambrose Fleming invented the thermionic valve — a vacuum tube with two electrodes, one heated, one cold — and by this means human speech could be sent out on radio-waves and be heard at the receiving end. In 1906, the American, Lee Forest, added a perforated metal plate between the anode and the cathode to make this weak current of speech much stronger, so the words could be heard clearly. (Any radio textbook will explain this more fully.) As a result of these inventions, there commenced at Chelmsford in 1920 a broadcasting service operating for half-an-hour a week, and which developed in 1922 into the present London British Broadcasting

Corporation (B.B.C.) with a daily 24-hour transmission. For though radio-telegraphy, whereby nation could send messages to nation, e.g. by Morse, had been a wonderful invention, radio-telephony, whereby nation could actually speak unto nation, was even more wonderful.

In 1948, a tremendous development occurred when valves were replaced by transistors. A transistor is a wire made of a metal containing impurities, with the result that it vastly increases the power of a radio signal travelling along it. It is very much smaller indeed than a valve or a vacuum tube, as well as lighter, with a longer life and using less power. Thus transmitters and receivers could also become much smaller — even indeed, no larger than a bean. A tiny transmitter could be swallowed by a patient, and send a stomach report to the listening doctor who therefore did not need to operate to discover what was wrong.

TELEVISION

But the history of scientific achievement was by no means exhausted. Radio-telegraphy, whereby nation could send messages to nation, e.g. by Morse, had been a wonderful invention; radio-telephony, whereby nation could speak to nation, was an even more wonderful invention; but there was to be yet a third stage of progress. For in 1924, John Logie Baird invented television, whereby nation could actually look at nation.

John Logie Baird (1888-1946) was a Scotsman, and it is no doubt fair to say that only a Scotsman imbued with all the dour determination of his race, could have succeeded amid the circumstances of his experiments. For here was a man not in the full health of life, working in a well-equipped up-to-date laboratory. Instead, he was a sick man, working in a Hastings attic, using tea-chests, biscuit-tins, pieces of cardboard, old motor engines from scrap heaps, odd spectacle lenses, all held together by pieces of string, glue, pins and sealing-wax, and spread out on an old washstand. It was with this equipment that, in 1924, Baird saw on his receiving screen a flickering, indistinct, but definitely recognisable reproduction of the Maltese Cross which had been sent from a few yards away — the first television picture.

Success spurred him on. He improved his pictures so that he had not only black and white, but half-tones, and in 1925 he achieved radio-television as well (picture and sound combined). Then he established a television studio at Long Acre in London in 1927, from where, in the following year, he was the first to send pictures across the

Atlantic. In 1928 his experimental work produced colour television. Hence he reached the height of his fame for, from 1929-1935, the B.B.C. used his systems for its television programmes. The sickly, poverty-stricken Scotsman had triumphed.

And at the same moment he faced defeat. For Baird used mechanical devices — motors and revolving discs — and a receiving instrument far more efficient than these had been discovered — the cathode ray tube. It was this instrument of television which replaced Baird's in 1936.

During the war, from 1939-1945, television programmes ceased, but when the hostilities were over this powerful instrument of education and entertainment began to dominate the life of the nation, and far beyond throughout the world. New ideas, new techniques and fresh inventions were developed; in 1954 an Independent Television Authority was set up, obtaining its income from advertising programmes.

Amid all these developments and interest, the name of John Logie Baird was forgotten — for such is fame. It was with a real bitter sadness that his widow transferred his mortal remains back to his native Scotland, for she felt he had no adequate honour in the country to which he had given so much.

Chapter X

Free Trade

In this chapter, we are going to trace the development of Free Trade, so first of all let us explain what is meant by 'Free Trade'.

If the Government of a country wish to protect their manufacturers and farmers from cheap foreign competition, they put a duty (or tax) on foreign imports, or stop foreign imports altogether. This action is called 'Protection', and was carried out in England from the 15th century until the Industrial Revolution.

If, however, a Government allows foreign imports to enter without paying any duty at all (or only a very small duty merely in order to gain money — revenue), then this policy is called 'Free Trade'.

The Industrial Revolution caused a great extension of trade between 1750 and 1834. Powerful steam-driven machines and sweated human labour produced more goods more quickly and more cheaply than at any previous time in English history. But there was still one obstacle to the onward march of progress — the heavy taxation on imports and exports. Raw materials coming into this country had to pay tax, and goods leaving the country were also taxed. Admittedly, the Government got money, but it meant that the price of articles increased, so that many of those who wanted to buy could not do so, while the manufacturer was equally dissatisfied because he lost his sales.

If we had no such taxes, i.e. Free Trade, we could import cheap food for our increasing population, and cheap raw materials for our factories. If we had Free Trade, we could also export cheaply the goods made by our Industrial Revolution.

So what could be done about these import and export taxes?

The answer to the problem, of course, was simple. Smuggling. The fast-moving vessels of the smugglers would meet incoming ships in the Channel, swiftly the chests and casks would be transferred, and the illegal cargo run ashore on to a deserted beach, or into dark caves when the tide was high. The goods were then carried into other caves, or into the cellars of private houses, or even into the church, for the local parson was probably a member of the gang.

And the word 'gang' itself was not to be used lightly. In the 18th century it often indicated an organisation both powerful and ruthless, until it achieved the situation where armed bands of 50 to 100 men loaded waggons and pack-horses on the open beach in broad daylight without interference. The weak, under-manned force of Customs officials, was powerless to stop them. As far as ruthlessness was concerned, there was the instance of a cargo of tea captured by the Customs officials in 1748 and taken to Poole Customs House. Kingsmill, the leader of the Hawkhurst Gang, at once organised a night attack upon the Customs House and recovered the cargo. Then, to prevent two witnesses of the attack from giving evidence against him, he had one flogged to death, while the other was flogged, had his nose and face slashed, and was then forced to walk into a well with a noose around his neck to hang himself.

Sussex was the particular stronghold of the smugglers, but the whole length of the South coast and the Fenlands also contributed towards an occupation in which as many as 40,000 people found employment. On a moonlight night, anyone could hear the sound of

> Four and twenty ponies trotting in the dark
> With brandy for the parson and baccy for the clerk.

Thus two-thirds of the tea, half the brandy and half the consignments of silk gloves brought into England never went through the Customs houses.

It was quite obvious that the surest way to end this smuggling was to make it unprofitable by reducing or removing the trade duties, or in other words, to allow Free Trade. This idea was strongly supported by Adam Smith (1723-90), a Glasgow Professor, in his book *The Wealth of Nations* in 1776 — a book that was almost worshipped by manufacturers, and had an equally strong influence upon the leading Ministers of the time. (For further details about Adam Smith, and the *Wealth of Nations*, see pages 140 to 141.)

A start towards Free Trade was made by William Pitt, the Prime Minister in 1783, who simplified the list of duties so that instead of a chaotic mass of regulations which even the Customs officials found almost impossible to understand, there was a straightforward, simple list of the amounts to be paid on different items. He also arranged greater free trade with France by the Eden Treaty 1786, so-named after the chief English negotiator.

The next step was by William Huskisson, President of the Board of Trade, 1823-27. He (i) reduced the duties on many imported raw materials; (ii) goods from our colonies paid less duty than similar goods from foreign countries, so this helped our overseas possessions; (iii) he permitted artisans to emigrate and machinery to be sent abroad; (iv) and by the Reciprocity Act, the Government made trade treaties with other nations (except with our trade rivals, Holland) on the same terms as they made with us. Finally, (v) the Navigation Acts (see later) were less strictly enforced.

The work was continued in 1842 and 1845 by Sir Robert Peel, the Prime Minister, who (i) reduced the import duties on 750 out of 1,200 manufactured goods; (ii) and then placed an import tax on manufactured goods of 20 per cent maximum (i.e. the tax was not to exceed 20 per cent of the worth of the goods), on semi-manufactured goods 12 per cent maximum, and on raw materials five per cent maximum. By 1846 the import of all raw materials, except timber and tallow, was allowed free; and all exports were also allowed free. The money thus lost to the Government was recovered by means of Income Tax, which was re-introduced in 1842. (It had first been introduced in 1798-1816 to pay for the French and Napoleonic Wars.)

There was still, however, one great obstacle to any further progress in Free Trade — the Corn Laws — and it seemed that these at least were too firmly established to be removed. After the Napoleonic Wars had ended in 1815, a flood of foreign corn had entered this country, so the land-owning Members of Parliament passed the Corn Laws to check such entry by imposing a duty. For if foreign corn was not allowed in, or if it was heavily taxed, there would be no competition with English corn and these landowners would thus obtain a good price for their own crops.

But there were others who realised that this was sheer selfishness. The Corn Laws had been passed for the land-owning M.P.s' benefit only. On the other hand, if foreign corn was not taxed when it came into England, it would mean cheaper bread to help the poor and to benefit the manufacturer (since he could pay less wages), and would also enable English ships to return with a cargo of foreign corn instead of empty.

So the manufacturers and traders opposed the landowners, and under the leadership of Richard Cobden and John Bright, the Anti-Corn Law League was founded in 1839. Richard Cobden (1804-65) was the Member of Parliament for Stockport, near Manchester, and a wonderful speaker; John Bright (1811-89) was a Quaker cotton manufacturer from Rochdale and also a Member of Parliament for Durham. By pamphlets, petitions, meetings and Parliamentary debates, these two men fought for eight bitter years against the selfishness of the landowners. 'I lived' said Bright, 'in public meetings'.

Famine settled the matter. In 1845 the terrible plague of potato rot attacked the chief food of the Irish people, and in 1846, over ¾ million Irish peasants died of starvation. Cheap corn from abroad was the only remedy, so in 1846 Peel repealed the Corn Laws.

Between 1853-60, William Gladstone, Chancellor of the Exchequer, completed the work of Huskisson and Peel by removing nearly all duties (except small amounts). Also in 1854 the Navigation Acts of 1651, which had insisted on the use of English ships for trade to, from and around England, or else the use of the ships of the country which sent the goods, were finally repealed.

Thus England became a free trade country, with the result that manufacturers could pay less wages (since their employees' food was cheaper). Cheaper goods meant more sales, especially abroad, and English shipping developed until this small island became the greatest trading nation in the world.

Disadvantages of Free Trade

At the same time, however, there were some people who realised the dangers of free trade. English agriculture was now faced with foreign competition, and the English farmer was utterly unable to produce corn as cheaply as the flood of foreign imports from Russia, America and Canada, so he turned to sheep-farming which needed less labour, and the unemployed agricultural workers had to drift to the already overcrowded towns. Worse still, it meant that England was not supplying sufficient food for her own needs. Instead, she had become dependent upon foreign imports, and if war broke out, these foreign imports might be stopped.

Then later on, as the 19th century continued, industry was similarly affected. America and Germany, aided by cheap iron ore in their own countries, and Japan, aided by cheap labour, began to develop their own resources with new methods, and poured an avalanche of their goods into this country. Thus English manufacturers had to face a very serious competition which threatened to ruin them.

Also, from 1899-1902, there was the cost of the Boer War which had to be met by heavy taxation, and many people felt that these taxes could be reduced by obtaining money from import duties instead.

At the time of the Boer War, the Colonial Secretary was Joseph Chamberlain. During his period of office from 1895-1903, he strove to strengthen and unite the great British Empire in which he so passionately believed.

One of his ideas was to allow Empire goods to enter this country in preference to the vast quantities of foreign produce (i.e. Imperial Preference). To do this, however, would mean imposing duties — a high duty on foreign goods and a lower duty on Empire goods — so ending Free Trade. For three years, 1903-6, Chamberlain urged these views. Unfortunately, the Empire sent us mainly food, and therefore the imposition of any duties, however low, would cause the price of food to rise — a very serious matter. For this reason, many of Chamberlain's own party (the Conservatives) and the nation as a whole opposed him. Defeated, he left politics in 1906, but the influence of his beliefs remained.

Thus the ideas of Free Trade began to appear of less benefit, so in 1915 import taxes were placed on certain goods — motor cars, clocks, watches, etc. — and from then onwards Britain reimposed still more duties, until we ceased to be a Free Trade country by the 1931-32 Import Duties Act.

Chapter XI

The Results of
the Industrial Revolution

The immediate result of the Industrial Revolution was to enable England to withstand the Napoleonic Wars. In a determined and desperate attempt to subdue the only country of importance in Europe which defied him, the French Emperor Napoleon I had passed the Decrees of Berlin in 1806 and the Decrees of Milan in 1807, forbidding the Continent to have any trade whatsoever with England. But the Continent of Europe desired the English goods which the Industrial Revolution provided, and smuggling caused the laws to have little effect. Thus, after a bitter twelve year struggle from 1803-15, we finally emerged victorious over France with our trade still far from crippled.

The Industrial Revolution, however, had results far more important than the winning of the Napoleonic Wars.

Economic results of the Industrial Revolution

First of all, the Revolution marked a turning point in English economic history — the time when this country changed from agriculture to industry. This fact must be most carefully remembered, for thenceforward the power and happiness of our country have depended upon our manufactures.

Then again, in industry itself, the Revolution marked three great changes:

Firstly. There was the change from the Domestic to the Capitalist or Factory System. Previously, the worker had been able to obtain a spinning wheel or a loom quite cheaply, and then operate them in his own home (the Domestic System). But this practice was no longer possible, for the new machines which had been invented were so expensive that capital was needed to purchase them. Also, these new machines could not suitably be used in a cottage, so factories had to be built to accommodate them. (Hence the Capitalist or Factory System.)

Secondly. English industry changed from wool to cotton manufacture. This was a most important change because for centuries our prosperity had depended upon the wool trade. Cotton supplies (from the Levant and the West Indies) had been uncertain, and the woollen manufacturers had used their influence to prevent the import or use of printed cotton goods in this country. In any event, cotton was so weak that linen had been used to strengthen the material.

But now, in the latter part of the 18th century, there came a plentiful supply of cheap cotton from the southern United States and Egypt, while the new machinery which we have described in Chapter III, produced a stronger thread so that linen was no longer needed for the warp (the long threads). At this same time the woollen industry was compelled to rely on the limited home supplies of raw materials, since only a little came from abroad, and, moreover, the woollen industry had been established so long that the owners resisted any change from the old methods to the new methods. As, they argued, we have become so wealthy under the old methods, why change to the new and untried?

It was not until after 1830 that the sheep runs of Australia and New Zealand increased our wool supplies, and the woollen firms began to realise the value of the new machinery, but by that time it was too late. The wealth of England had by then become dependent upon cotton. It was a considerable wealth too, for the vastly increased production of manufactured goods enabled British trade to expand to all parts of the globe, and to gain a lead over all industrial rivals. For 25 years, indeed, from 1850-75, this country was 'the workshop of the world'. You can read the account on pages 54 to 55.

Thirdly. Not only did cotton become a new industry, but also coal. Coal was now required for warmth, for steam power in industry and transport, as well as to smelt iron. Thus, whereas in 1750 only about five million tons were mined in England, by 1830 the amount was twenty-three million tons. The story of this development is fully explained on pages 36 to 41.

So much, then, for the economic consequences of the Industrial Revolution.

Social results of the Industrial Revolution

Now let us consider another aspect of the matter — the social effects. How did the new machinery and conditions affect the lives of human beings?

Socially, the results of the Industrial Revolution were also extremely important, for they altered the face and the life of England. An amazing and an enduring change passed over the surface of our country, and what a difference it made!

In the first instance, no longer was wealth to be sought upon the rich pastures and the rolling downs of the south; instead prosperity now lay amid the fast-flowing mountain streams whose soft water did not fur up the engine boilers, amid the damp cotton climate, and amid the coalfields — all of them to be found in the north.

Previously, Norwich had been the centre of worsted manufacture, with the most important woollen centres in the West Country (Gloucestershire, Wiltshire, Somerset and Devon), and cheaper cloths being produced in the West Riding of Yorkshire. But now industry migrated to the north in full force, and as it did so it moved in a grim and hideous way. The Midlands became the Black Country, with chimneys belching dense, filthy smoke into the blue sky, and the beautiful countryside covered with ugly slag heaps. The bleak moorland and lonely vales of Lancashire and Yorkshire were filled with manufacturing towns growing larger and even larger till it seemed there could be no end to their expansion. Thus Manchester, whose population in 1700 was only 8,000, had swollen to 84,000 by 1800; and in that same period, 1700-1800, Liverpool had increased from 5,000 to 77,000. To express the situation in a different way, we could state that in 1750, eight out of every ten people lived in the countryside; in 1850 only five out of every ten.

This urban development was inevitable. Once a factory had been established it was necessary to have homes for those who were employed there. For hundreds and even thousands of work people, accommodation had to be found somewhere. So, like an ugly fungus growth across the green fields surrounding the factory, there spread the grim brick houses, the rough shacks, and the rude hovels of the workers. Naturally, everyone wanted to live as close to their work as possible, to avoid the time and trouble of walking a great distance, so the rows of houses were built back-to-back as closely as could possibly be. No organisation or planning restrained the chaos that resulted, and as more and more workers arrived, the overcrowding reached an appalling and unbelievable state.

To mention but one example, the population of Nottingham doubled between 1800-50, but the town did not increase in size. You have all seen a running-track, haven't you? And you have all seen the 220 yards course, no doubt? Now try to fix in your mind the length of that

220 yards track, that is to say, try to imagine a stretch of ground 220 yards long. Now try to imagine another stretch of ground also 220 yards long, but at right-angles to the first, and then complete the figure so that you have a square 220 yards by 220 yards. Fix that picture firmly in your imagination. Keep it there. You wouldn't think, would you — you wouldn't think that in that area of ground, 220 yards long by 220 yards broad, *over* 4,000 *people* could live.

But they did in Nottingham.

A 'typical town' of the Industrial Revolution was thus the nearest approach to an earthly purgatory that one could conceive. If you dare, indeed, let us visit one of these towns . . . to see what it was really like . . . to enter the inmost depths of its slums . . . and to learn about the people who lived there. You will never forget this visit. Never. However long you live . . .

The town itself was entered by a number of narrow, filthy streets, which sub-divided into vile-smelling lanes and dark back-alleys. Along these passages ran the drains — open gullies carrying their filth to a river so black and polluted that no fish could live there.

The grim, smoke-blackened houses on either side were built round courts — a court being an open, flagged space surrounded by the tall buildings, and containing, perhaps, a single lavatory to serve 150 people (in one part of Manchester there were 33 lavatories for 7,000 people — an average of one lavatory for 212 persons). This lavatory was a rough seat over a dung heap or cesspit, and as the heap gradually grew larger it overflowed, oozed over the court, down the passage, and into the street. Thus, in some cities the heaps of sewage were piled up to a total of 35,000 tons.

Here and there on the roadside you might notice a tap, each tap serving about three streets and operating only at certain hours on certain days of the week. In Westminster, London, one tap served sixteen houses and on a Sunday operated for only five minutes. As there was no other water supply either for drinking or washing, to quench the thirst was difficult and personal cleanliness was impossible.

If such were the terrible conditions outside the houses, it could hardly be expected that there would be anything better inside the homes. Indeed, the conditions inside were often worse. Behind the cracked and broken door panels, behind the dirty windows tight-closed against the outside stench from the streets, it was not uncommon to find three families living in a single room. Thus in parts of Manchester in the 18th century there was an average of ten persons per room. In Sunderland there were instances of as many as 150 people in a house, sleeping five in a bed. Most of these rooms, be it remembered, were cellars — damp, airless, filthy beyond description, and crowded with pigs, fowls and horses, as well as human beings. The grimness of the squalor exceeded all limits. The stench of unwashed bodies and the vile aroma from lack of sanitation caused a sickening, suffocating atmosphere to hang heavy about the room. Across the damp ceiling the mosses and lichens spread; lice could be scraped in handfuls off the walls. Such was the place which some people called 'home'.

The whole situation is brought into numerical horror by the fact that in 1840, in Liverpool alone, 40,000 people lived in cellars and 86,000 in courts.

The imagination becomes powerless to consider life under such conditions. But is it to be wondered, therefore, that an unhealthy vapour hung over the whole industrial slum, and could be seen from the distant hills like a darkish cloud above the city.

Others who were *not so fortunate* as to live in houses, occupied rough shacks and hovels where they existed in the most primitive of conditions, where for a table there was a box, and a chair was a piece of stone. So grave was the poverty of such people that a day's meals consisted of oatmeal for breakfast, flour and water for dinner, and oatmeal for tea. Nettles, rotten apples and swedes were also eaten to check the pangs of hunger, while the most desperate cases had to be content with one meal per day, or meals only on alternate days. Under such circumstances three out of every four children born, died before the age of five, and the survivor could look forward to another 35 years before death released him from his suffering. The body was then thrust into a grave packed with a dozen or more others, in a cemetery so crowded that bones could be seen on the surface of the ground.

From these terrible home conditions in slums, courts, cellars and hovels, the worker then set out to his work. The cotton factory was a huge building seven storeys high. The windows were closed and the air stifling and thick with cotton dust, not to mention the stench from the open lavatory buckets along the walls. In some rooms the atmosphere was so drenched with steam that the operators were wet through — conditions which led to both rheumatism and consumption — the one crippling, the other killing.

In circumstances such as these the wretched employee toiled for $12\frac{1}{2}$ to 14 hours per day, from Monday to Saturday, with four hours on Sunday, and no holidays except Good Friday and Christmas Day.

No longer was he his own master. Gone was his old freedom to work as and when he wished in his own home. Instead, he was the slave of a machine whose wheels determined his activity, and where a bell ordered him when to start and when to stop. He must give all his attention to those whirling wheels and revolving bands — yes, all his attention indeed, for he was fined if he even whistled at his work. So his health was ruined, his body deformed, and his spirit crushed.

And all the while he was full of the fear of unemployment, for there were relatively few jobs and many applicants, especially since women and children could also undertake the tasks, or cheaper Irish labour could be used. In any event, the hatred between the very rich factory owners and the very poor workers caused strikes, and there was further unemployment when trade was bad and the factories closed down for a while. Above all, it must be realised that the worker was utterly at the mercy of the employer who owned both the materials and the machines upon which the employee depended for his work.

Or perhaps the worker was employed in the coal mines. Before the Industrial Revolution, coal had been mined on or near the surface ('open-cast mining'), but the new increased demand now meant deeper working. Here, explosive gas was encountered, there was the threat of collapsing walls and the menace of flooding — in fact, mining accidents were so common that before 1815 inquests were not usually held. Some idea of the dangers of mining may be gathered by the record that in 1708 at the Wear coalfields 69 people were killed, three of them (one a woman) being blown right out of the pit. In 1719 an explosion at Gateshead pit blasted 70 men out of the pit together, with their bodies horribly mangled.

For working in conditions such as these, the miners received low wages and had to agree to remain at the mine where they took service. Also they had to buy their food at the mineowner's shop where they were charged outrageous prices. Many lived in 'tied' cottages (i.e. they could occupy the cottage only so long as they were working at the mine), so if there was a strike they were turned out of their homes.

If life was thus so grim for a man, it was far worse for his child. The factory-owners were only too pleased to employ youngsters, for they could work for less wages. Many parents, too, regarded children as an investment and reared large families not for love, but for the sake of the extra income from their earnings. Other parents wanted to be rid of their children, while yet others in sorrow and terror, had to send them to work so that the money they earned would save the family from starvation. But whatever the reason, the youngsters were condemned to labour.

Of all these children, pauper children (either orphans or with pauper parents) were regarded as the most suitable for employment. The Overseers of the Poor Law were only too glad to send them, for their departure would lessen the Poor Rate, and of course the Overseer himself received so much from the factory-owner. The factory-owner was equally glad to have them as there would not be any awkward parental questions to answer if the children died while at work. So, in cart-loads of a hundred or so at a time, they were taken to the mills—and occasionally it was part of the agreement that one in every twenty should be an idiot so that the workhouse would be rid of these unfortunates.

Children in the cotton mills could commence work at the age of four, crawling under the whirling machines to collect the cotton waste. Other pauper children began work about the age of seven and were bound (i.e. made apprentices) until 21. At ages so young, they stumbled wearily along to the factory in the early hours of the morning, well knowing that the penalty for lateness was the strap. Ahead of them lay 14 to 15 hours' work per day, with half-day on Sundays. Two hours' work was done before breakfast, for which meal, as well as for dinner half-an-hour was allowed. So that no time should be wasted, their meal was often sandwiches, which had to be eaten while they continued to clean the machinery, and the dust, oil and filth of the workroom fell on the bread. Their work was often to mend broken threads — a task which skinned their fingers, and which also involved walking the equivalent of 20 miles a day. It is to be wondered, therefore, that the children fell asleep over the machines, or as they stood, and to prevent such idleness the overlookers employed for the purpose strapped, hit, kicked or poured cold water over them. Sometimes, however, they were too late; the sleeping children fell into the machinery, and the gears and wheels ripped them to a merciful death.

At the end of the normal 14 to 15 hour day (in rush periods, indeed, they had to work from 3 a.m. to 10 p.m., i.e. 19 hours a day) they then stumbled back to the dormitories to occupy the beds just left by the children going on night shift work. The bed consisted of two blankets — one to lie on and the other to cover.

Or the children could be employed in the coal mines, for from five to eight years of age they were quite capable of spending twelve hours alone in the dark, opening and shutting the ventilating doors. After that age they had to go along the corridors and the galleries until they reached where the miner was hacking away lumps of coal and putting them into trucks. Each child had a broad leather belt round the waist and to this belt was attached a chain passing between the legs and fastened to the truck. For 16 hours a day the child had then to pull the truck along the galleries from the miner to the collecting centre and back. Many of the gallery passages were only 28 inches high (just measure this height from the floor), and worse still, they were uneven, so that extra effort was required to crag the load uphill, while downhill the child had to move faster lest he be overrun and crushed by the truck. All the time, of course, the rough chain chafed savagely into the flesh of the legs. Bent and crippled, haggard and aged beyond their years, were these offspring of the coal mines.

Hardly more fortunate were the child chimney sweeps, or Climbing Boys as they were called. Starting work at the age of four, they were compelled to climb up dark and suffocating chimney passages until their elbows and knees were raw, sooted and calloused. If they were slow, a fire was lit beneath them; if they were unskilled, they might be jammed in the chimney and the whole chimney would have to be pulled down. If the soot collapsed they were buried and died of suffocation. If they failed to do their work properly, they might be flogged to death. They received a wash once a week, and some not at all. It is left to your imagination to picture them in their wretchedness.

The real tragedy of all this was, however, that labour was plentiful. The Industrial Revolution witnessed a great increase in the population, as you can read in Chapter XIV. Thus the population of England and Wales increased between 1700 and 1800 from nearly $5\frac{1}{2}$ million to nine million, and by 1851 it had risen to 18 million. So the whole ghastly evil of employment was worse.

Let us, however, be strictly fair in our judgment and condemnation of the Industrial Revolution.

To balance the picture of misery which has just been portrayed, it should be noted that the Industrial Revolution was a slow process. There was no sudden catastrophic upheaval as the new replaced the old. On the contrary, the old Domestic System lingered on for a time — the wool-weaving hand loom and the water-wheel continued in use till the mid 19th century.

Then again, despite the evils of the factory, the Domestic System itself was not always such a state of perfect bliss that many people have imagined. The old-fashioned cottage may have looked very pretty with its thatched roof and 'roses circling round the door', but inside, very probably, the roof leaked and the ceiling was low, the floor was of earth, the rooms ill-ventilated, and the family driven to exhaustion to earn their living at the loom. The hours of work and the conditions of labour at home could be even worse than in a factory. In this respect the Factory System proved a real advantage, for the workers were better able to combine and form unions — trade unions — to improve their hours of work and rates of pay.

Later on, much later on, the Industrial Revolution produced more and cheaper clothes, so the poor could change clothing, more and cheaper soap, so people washed more often, more and cheaper houses; while the railways brought more and cheaper food (particularly meat, milk, butter and sugar), as well as providing work or transport to work, and enabling holidays to the country or to the sea. So the Revolution thus assisted the improvement in public health and happiness.

This improvement, however, only came later; the immediate effects upon mankind were terrible, as we have learnt.

But why, amid such misery and suffering, did the poor not revolt? Why was England not torn by riots and little wars? What force prevented a successful revolution by the working class?

The answer was: the Law.

Chapter XII

The Law

After the Napoleonic Wars, England was a country which literally seethed with discontent. For this, there were several good reasons.

In order to pay for the Napoleonic Wars, the Government had borrowed money (the 'National Debt' as it was called — the debt owed by the Government to the people of the nation) — and the amount thus owed rose from £241 million in 1783 to £834 million in 1815.

To try to pay off this debt, the Government imposed heavy duties on goods, and also Income Tax in 1798. These measures roused great opposition, for the manufacturers, who were the people chiefly affected by the duties and the tax, were already hard enough hit by other difficulties. In the first place, after the wars, people were too poor to buy goods, and at the same time, cheap foreign imports again became available. So the English manufacturers had sufficient difficulty in selling their products as it was, without having to suffer from heavy duties and Income Tax as well.

Then, into this discontented world, came a flood of discharged soldiers, and men from the factories which were no longer required to make weapons and uniforms. All these people wanted jobs, but unfortunately no jobs were available, so groups of unemployed and discontented men drifted about the streets.

Just as dissatisfied, were those who were employed. In agriculture, the enclosure of the fields had caused the labourer to lose the common land and waste land so valuable for grazing and fuel, to lose his regular employment, and to have the rent of his cottage increased, thus reducing him to a poverty which was really terrible.

Under the circumstances, he might decide to move to another village where the prospects of work seemed better. But here again, he was checked — checked by the Laws of Settlement which had been passed as far back as 1662. By 1697, a worker who wished to leave his native village had to obtain from the parish a certificate accepting full responsibility for him if he became a charge on the poor rate of the place to which he was going. Unless he had such a certificate, the new

129

area had legal power to return him, and generally did so, for obviously no parish would allow a newcomer to settle there if they risked having to pay for his upkeep. An Act of 1795 did, indeed, allow a man to stay in another parish until he actually became a charge on the poor rate, but the moment he did so become — the moment he was out of work and destitute — he was immediately sent back to his former home. So a poor man's parish became his prison; he could not leave, for nowehere else would have him.

Moreover, all attempts at relief had failed. (Read ahead pages 202 to 203, and then read the following summary).

Already, each landowner in the parish had to pay a poor rate to help the poor.

Then, in 1722, the Workhouse Act allowed parishes, if they wished, to establish a workhouse where all poor relief was to be given, i.e. there need be no outside relief whereby people received money from the parish while still in their own homes. If you were poor, you had to enter the workhouse for assistance . . . But this new system failed, because the workhouses were often farmed out — that is, offered to the highest bidder, who then naturally tried to recover the cost of the deal and make a profit. Thus if the workhouse owner was paid a lump sum by the parish to cover all the costs of organising a workhouse, he admitted as few as possible, and made life as unpleasant as possible. If he was paid for the work the inmates did, then they toiled until exhausted. In any case, all types of character, good and bad, were mixed together, so there was a general decline of standards.

Next, in 1782, Gilbert's Act, which became compulsory in 1795, saw the parishes establish workhouses for the infirm, and encourage the able-bodied to find work even to the extent of supplementing their wages if necessary. This effort did not succeed, either, and worse was to follow. The Speenhamland system, 1795, based the amount of relief according to the price of bread, and the size of a man's family, while also increasing low wages from the poor rate. This merely encouraged the employer to lower wages, and made a man need to be a pauper in order to be given work, for only paupers could have low wages made up from the poor rate. Moreover, since children were a good investment for poor relief, illegitimacy was encouraged.

Other systems were employed in the country. Under the Gang System, groups of paupers were employed on the roads or at farming. Under the Roundsman System, paupers were hired at weekly auctions to farmers at low wages, the rest of the wages being paid by the poor rate. Sometimes agreements were made that each farmer should employ a percentage of paupers instead of paying rates. In some cases even, the poor were subjected to the humiliation of being harnessed to a cart, and then being sent round to beg for relief. What greater indignity could you inflict on a man?

Thus the labourer was degraded to his unhappiest existence in History. He was, indeed, starving and desperate . . . yet when he poached or stole in order to live, the severe Game Acts were passed — even extending to the death penalty if he offered armed resistance.

The industrial worker was no better off. He lived in slums, courts, cellars and hovels, and worked long, boring hours in unhealthy factories where he was the slave of a machine. Or he toiled in a coal mine amid the dangers of flood, fire, explosion and roof-fall. The wages he earned scarcely enabled him to live, and he had no means to increase them. The Statute of Apprentices, passed in 1563 in the reign of Elizabeth I, had ordered a seven year apprenticeship for trades, and that the Justices of the Peace should determine wages according to food prices. But this well-meaning Act had long been neglected, and when the workers tried to have it revived, the Government officially ended wage regulation in 1813, and the apprenticeship conditions the following year.

It was the same Government, too, which kept the price of essential food and goods high, by taxing them to pay for the war. It was the same Government, too, which would not allow the workers to form unions to get better working conditions, because there was a fear of revolution. It was the same Government, too, which did not allow the workers to vote or to be represented in Parliament, because the rich land-owning M.P.'s wished to remain in power.

Thus the unemployed, the agricultural labourers and the industrial workers were so discontented that it is not surprising that riots and revolts broke out. Most of these disturbances were directed against the new machines which the workers regarded as being responsible for their unemployment. Thus in 1779, Arkwright's spinning machine was smashed, and similar wreckings continued at intervals until they reached the riots of 1811-12. It was then, in 1811, that the real Ned Ludd, an apprentice, refused to work, and was whipped by order of the magistrates. Thereupon, in a fit of anger, he smashed a stocking frame with a hammer, and this so inspired his fellows that groups of men, calling themselves Luddites, wrecked over 1,000 frames in Nottinghamshire. Who really organised this destruction, we do not know, for the so-called 'Ned Ludd' who used the name and led the rioters, has never been identified. However, the movement spread to Lancashire, Yorkshire and Cheshire, where one or two mills were burnt as well.

The upper class of England arose in anger to oppose this mob violence. Such a state of affairs could not for a moment be tolerated. It was a scandal that the calm of the country should be so rudely shattered by such acts of hooliganism and wanton destruction.

In fairness to the upper and middle classes, however, it must be admitted that they could honestly see no reason at all for the revolts and the rioting. This appears unbelievable, but it was true. In the first instance, the new wealth of the richer classes had blinded them to the misery which had produced it, and if they did chance to meet any signs of poverty, they regarded them as exceptional, and satisfied their conscience with occasional acts of charity. Then again, not only their wealth, but also their religion, blinded them. Any attempt to upset the proper order of Society was not only riotous, but was positively ungodly. In the church hymnal, you can still find the hymn by Mrs. Alexandra, commencing with the words, 'All things bright and beautiful', and including the verse

'The rich man in his castle,
The poor man at his gate,
God made them, high or lowly,
And order'd their estate'.

Here was thus expressed the sincere belief of upper and middle class England in the 19th century. The order of society was divinely established, and any attempt to alter or upset that order was an act against God.

Furthermore, as far as the rich were concerned, poverty was the consequence of idleness, of thriftlessness, of drunkenness, or of any other vice you cared to mention. The path of virtue, of course, led to wealth.

So these higher classes rose up in anger to oppose the violence of the mob. They also rose up in fear. No one was more conscious than they were of the absence of a police force, or of any other organisation which could fulfil such a function. There was, it is true, the local militia, but they were more likely to side with the mob. After that, and then only in cases of exceptional danger, it was necessary to call upon the army, but this again was made up of the scum of the world — utterly unreliable, and likely to be more occupied in rioting than in suppressing riots. So unsatisfactory was the discipline of the army, indeed, that the soldiers had to be kept to themselves in barracks, and moved about from district to district. The only reliable force to deal with the mob was the yeoman cavalry, drawn from the middle class itself.

So the authorities of England followed a desperate policy of repression. At all costs, whatever happened, this mob violence must be quelled. And grim indeed was the method of quelling it. After the riots in Lancashire, Yorkshire and Cheshire between 1811-12, in which one or two of the mills were burnt, there were over 20 hung and many transported.

In 1816, riots occurred in Spa Fields in London, and were suppressed. Shortly afterwards, when a band of hungry stocking-makers marched on Nottingham, the authorities called out the cavalry, hung three ringleaders, and transported others.

Then in 1817, the Government suspended the Habeas Corpus Act — an Act which said that an accused person, imprisoned while awaiting trial, had to be brought before the magistrates to be tried without delay. Under the Act, a person could not be imprisoned, or only for a short time, before being tried. The suspension of the Act, of course, meant that people could be imprisoned for a long time without trial.

Also in 1817, there occurred the 'March of the Blanketeers' — so called because the men carried blankets in which to sleep at night. They intended to march from Manchester to London to present a petition, but they were stopped at Derby. Only one man reached London.

Two years' later, in 1819, however, there occurred a far worse instance of repression. At St. Peter's Fields, just outside Manchester, a great reform meeting was planned. The people in charge took every precaution to ensure order, and the chief speaker, whose name was Henry Hunt, offered himself to the magistrates as a security for the good behaviour of the crowd. Some 60,000 people, about one-third of whom were women, thus gathered on the fields of Manchester. They wore their Sunday clothes, and stood respectfully while the band played 'God save the King'. Anything less like a revolutionary gathering could scarcely have been imagined. Yet Hunt had hardly began to speak when, on the magistrates' order, the Yeomanry advanced to arrest him, and then the Regular Cavalry charged the crowd with drawn swords.

The panic that followed was almost indescribable; it can only be imagined by stating that *within ten minutes* the field was deserted save for the dead and wounded. Eleven people were killed, and 400 injured. It was a terrible enough event, but what made it worse was that the Government publicly thanked the magistrates for what they had caused to be done, and Hunt was imprisoned for two years. In grim and bitter mockery of the victory at Waterloo, this incident at St. Peter's Fields was ever after called the 'Massacre of Peterloo'.

Immediately afterwards, the Six Acts were passed:

(1) no unauthorised military drilling.
(2) heavy penalties for libels (written statements tending to bring a person into contempt, hatred or mockery).
(3) duties on newspapers were increased so that the cost would reduce their circulation, and they could not thus spread revolutionary ideas so widely.
(4) private meetings were checked.
(5) magistrates could seize private arms.
(6) justice could be hastened in the case of crimes of violence.

To add to these measures against the poorer classes, the Napoleonic Wars had ended, and the price of English wheat fell from £6.25 to £2.25 per quarter when foreign supplies were once more able to enter this country. Thousands of small farmers thus became bankrupt, and even more thousands of labourers became unemployed. Many indeed, emigrated — 34,000 in 1819 alone — but the others remained, dissatisfied, discontented and rebellious.

The storm had to burst, and it came in 1830, the year when rot killed two million sheep, ruined more farmers, and caused still more unemployment. In that year, the desperate agricultural labourers in Kent revolted. They stormed into the farmyards and the farm houses, they wrecked the threshing machines, and they set fire to the ricks. The rioting spread rapidly. It spread to Sussex, to Berkshire, to Hampshire and Wiltshire. It spread beyond thence to Dorset and Gloucester, and on to Norfolk, Suffolk and Essex. Everywhere, threshing machines, ricks and work houses were destroyed, and terrible indeed was the desperation behind it all. At Ely, 1,500 peasants fought the trained soldiery of England for a whole day, battling desperately with their crude and primitive weapons, and beneath a great banner with the ghastly inscription "Bread or Blood".

Equally grimly and equally desperately, the upper class replied. The Government was deluged with appeals for troops. Arrests were made wholesale, and so great was the number that the Law Courts could not hope to deal with all the cases awaiting trial. Accordingly, special Commissions were appointed to cope with the over-crowded jails, and grimly they set the law against the rioters. Even though, during the whole of the outbreak, not a single person had been killed, the punishments inflicted upon the rioters included nine hanged, 450 transported and 400 imprisoned.

It might be as well at this stage, to see what happened at the trial of these persons who were arrested for breaking the Law. So let us now take a typical prisoner as he faced the magistrates in the grim courtroom — some poor labourer gaunt and famished, with the light of desperation or the dull glaze of hopelessness in his eyes. There he stood, awaiting his fate.

It was obvious from the start that the magistrates were against him — indeed, they were probably the owners of the farmsteads and mills which had been burnt. He was, it is true, allowed to have a lawyer, but the lawyer could not speak on his behalf; the lawyer could only cross-examine witnesses. So the accused, therefore, had to defend himself. This was a very difficult and nerve-racking experience even for an educated man, but what chance for some poor labourer who could neither read nor write? Even while trying to defend himself, he was not allowed to give evidence on his own behalf. If he was found guilty, he was rarely allowed to appeal.

So the poor labourer, who was as good as convicted before he had been tried, faced his punishment. The prisons were the prisons that the 19th century knew . . . gaol fees to the warder, shackles, over-crowding, filth, gaol fever.

But imprisonment, it must be noted, was only for very minor offences indeed. For petty theft, for horse stealing, sheep stealing — *in fact for a whole catalogue of over 220 crimes* — the penalty was not imprisonment — but death. It was a terrible code of law that was thus laid down. If you committed murder, you could be hung, admittedly; if you committed treason, the penalty was death, too. But if you stole goods to a value greater than 25p, the penalty was death; if you shot rabbits or cut down young trees, the penalty was death; if you impersonated a Chelsea pensioner, the penalty was death; if you scribbled on Westminster Bridge, the penalty was death. No wonder men said it was as well to be hung for a sheep as for a lamb — in other words, if you were going to be hung, it might as well be for some great crime (a sheep) as for a small one (a lamb).

And this grim law of death was as grimly enforced. Anyone could see that, for England was littered with gallows. They stood at intervals along both sides of the River Thames; the main gallows of the city of London were at Tyburn, (near the present Marble Arch) and later at Newgate Gaol; and everywhere, in the towns and on the commons, were the gibbets. (In 1846, movable gallows were introduced so that the criminal could be hung at the scene of his crime, and as swiftly as one day after being convicted).

Hanging, of course, was a public spectacle. The condemned man, in his best clothes, with a natural or drunken bravado, was driven through the streets in a cart, amid the wildly cheering crowds, and when he arrived at the gallows, a vast throng, many of whom had spent the whole of the previous night there, were waiting to glory in the sight. So unbelievably dense were these crowds that in 1807, 100 people were crushed to death at one of the hangings. Yet the Law provided a full enough supply of this grim and morbid entertainment. Sometimes as many as 11 were hung at a time. The ghastly spectacle, in truth, was always varying, particularly since the law spared neither sex nor age. Women on their way to execution carried their babies at their breasts; in 1837, a boy of nine was hung at Chelmsford for setting fire to a house.

After the hanging, the dead bodies were frequently taken to the medical colleges for surgeons to practice operations thereon; or else the corpses were exhibited in public as a warning to others. It is also on record that men who had been hung were then flayed, and the skin used as parchment for documents. It must have been gruesome to write on human skin.

However horrible all this may seem, there was still one punishment that was even worse than death — and that was transportation.

Under the terms of this penalty, men were sent to Australia (for the American colonies were no longer available after the War of Independence 1775-83). About 500 a year between 1787-1810, 2,500 a year from 1811-30, and a further 100,000 altogether until 1868, were condemned to a fate that marched them down to the docks with weeping relatives gazing upon them for what was in most cases, the last time.

Then the dark, dank convict ships, with their cargoes of men, naked and chained, set out on the 12,000 mile journey to the far side of the world. On the long storm-tossed passage, several of the prisoners — one out of every five sometimes — died, but their deaths were concealed in order that the living could get the dead men's rations. It was worth enduring the stench of rotting corpses in order to get more food. At the end of the journey at Sydney, Hobart or Botany Bay (Port Jackson), the living were slung over the ship's side and carried ashore, for they were usually unable to walk. The only hospital treatment they could receive, however, was on the open beach with one blanket shared among four men.

If they survived the voyage, they were granted out to the local farmers in the area. These farmers were free settlers, for whom the British Government had provided a free passage to go to Australia, as well as sheep, cows, two years' supply of food, a grant of land and a number of convicts. The convicts were leased to the farmers as slaves, and their fate was the fate of slaves. They were whipped without mercy for the slightest offence — whipped until the law of nature began to operate, and the lash ceased to hurt, for they had become numb with pain. Until then, the shrieks and screams were terrible. Sometimes the whipper moved forward a few paces for each blow, then the heavy whip-cord whistled through the air and ripped through the flesh, to leave a deep channel rapidly filling with blood. As many as a total of 100,000 lashes a year were given.

Despite such savagery, however, there were still some convicts whom not even the lash could break. For men of this type, therefore, penal settlements were established. What happened there it is not proposed to write about. Suffice it to say that men arranged to be murdered, so that one would die thus, and the other would die by being hung for it, and the murder was then accomplished in full view of the guards. Those who attempted to escape did so in groups . . . in order that the carcases of those who died on the journey would provide food for the others.

These penalties and punishments of transportation, remember, were given for such offences as stealing three hares and a pot of sausages, or for killing a partridge.

Undoubtedly one reason for the outbursts of crime and the severity of punishments was the fact that England possessed no Police force. In the Middle Ages, towns had had Justices of the Peace, as well as petty constables, and in the 16th century the Tudors also employed Justices of the Peace and constables, to keep order.

But in those days, the towns were relatively small, and some degree of order could thus be maintained. By the 18th century, however, the towns had become so large that the old system broke down completely.

Even at the best of times, the office of constable had not been a popular one, and there was a serious shortage of volunteers. Though legally, any man could be compelled to serve for a year as a constable, in practice the richer people hired deputies of any quality whatsoever who would take their place. In addition to that, many a person was appointed a constable in order to prevent him from becoming a charge on the poor rate. So the 'police force' was a laughing stock of aged, infirm and rascally characters, who were either ignored by, or in league with, the criminals.

The results may be judged by the fact that crime — theft, burglary, pick-pocketing and violence — flourished openly and continuously in the streets of London. Gangs of young rioters called Mohocks, overturned the watchmen's boxes, pressed their victim's nose flat with his face, bored out people's eyes with their fingers, slit noses with their daggers or encircled their captive and pierced him with swords. Nor was such crime any respecter of persons. Even the Prime Minister, Lord North himself, was held up and robbed in Piccadilly . . . in broad daylight. So serious did the robberies and murders become that the wealthier citizens converted their houses into small fortresses, with solid iron doors, iron-barred shutters, man-traps in the garden, and an armoury of weapons beneath their pillows.

The first improvement in the situation was due to the novelist, Henry Fielding, also magistrate of Bow Street Police Court. It was he who, about 1750, organised the Bow Street Runners — a group of strong courageous men, who had no fear of the well-organised gangs of thieves they had to oppose, and who were well rewarded for their success. Their fame spread, particularly after they had rid the outskirts of London of some of the worst of the highwaymen.

The next improvement in the situation was the founding of the London Police Force, by Sir Robert Peel in 1829. Clad in top hats, dark blue tailcoats and white breeches, the men patrolled the streets carrying their only weapon — a wooden truncheon — together with a rattle to summon assistance. The instructions which they received have governed the police force ever since: 'The object to be attained is the prevention of crime. Be civil and obliging to all people of every rank and class. There is no qualification so indispensable to a police officer as a perfect command of temper'. And when you compare the British Police Force nowadays with those in other parts of the world, you will realise how well these instructions have been upheld.

The example of London was copied by the large provincial towns, and to encourage them, in 1856 a Government grant was made payable to efficient local forces. The smaller towns and the countryside followed more slowly, until in 1890, the Police Act made the policing of such areas the joint responsibility of the County Councils and the Justices of the Peace.

Meanwhile, in 1878, the Criminal Investigation Department (C.I.D.) was founded, and in 1891, the headquarters of the London Police moved to New Scotland Yard. From then onwards, all the resources of the finger-print system and scientific analysis have been brought to bear upon the problems of preventing crime and capturing the criminal.

Chapter XIII

Laissez Faire

We have told the story of the Industrial Revolution. We have seen the terrible effects which it had upon the working class, and how the law dealt with those poor workers who, in their desperation, tried to revolt.

Yet, we may well ask, why was it that no one ever attempted to *help* these unhappy workers? Why, for example, did the Government not make at least some effort to improve the wretched conditions of their existence?

The reason is not difficult to understand. A certain French business-man was said to have once been asked 'How could the French Government best help French industry?' His reply was short, simple, and without hesitation, 'Laissez faire' — 'leave it alone'.

This idea that the Government should leave industry alone spread to England where it was developed by Adam Smith, a Glasgow Professor, in his book, *Wealth of Nations*, published in 1776. According to Adam Smith, the best way to help industry was to let it alone. In that way you would have a happy, wealthy country.

Everyone should be free to follow his own interests (unless, of course, this was dangerous to others, immoral, or against the State), and each man should specialise in one craft or one process only, not in several. (This is known as the 'division of labour' — one man to one particular job only.)

If industry was the left alone, the price of goods would reach a proper price according to the law of supply and demand. If industry was left alone, the wages that were paid would reach a correct level according to the number of people there were to be employed. If there were too many people trying to obtain work, some would starve to death, and so each of those left would have a reasonable wage.

At the same time, of course, there should be Free Trade. Every country should produce what it could make best, and then exchange with other countries. For example, France could produce plenty of cheap wine; England could produce plenty of cheap cloth. So let each country concentrate on making its best product only, and then exchange without interference — French wine for English cloth. Customs duties would be unnecessary.

Thus the Government need not regulate prices, wages, production or international trade. Everything would look after itself, provided it was left alone to do so.

On the contrary, if the Government did interfere in industry, there would be nothing but muddle and mess. After all, the Government knew little about industry, so let the people who *did* know something about it, that is, the industrialists themselves, let them control the business.

The British Government agreed with all this, and so the Industrial Revolution continued without any Parliamentary hindrance to its activity. This, of course, meant that Parliament did not attempt to help the poor. The problem of the poor would sort itself out, if only it was left alone to do so.

It it easy to see what was wrong with Adam Smith's ideas of 'laissez faire'. If everyone was left alone to do as he wished, the weakest would immediately suffer, and only the strong would be successful. That is why Adam Smith's ideas were so popular, for they were naturally supported by the powerful industrial manufacturers. Let every one of them do as *he* wished, of course. But what of the poor worker? Oh, he didn't matter.

Supporting Adam Smith were the grim, gloomy views of Thomas Malthus, 1766-1834, Professor of History at Cambridge University. In 1798 he published his *Essay on Population*, with its dismal statement that there were more people than food to feed them. It was essential, therefore, to reduce the population, and this could be very effectively achieved by such means as war, famine and disease, while less effective methods were by not marrying or marrying late in life, so having fewer children. In the main, however, the problem of poverty would be solved by people dying until the amount of food available could support the survivors.

From ideas like these it followed that private charity was a sin, and public assistance was a crime. Such misplaced kindness merely hampered the process of reducing the population.

It is easy to see what was wrong with Malthus' ideas. His views were true of his own time, especially when we remember the results of the charity of the Speenhamland system. In later years, however, emigration was to reduce the number of people, more food was produced from the same amount of land as a result of better cultivation, and more goods were made which paid for more food imports. So the poor survived.

But Parliament at the time agreed with Adam Smith and Malthus. The problem of the poor would sort itself out, if only it was left alone to do so. Laissez faire.

Chapter XIV

The Growth of Population
1700 — 1850

Between 1700-1850, the population of England and Wales increased dramatically. In two vast accelerations, the estimates read:

1700	..	..	..	$5\frac{1}{2}$ million
1801	..	..	..	9 million
1850	..	..	..	18 million

So let us see what this means.

The Great Britain of 1700 was a land of open space. The most densely populated area was in the agricultural south, between a line from the Severn to the Wash and a line from the Bristol Channel to Kent. Within these limits lay the great capital city, London, with a total population of about 700,000. Microscopic this might seem in comparison with the present eight million, but in 1700 London existed without a rival. The second city of the kingdom was Bristol, with only about 30,000 inhabitants at most, and owing its status to trade with America and shipbuilding. After that, third came Norwich, the centre of the worsted industry.

By 1800 the picture had changed considerably. The most densely populated area then was the industrial western half of the country, from central Lancashire to the Bristol Channel. London still retained its supremacy with a population of about 960,000, but the runners-up now were Manchester with 84,000 and its attendant port of Liverpool with 78,000.

In 1851 the picture remained the same, but more intense. Durham, South Yorkshire, South Lancashire, the Black Country and South Wales were the main areas of population. London was now a city of 2,400,000 inhabitants, while its successors were still Liverpool (376,000) and Manchester and Salford (366,000).

The increase in population is therefore clear, but the reasons for it are not so clear.

However, let us first consider the period 1700-1800.

POPULATION 1700
Shaded areas show greatest density

POPULATION 1801
Shaded areas show greatest density

One reason for the growth of population in this century was the rising birth rate (i.e. more babies were born). The rate rose till about 1750, then remained steady. Men now married at a younger age, and therefore probably had more children. True, the Statute of Apprentices of 1563 — and still legal — had ordered a seven year apprenticeship, and the apprentice did not marry until he had completed his contract. But by 1700 the Act was not seriously enforced, so the apprentice earned more money, married and had children. In many industries— such as mining, or building canals or railways — it did not require long for a man to be capable of full quality work, hence he earned full pay early and so could afford to marry while still young.

But it seems more likely that the population increase from 1700-1800 was really due to a declining death rate (i.e. fewer people died). For these fewer deaths there were many reasons.

Thanks considerably to Dr. William Smellie (1697-1763), proper training was provided for doctors and midwives. Thus, in particular, the midwife became a member of a profession with recognised standards, instead of some ignorant woman called away from her cleaning, to use her rough and ready methods with unwashed hands. Far more children now survived their birth, as well as the first few and difficult years of life.

And for those children who thus survived, let us not forget Captain Thomas Coram who, in 1741, set up the Foundling Hospital in London for unwanted and deserted babies. It was an act of mercy that drew attention in his own time and has lasted until this.

Better food then contributed to less deaths. The Agricultural Revolution, with its enclosed fields, provided more produce. Previously, too, many cattle had had to be slaughtered in the autumn as there was insufficient food to keep them during the winter months. But now, root crops provided winter cattle food, so that fresh meat, or more milk, butter and cheese were available throughout the year. Increasing supplies of sugar enabled more fruit to be preserved for use in winter.

Better drink was available. The vile curse of cheap gin was ended by the Act of 1751 which placed a heavy tax on spirits, and limited the number of gin shops. Tea gradually became a substitute.

Better transport — turnpike roads and canals — brought food to the growing population of the towns.

Better clothing also improved the prospects of life, for cotton clothes could now be worn in preference to the thick, filth-harbouring woollens.

Better hygiene, however, was developed not only by cotton clothing, but also by cheaper soap, so that the poor could wash more frequently. In addition, attempts were being made in the 18th century to dispose of sewage and to improve water supplies.

Finally, for those who were ill, more hospitals were built throughout the country — from 1700-1825 about 154, indeed. Most famous of them was the one erected in London in 1724 from the profits made by Thomas Guy, a wealthy bookseller, and his establishment remains to this day. In some of the best hospitals the floors were cleaned, cleaner cotton sheets replaced the woollen ones which collected dirt and vermin in the thick material, while iron bedsteads replaced germ-infested wooden ones.

Of real help, too, were the dispensaries which, from 1769, gave medicine and advice to the poor.

We must, however, estimate correctly the real value of all these improvements. None of them raised the standards to anything even remotely acceptable today. The food of the people was still poor and inadequate, the transport system was inefficient, the sewage was still heaped in the streets, the hospital death rate was appalling. But at least efforts to improve were made, and they created a situation better than it would otherwise have been. To these efforts, therefore, the increase in the population could be considered very likely due.

Now let is consider the period 1800-1850.

After 1820 the death rate began to rise (i.e. more people died), and there were fewer births after 1840 — both due to the slum conditions of the Industrial Revolution. Despite this, however, the population continued to increase, nearly doubling itself in half a century, so here again we have to search hard for the reasons.

The Speenhamland system of poor relief certainly encouraged people to have more children for the sake of the extra money, but overall it did not really affect the increase in population. Similarly, although immigrants from Scotland and Ireland came here to find better working conditions than in their own areas, their arrival did not account for so great an increase in the population.

The reason, then, would seem to be in the improvement in public health.

First and foremost was Dr. Edward Jenner's discovery of vaccination in 1798 — one of the greatest 'breakthroughs' in medical history. At the same time we must also mention the work of James Lind, a naval surgeon, who discovered the cure for scurvy was fresh fruit and green vegetables.

Local government, too, became more active in improving health standards, firstly by arranging for sewage disposal, and secondly in securing better water supplies. In 1835 the Municipal Corporations Act allowed local authorities to pave, light and cleanse the streets if they wished. In 1848 the Public Health Act enabled local authorities to appoint surveyors and medical officers; to pave, light and cleanse streets; and to provide clean water and drainage; if they wished. Although these activities were voluntary, many local authorities made at least some effort to improve public health conditions, and these improvements must have resulted in an increase in the population.

PART TWO

FROM WORKHOUSE
TO WELFARE STATE

Chapter XV

An Introduction
to this Part

We know that one of the worst results of the Agricultural and Industrial Revolutions was the suffering of those human beings who were at the lower end of the social scale, — the poorer working class.

Before and during the Agricultural Revolution, i.e. in the period 1660-1790, many a small owner-farmer declined, for he could not compete with the large farms.

Then his situation worsened. After the Napoleonic Wars ended in 1815, trade was bad, and Government taxes to pay for the war were high. In addition, the parish levies of a poor rate (to help the poor) and a highway rate (to repair the roads) were paid mainly by the farmers. Faced with all these costs and taxes the small farmer had to sell his property, and he became a tenant, a labourer, a worker in a nearby factory, or, in rare cases, a pauper.

Not was it only the small farmer who suffered. The enclosing of the land had caused the ordinary labourer to lose the common and the wasteland so valuable for grazing and fuel. He also lost his regular employment or occasional work at the same time as the landlord increased the rent of his cottage and the price of food more than doubled. He was thus reduced to a poverty that became truly terrible.

The 'squatter', who had no right at all to the land on which he had built his hovel, was turned adrift to die.

And how could the poor countryman improve his situation? There was little work available on the farms, for the increasing population could not be absorbed by agriculture. Local industries, such as spinning, weaving, dyeing, tanning, etc., which at one time had helped him to earn a living, were now being carried out in the factories of the newly-created towns. Perhaps he might decide to move to another area where the prospects of employment seemed better. But here again he was checked — checked by the Laws of Settlement which allowed a parish to return any destitute newcomer to his former home. So a poor man's own parish became his prison; he could not leave because no where else would have him.

151

Meanwhile, what the Agricultural Revolution inflicted upon the country people, the Industrial Revolution did to the town dweller. Indeed, conditions in the factory cities were far worse than in a farming village. The town worker lived in slums, cellars and hovels, amid an atmosphere polluted with grime and suffocated with stench. There were no good water supplies, very little sanitation, and constant disease.

He then had to work long, boring hours in an unhealthy factory where he was the slave of a machine, or he could choose to toil in a coal mine amid the dangers of flood, fire, explosion and roof fall. Whatever wages he earned in either occupation scarcely enabled him to live, yet he dare not complain. Irish immigrants, accustomed to even worse conditions in Ireland, where they shared their hovels with cattle and pigs, were prepared to accept such low wages should he make any complaint.

Even at the best of times, the hatred between the very rich factory owner and the very poor workers caused strikes, and there was a further loss of wages when trade was bad and the factories closed down for a while.

All the time, indeed, the worker feared the threat of unemployment. In the grim factories, machines were replacing men, and women and children could also undertake his task. Only too clearly did he realise that he was utterly at the mercy of the employer, who owned both the materials and the machines upon which the employee depended for his work. It was this division of society into the 'haves' and the 'have-nots' that caused the suffering of the lower class.

The problem of unemployment gradually became worse. In the course of a century, the population of England and Wales increased from $5\frac{1}{2}$ million in 1700 to nine million in 1801. But there were no jobs for these people. Then, after the Napoleonic Wars ended in 1815, there came a flood of discharged soldiers and men from the factories no longer required to make weapons and uniforms. All these people wanted work, but unfortunately, no jobs were available.

Also after the Napoleonic Wars, there was heavy taxation on essential foods and goods to pay for the cost of the fighting — and these taxes weighed heavily on the poor.

Yet what could these poor and unemployed people do? There was no way by which a worker could improve the conditions of his existence. Admittedly, the Statute of Apprentices, passed in 1563 in the reign of Elizabeth I, had ordered a seven year apprenticeship for trades, and that the Justices of the Peace should fix wages according to food prices. But this well-meaning Act had long been neglected, and when the workers tried to have it enforced, the Government officially ended wage regulation in 1813, and the apprenticeship conditions the following year. At the same time, the worker was not allowed to join a union to obtain better conditions, because there was a fear of revolution. Nor had he a vote, so he could not have any influence on Parliament.

The Government itself made no effort to prevent the poverty and distress. This, indeed, was the great age of *laissez faire* ('leave it alone') — a belief that was to last for over a century. Everything — whether prices, wages, unemployment or poverty — everything would sort itself out, if only it was left alone to do so. If agriculture and industry were left alone, the price of goods would reach a proper price according to the law of supply and demand. If agriculture and industry were left alone, the wages that were paid would reach the correct level according to the number of people employed and the amount of money available. If there were too many people trying to obtain work, some would starve to death, so those left would have opportunity for employment. The problem of poverty would be solved by letting people die until the amount of food and money available could support the survivors. *Laissez faire*, then; leave everything alone . . . and that, of course, meant leaving the poor worker to his fate.

But gradually, as time went on, it began to be realised that the poor working man should not be left to his fate, and that somehow or other, he would have to be helped. The belief in 'leaving things alone' began to fade, and in its place came more and more interference with agriculture and industry in order to help the poor. This interference was undertaken firstly by humanitarians (people who wanted to help their fellow humans), then by the workers themselves, and finally by the State.

So in this book, let us now trace the decline of the idea of *laissez faire*. Let us follow the rise of the new interference with the affairs of agriculture and industry in the following chapters:

Religion Other humanitarians	Humanitarians
Trade Unions Chartists	The workers themselves

Factory Laws
Poor Laws
Health
Housing   }   The State
Education
England amid the wars
The Welfare State

Chapter XVI

The Methodist Revival

The poor and the church

From our reading of the previous chapter, we can realise the terrible condition of the lowest classes in England in the 18th century. They had, in truth, reached the utmost of misery and despair.

It is at times such as these, when troubles and sorrow overwhelm, that the human race turns to whatever faith it worships, in an effort to obtain the consolation and strength needed to make life bearable. So if there was to be any hope at all for the unfortunate poor . . . if they were to receive any real help whatsoever . . . such could come from one source only . . . religion. Their salvation depended on the church.

But in the 18th century, unfortunately, the church and its beliefs were at a low ebb.

This is hardly surprising when one realises that the Parliamentary party known as the Whigs used to appoint the bishops as a reward for their political services rather than their religious enthusiasm. So a highly irreverent, but very capable supporter of the party, might find himself in possession of a rich church living for no other reason than to appreciate his services to the Whig Government. His sole interest, therefore, in the whole of the church building was limited to the collection plate, and his only prayer to God was in the form of counting the money.

Thus, one Bishop of Llandaff never even lived in the diocese, and the example spread to the other ranks of the clergy. On general average, it is safe to say that three out of every five vicars did not live in their own areas, but appointed a cheaply-paid curate to do the work there for them.

Even when the vicar did reside in the parish of his living, he was usually a mere follower of the rich, adjusting the time of the service and the length of the sermon to suit the local wealthy, dining at the squire's table, and drinking and hunting with the gentry. Indeed, he often came to church in his hunting dress, and left his gun in the porch. Such clergy knew more about gambling than Godliness, and were better acquainted with the bottle than with the Bible.

The lowest clergy of all — those who toiled in the poorer areas — were very ill-paid, and at their hard-working best had only a limited effectiveness in inspiring people to be Christians. Moreover, the new industrial slums, which developed outside the old parish boundaries, quite frequently had no priest at all.

If some of the clergy were not too religious, neither was any other section of the community. Among the upper class, disbelief was fashionable. Indeed, it could hardly have been otherwise when gambling and immorality formed the recognised occupation of higher society. The middle class, for their part, lacked any enthusiasm for worship, being more concerned with earning money.

So the poor received very little help from the church, or from anywhere else.

Methodism

Then into this world of religious indifference, there suddenly came the dynamic driving force of a mighty crusade, spear-headed by three men — John Wesley, Charles Wesley and George Whitefield.

Born at Epworth, Lincolnshire, the son of a rector, John Wesley (1703-91) was educated at Oxford. It was here that the Methodist movement was founded, being so-named because its originators lived very methodical, well-arranged lives.

It was from Oxford also that John Wesley commenced a religious career in which he travelled 250,000 miles and preached 40,000 sermons. Though he failed to impress the American colonists in Georgia or high society in London, his success in other spheres was immeasurably outstanding. To the tin-miners of Cornwall, to the factory workers in the slums of the north, he brought the sincerity of his faith and the power of conversion.

When the Church of England was not prepared to tolerate his beliefs, and closed the church doors against him, he was driven more and more to the world beyond the Church of England parish boundaries — a wider and rougher world which knew no definite God. Sometimes he was robbed, sometimes he was stoned, but he was never seriously hurt — a fact which increased his belief that he was under God's protection in the performance of God's work. So he continued his work undaunted, for a full forty years of his life.

Perhaps there were three aspects of his character which ensured success.

In the first instance, he was an amazing preacher. He had no wonderful eloquence, but his plain simple language, and the obvious sincerity with which he spoke, impressed the lower classes of the 18th century far more than any power of oratory. When he spoke to the miners at Kingswood, near Bristol, the tears left white channels down their coal-grimed faces.

He was fearless — a quality tested to the utmost when facing a mob desperate from weeks of starvation or frenzied with the success of several hours looting. Into the midst of the rioters, he walked . . . and talked them into calmness.

Thirdly, he had a wonderful charm of manner — a man who did not lose his temper, a man of wit and humour, a man who believed the work of God to be far more important than his own personal vanity.

So he travelled on, preaching, and above all . . . above all . . . *organising* the new religion. 250,000 miles . . . 40,000 sermons . . . first class organisation.

His brother, Charles Wesley (1707-88), was the 'sweet singer', and it has been said that Methodism owed as much to the hymns of the one as to the sermons of the other. There is a wonderful triumphant majesty about 'Hark the herald Angels sing', a great tenderness about 'Jesu, lover of my soul', and a deep sense of wonder in 'Love divine, all loves excelling'. How greatly song has played a part in human civilisation has yet to be fully discovered, but there is no doubt that it proved a very powerful influence in converting people to the Methodist faith. During his life, Charles Wesley wrote some 6,500 hymns.

It was, however, in the field preaching of George Whitefield (1714-70) that the real tremendous force of the religious revival was to be found. For 34 years, Whitefield remained in the Ministry, and he gave an average of about 10 sermons per week. Not only his mind, but also his voice, was ideally suited to the task, and to be present at an open-air service where his sermon, with its peculiar vividness of description could be heard by 30,000 people, was an experience never to be forgotten.

The movement was further strengthened by the establishment of chapels and the employment of lay preachers. The whole country was divided into districts called 'circuits', and the ministers journeyed from circuit to circuit every three years to supervise the bands of Methodists who formed energetic, deeply-religious communities in every area. Thus though John Wesley himself remained a member of the Church of England all his life, it is not surprising that the two religions parted after his death, and the lower and lower middle classes (the latter being the skilled or partly-skilled workers, small shopkeepers, etc.), won over by the fervour of the new faith, proclaimed it independent in 1795.

What, then, was this new faith, so powerfully proclaimed, and so well organised ? And why did it attract people ?

Methodism was essentially the religion of the New Testament. It stressed the love of God, His mercy, His forgiveness, and the hope of being saved. It was a vital, dynamic religion, which emphasised the value of good deeds, and taught industry, thrift, selflessness and similar virtues. To the wretched poor, it offered a chance of salvation which the Church of England never offered; it gave them a feeling of security in an age of violence and drunkenness; it gave a sense of purpose to their existence to save them from drifting aimlessly through life. For these reasons, therefore, it lessened the likelihood of riots and revolutions in the grim years of the 1790s and 1800s.

On the other hand, it was a very superstitious movement — John Wesley himself firmly believed in witches and devils — and it converted people by playing upon their emotions. After hearing an extremely vivid and dramatic sermon by Whitefield on the horrors of Hell or the love of God, a vast wave of emotion would sweep over the audience, and a near-hysterical crowd would enter the Methodist faith in a frenzy of fear or an orgy of hope. Nor did Methodism help the most helpless of all — the very virtue of hard work urged young children into the appalling conditions of the factory and the mine.

Evangelicals

The influence of Methodism then reached the Church of England, and it thereupon divided that organisation into two groups.

The first group was called the Evangelicals, or Low Church, mainly the upper and upper middle class of society, the power of whose religious beliefs raised them to be the greatest influence in Victorian England. In fact, they *were* Victorian England, and all that that implied.

As far as religion was concerned, their views were grim, like the Puritans of old, for they wanted a strict Sunday observance, and no elaborate ceremonies. They believed that the way to Heaven was by hard work, thrift, soberness, and by high standards of morals and duty. It was truly a hard faith, utterly merciless to sinners, and it produced an intensely self-confident, self-satisfied race of people, certain that they, and they alone, were right. But likewise it drove these people to great achievements in the face of incredible difficulties;

it sent them to the four corners of the world to spread what was believed to be the 'White Man's blessing'; it made England a great nation. Indeed, this country became the 'Workshop of the World'; it clothed the world, it financed the world; there was no outpost of the universe which did not know its engineers, labourers, scientists, soldiers and missionaries. You are a fool if you scorn a faith which achieves results like this.

So now, in the lives of seven persons in particular, let us see the influence of this Evangelical movement.

John Howard

The first of these seven was John Howard (1726-90). In the year 1756, on a voyage to Lisbon, he was captured by French pirates and flung into gaol. It was a terrible experience, which included the knowledge of 36 fellow prisoners buried in one day. Later the young traveller was freed, and when he became High Sheriff of Bedfordshire, he resolved to visit the gaols in England, to make comparisons. There was no shortage of opportunity, for each county and town in those days had its own place of confinement, sometimes specially built, sometimes in an old gateway, or an old fortress, and Howard toured England four times, visiting every possible prison, and carrying a small bottle of vinegar as a disinfectant.

Grim indeed were his discoveries. Men were imprisoned for years, merely in order to await their trial . . . for in the early 18th century, the Assizes were held about once in seven years. As soon as a man entered the prison, he had to pay an entrance fee to the gaoler or he would be placed in irons. During his time in prison, he had to pay the gaoler if he wanted a bed, or even the minimum of comforts — food, exercise, admission of relatives, friends, etc. — and before he could leave he had to pay a release fee. The root of this evil system lay in the fact that the gaolers received no wages.

Inside the prison, men, women, and children were herded together — as many as 30 to 60 in a room, and the rooms were small and filthy. The cells where the prisoners slept were often below ground level, with floors half-covered with water; sometimes, but not always, a rough wooden board or a little straw was provided for a bed.

The stench of the prisons was terrible, and amid the vile conditions a grim disease flourished — gaol fever. This fatal plague developed so rapidly that it threatened to revenge the prisoners upon the law, for it was brought into the courts and trial chambers. In vain were herbs and disinfectant scattered about the places of justice; in 1750, at the old Bailey Court in London, four out of the six judges died, and 40 other persons also, including counsel and jury — all victims of gaol fever. To this day, flowers (herbs) are carried in the judges' procession to the Assize Courts as a survival of the ancient custom.

With evidence such as this to support him, John Howard persuaded Parliament to pass Acts in 1774, for prisons to be whitewashed once a year and for gaolers to be paid a salary. At his own expense, he had leaflets printed and distributed to notify each gaol of the new regulations. So he set in motion the movement for the reform of England's inhuman prisons, and continued his work at home and abroad until, by the irony of fate, the gaol fever which he had striven so hard to suppress, seized hold of him, and he died in 1790.

Elizabeth Fry

His work, however, was to be continued by one of the true saints of History — Elizabeth Fry (1780-1845), and about her we must certainly have some knowledge.

Elizabeth Fry was a Quaker who, as allowed by her religion, became a minister. In her early life, she visited the sick, the schools and the workhouses, as well as holding Bible classes and preaching, but her real contact with the lowest of humanity was when she visited Newgate Gaol in 1813. There, indeed, she found a place more greatly in need of her ministrations than anywhere else in the realm, and not even the brevity of the following account can disguise the horror which she had to face.

In that infamous London gaol, the women's side was a ghastly nightmare. For utter squalor, filth and degradation, it has never had an equal in England, and the effect upon the inmates was terrible in the extreme. Within an area only 190 yards square, 300 prisoners were confined like beasts in a cage . . . and like beasts in a cage they behaved. Filthy, half-naked women clung to the railings, shrieking and screaming; others gibbered and moaned in half-mad despair. Some sat on stones, ugly and bestial, while since the law did not recognise criminal lunatics, these went raving about the wards. Some of the prisoners had heavy leg-irons, riveted at the knees and ankles — irons which caused a terrible inflammation as they chafed the flesh, and the victims cried out in the agony of every movement. Indeed, the shrieks, the cries and the moans rang out in a veritable pandemonium, while all the time the stench as of a slaughterhouse and a sewerage rose into the air.

In these circumstances and in that atmosphere, the wretched women were condemned to remain for years, and of course, it is not difficult to realise what had to happen. These human beings were gradually stripped of all humanity, until they had returned to their primitive wildness. The whole place was thus bluntly described as 'like a den of wild beasts', or even more aptly and accurately as 'the hell above ground'. It was a place so savage, indeed, that not even the Governor himself, dared to enter without a guard.

Elizabeth Fry entered alone and unafraid.

Slowly and surely . . . slowly and surely — the amazing wonder of it! — her influence made itself felt. She knitted dresses and other clothes for the prisoners. She comforted those who had been condemned to die, and were frantic with terror or hopeless with despair. Then, in an empty cell, she commenced a school for children, and after that held religious services for the adults.

But Newgate was not a permanent home for most of those sent there; some would be set free, others were awaiting transportation to Australia. So Elizabeth Fry arranged for contractors to supply the prisoners with sewing and knitting, and the profits provided food and a start in life after they had been released. For those who were to be transported, she saw to it that instead of going in carts, chained together, and then herded into ships like cattle, they should travel in hackney coaches unchained, and be given some occupation such as sewing on the long voyages. That was the essence of her saintliness — she not only talked of hope . . . she provided it.

The results were almost unbelievable. The attitude of the wretched prisoners changed completely — they were happier and more orderly — and the authorities were so impressed that Fry's system spread throughout England. She was received in audience by the Queen, and interviewed by Members of Parliament and distinguished foreigners, the latter being only too pleased for her to visit their countries to teach her ideas. Not until 1845, did she die, after 30 years of life spent in the service of her God, in the gaols.

Robert Raikes

The next person we shall mention here is Robert Raikes (1735-1811) who, at Gloucester in 1780, commenced his Sunday School, to relieve the misery and the ignorance of the poor children of that city. He lived to see such schools extend over the whole of England.

F

Clarkson and Wilberforce

But the influence of Evangelism was still not exhausted, for at this time there lived Thomas Clarkson (1760-1846) and William Wilberforce (1759-1833).

It was these two men who saw a nightmare vision even more ghastly than that seen by Howard and Fry in the English prisons. They saw, indeed, a terrible scene set in the dense jungle of tropical Africa, many thousands of miles from white civilisation. There, stealing along the narrow trackways, were a band of armed natives with the hours of darkness around them. Swift and savage was their attack upon the unsuspecting village, yet for all their savagery which left the huts a charred and ruined scene, there were but a few casualties. The aim indeed, was to capture, not to kill.

The human spoils of war were then herded together to await the Arab slave-dealers coming from the coast. In exchange for Manchester cotton cloth, guns and gunpowder, brandy, gin, beads and trinkets, the slaves were handed over and began the manacled march, along the death-lined trails, from the interior to the coast. Down the sweltering rivers moved the canoe loads of captives, and not even the singing and the trumpet notes of the cheerful slavers could drown the screams of those tortured by the whip. Any slaves who seemed likely to die were turned loose for the merciless beasts of the jungle.

So the survivors reach the coast, where they were herded into slave pens. In 1791 there were recorded at least 40 of these great slave stations on the west coast of Africa — 15 Dutch, 14 English, 4 Portuguese, 4 Danish and 3 French. Here the slaves were fattened for sale.

In due course, the slave ships arrived and the human cargo, each branded by a red hot iron with the captain's trade mark, were packed on specially designed decks, and the overladen vessels began the horrors of the 'Middle passage' as the voyage from West Africa to the West Indies was called. The conditions were appalling. As many as 600 slaves, chained together, would be packed into a space 70 feet by 26 feet by four feet in height, and only occasionally were the water hoses turned on them to remove the filth and stench. In consequence, they died from suffocation, disease, suicide, insanity and sheer lack of desire to live.

On arrival on the far side of the Atlantic, the dead were unshackled from the living and flung overboard to the sharks, while the rest, after being washed, oiled and fattened, were sold by auction to labour on the tobacco, cotton and sugar plantations.

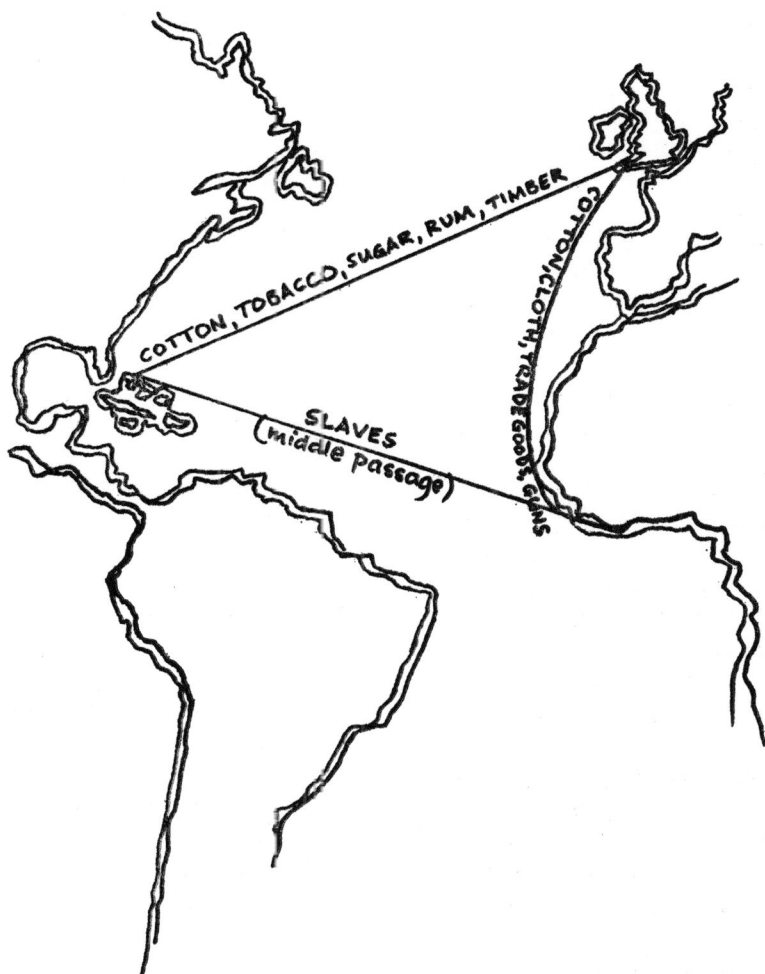

The triangular trade.

Such is a swift survey of the slave trade. It was an amazing and an appalling traffic. England alone, from 1680-1780, imported an annual average of 20,000 slaves to America and the West Indies, and other European nations were concerned as well. It is not too high a calculation, therefore, to estimate the number of Africans thus transported as reaching the terrible total of some eight million.

The horror of all this might seem to have made the task of Clarkson and Wilberforce easy, but their attempts to abolish the slave trade faced powerful opposition. In the 18th century, there were about 15,000 slaves in England alone, whose masters opposed abolition. In addition, the ship-owners of Liverpool, the cotton manufacturers of Lancashire, the makers of muskets and trinkets in the Midlands, all depended upon the slave trade for their prosperity — and indeed, so great was their interest, that Liverpool Corporation voted £10,000 to oppose the abolitionists. And well it might, for the port of Liverpool owed its development to the slave trade. By 1780, one half of the world's trans-Atlantic slave traffic was carried in Liverpool ships. By 1830, the docks of that city extended over two miles.

Equally involved with the trade were the West Indies' planters, whose great wealth depended upon slave labour, so they used money and Parliamentary influence to check any moves to free the slaves. Nor were English people in general unduly concerned about the fate of others not of their own race and thousands of miles away.

But Clarkson and Wilberforce continued the struggle. Already in 1772, Lord Mansfield, the Lord Chief Justice, had declared slavery illegal in England, and those who were thus freed were settled in Sierra Leone in West Africa. Thus encouraged, the Abolitionists gathered together their evidence, printed thousands of pamphlets, organised anti-slavery societies, public meetings and petitions to Parliament, and had sermons preached by eye-witness missionaries, until slowly the horror of slavery penetrated the general public.

At last, 20 years of toil reaped their reward. In 1807, England abolished her slave trade, and in 1833, slavery itself in the British Empire was ended. The planters were paid £20 million compensation for the loss of their slave labour — an average of some £37 per slave.

Lord Shaftesbury

The next of the great Evangelicals was Anthony Ashley Cooper (1801-85), Earl of Shaftesbury. He it was who saw yet another kind of human misery, one that many people ignored, and others deliberately increased.

Although a rich Dorset landowner, he was nevertheless well aware of the pitiful procession that passed daily through the slum streets on its way to the factories. Ragged children, half-starved and filthy, bent, stunted in growth, hopelessness written deeply upon their faces — children old before they had even had the time to be young — stumbled wearily and wretchedly over the rough, cobbled stones. The hours of darkness were still around them when they commenced work, and they well knew that the penalty for lateness was the strap. Ahead of them was their daily 15-hour toil.

The conscience of Lord Ashley was stirred. His influence lay in his personality. It was impossible to accuse him of being a mere rabble-rouser, a gutter-bred revolutionary or a starry-eyed idealist. On the contrary, he was a deeply religious person, a peer of the realm, and a man of acknowledged commonsense. Furthermore, he possessed the wonderful gift of oratory, a truly marvellous speaker who could command the attention of his audience. On one occasion he spoke for two hours on the conditions of children condemned by the hell of their employment. Carefully he marshalled his facts into a truth which no-one could deny, and for two hours the Members of the House of Commons listened to him . . . and they wept. When he had finished, one of his greatest opponents, a person who believed that the commercial prosperity of England would be ruined without the help of child labour, walked across the floor of the House to shake his hand in open congratulation. With a terrible brilliance of descriptive power, it was Shaftesbury who, when they appeared before him, referred to the workers in the factories as 'like a mass of crooked alphabets', so bent and twisted were they by their deformities.

Such was the man who now entered the fight against the employers of young children in the textile mills.

By an Act of 1833 (known as Althorp's Act from the then Home Secretary), inspectors were appointed in all textile factories (except silk) to ensure that:- those under the age of nine — no work; 9-13 — a 48 hour week (and in addition two hours education per day); 13-18 — a 69 hour week. The Act was a good attempt, but the employers of child labour, however, merely laughed. 9-13? 13-18? . . . how could anyone discover the age of a child in days when there were no birth certificates. Compulsory registration of births was not established until 1837, and since the children were starved and stunted in growth, appearance was no guide. As for education — the factory owners merely converted the stoke-hole into a classroom, and when the stoker had a few spare moments . . . he became a schoolteacher.

Undeterred however, Shaftesbury continued his efforts in three further Acts of Parliament.

In 1842, the Mining Act prohibited female or child labour underground.

In 1844, Peel's Factory Act ordered that, in textile factories, children from 8-13 should work $6\frac{1}{2}$ hours per day; those from 13-18 and all women 12 hours per day. The 8-13 year-olds also had to have three hours education per day, or work a 10 hour day in the factory and then attend a day at school, and so on alternately. Or in some areas, the children worked half a day in school, and the other half day in the mill. This was called the 'half-time system'. A further requirement of the 1844 Act was for factory machinery to be fenced.

Then, in 1847, came the Ten Hours Act, limiting the work of boys 13-under 18 and all women to 10 hours per day.

But the employers were still at least smiling. Since the number of hours of work were laid down, they evaded the regulations by shift work, which made it difficult for the Inspectors to discover when any particular person actually began or finished work.

Accordingly, by the 1850 Act, the actual times of work were laid down:- 6 a.m. to 6 p.m. in summer; 7 a.m. to 7 p.m. in winter, including $1\frac{1}{2}$ hours for meals. Saturday was a half-day. As this Act applied to women and young persons, and was extended to children in 1853, it also, in practice, applied to men, for it was no use to work the factory when perhaps half the staff, i.e. all the women and children, had left.

But the full measure of the great-hearted nobleman had still not been shown. For 35 years, he fought for the unhappy children who had to sweep the chimneys. For 35 years he fought, until finally in 1875, an Act was passed which effectively ended the misery of these poor climbing boys.

At the same time, Shaftesbury played a leading part in the development of what were known as the 'Ragged Schools' for poor children. By 1850, about 80 of these schools did their best to educate and help over 8,000 pupils from the most destitute of society.

Another present-day organisation of which he was one of the founders in 1844 is the influential Y.M.C.A. (Young Men's Christian Association), which by 1955 had some four million members in 76 different countries.

He exposed, too, the terrible conditions in lunatic asylums, where the unfortunate inmates, chained and shackled, were exhibited to the general public on payment of a fee to the gaoler. As a result of his efforts, these unhappy people received a kinder treatment, and a better understanding of their illness.

Remember, then, Lord Shaftesbury — a nobleman who could have lived a life of luxury and ease, untroubled by care, but instead chose to devote himself to the service of others in a grim unflinching fight. Without him, indeed, your early life might have been spent in a factory, in a mine, or sweeping chimneys, and there is no doubt that when this truly great man died, the existence of the lowest and most distressed of human beings in this country was far happier than it would otherwise have been.

Perhaps few people know that Lord Shaftesbury is commemorated by the statue of Eros, in Piccadilly Circus in London.

Dr. Barnardo

Thomas John Barnardo (1845-1905) was a London doctor and preacher who had intended to become a medical missionary. But as he travelled along the streets and past the slums, he likewise, saw the perfect misery of those who were too young to help themselves, and who had no-one else to help them — children whose whole world was bounded by squalid houses and a playground in the gutter. In 1870, therefore, at the early age of 25, he founded the first of his homes to feed, clothe, and educate these homeless, almost lifeless children. Between 1867 and the year of his death in 1905, no fewer than 60,000 of them were given a fair start in life, and the challenge which Dr. Barnardo's Homes flung down to private charity still echoes to this day — 'No destitute child ever refused admission'.

William Booth

A different character altogether was William Booth (1829-1912). He was originally a Methodist Minister, who later worked in an Evangelical mission in one of the most degraded areas in the country — the East End of London. It seemed to him that only an organised campaign of determined warfare could clean the vileness which he witnessed. So in 1865, the Salvation Army was formed, run on semi-military lines, with William Booth as 'General'. To those who smile or sneer at the brass bands at street corner meetings which are so noticeable a feature of the Salvation Army, there should also be noted the night shelters, the homes for the destitute, the training establishments and the emigration schemes which are also the activities of the Salvation Army.

In the lives of these seven people in particular therefore, we have seen the influence of the Evangelical or Low Church movement.

High Church

The other group in the Church of England was the Oxford Movement, or High Church, so called because its leaders, John Henry Newman, John Keble and Edward Pusey were all Fellows of Oxford University. They wanted elaborate ceremonial and beliefs closer to the Roman Catholic faith — indeed Newman later became a Roman Catholic.

Other Faiths

At the same time, however, as the Church of England continued its progress, other religions were also permitted to flourish. In 1828, Noncomformists (i.e. those who did not conform to (agree with) the Church of England) were allowed to take part in local and national government; in 1829, by the Catholic Emancipation Act, Catholics could enter Parliament and hold Crown offices except those of Monarchy itself, Lord Chancellor, or Viceroy of Ireland; and in 1858, Jews could become Members of Parliament, for they were then no longer required to take the oath 'on the true faith of a Christian'. In 1871, Nonconformists were admitted to the universities of Oxford and Cambridge.

In other words, during the 19th century, religious toleration became an officially recognised fact. No longer was a person to be prevented from obtaining high or important posts merely because he was not a member of the Church of England.

Decline of the Church

But by the late 19th, and in the 20th century indeed, both the powerful Low Church Victorian religion and the High Church Oxford Movement had faded. There was a decline in religion altogether, for which at least four causes could be traced as far as the Church of England was concerned:

(i) Poorer preachers. University graduates, who had been accustomed to make their career in the Church, now found that better opportunities existed in education, business and scientific work.

Also, the low salaries paid to Church of England ministers meant that aged preachers, afflicted by deafness and other disabilities, tottered about the chancel, mumbling the prayers, and proceeding with painful effort through a scarcely-audible, ill-contrived sermon, yet refusing to retire because they had no money to enable them to do so.

(ii) The growth of doubt — the challenge of science which made life seem less a miracle of God than a complicated, but understandable, scientific cause. It began to appear as if everything that occurred in the world was capable, or would in the end prove capable, of scientific explanation without any need of religious assistance.

(iii) The increase of pleasure led to indifference to religion. Sunday had always been a day of leisure, but whereas at one time the Church was the only way of spending that leisure, gradually other attractive occupations became available — Sunday golf, Sunday cinemas, museums, and art galleries, Sunday railway excursions.

(iv) War. There have been three wars in the late 19th and 20th centuries — the Boer War (1899-1902), but more particularly the First World War (1914-18) and the Second World War (1939-45).

Now these wars presented the greatest opportunity to promote religion that the Church of England has ever had. They resulted in the greatest opportunity that the Church of England has ever lost. War filled the cathedrals and the village churches, it packed them with hundreds of thousands of people all driven there by one of the greatest of forces — fear. But the Church could not even give a definite answer to the question 'Is it right to kill?' Nor was it able to convince some how a God of Love could permit $22\frac{3}{4}$ million persons to be killed in the First World War, and 55 million in the Second World War, while yet a further 55 million from these wars endured the agony of their wounds.

Thus war swept away not only the churches, the clergy and the congregations, but also the faith itself.

On the other hand, it has been pointed out that religion is the power that tries to raise us above the rest of the animal world. Man, remember, is the only animal that prays. If he ceases to have any religion at all, the question is asked 'What will happen?'

Chapter XVII

The Humanitarians

There were other humanitarians (helpers of human beings), however, apart from those who were inspired by religious beliefs. In this chapter, even though briefly, we must learn about some of them, for it must always be remembered that these were men who tried to help their fellows. It does not matter how greatly they succeeded — the fact was that they tried.

Who, then, were these helpers of others in the 18th and 19th centuries?

Firstly, there were the poets — men such as Robert Burns (1759-96) and William Wordsworth (1770-1850) — the rhythm of whose words throbbed out a deep love of freedom — freedom from wrong, freedom from fear, freedom from oppression. Perhaps they had only a little influence — hard-bitten factory owners and overseers had no time for poetry — but nevertheless, upon the upper classes who read and appreciated the wonders of verse, they must surely have made some impression.

More influential than the poets were the prose writers. No man could have exposed more effectively the conditions of poor children, the life of the workhouse and the underworld, than Charles Dickens (1812-70). We all know the starving pauper child who asks for more in *Oliver Twist*; the wretched snivelling schoolchildren at Dotheboys Hall in *Nicholas Nickleby*; and in *Bleak House*, Jo the pitiful and heart-rending slum-child. Grimly and ruthlessly, the great novelist penned his true-to-life stories, and the Victorian world read, considered and commenced to act.

Also effective was Charles Kingsley (1819-75), who chose the title of the *Water Babies* to describe the life of a climbing boy who had to sweep the chimneys of the richer folk. He ran away from a cruel master, and fell into a stream, where he was turned into a water baby by the fairies. Except for the happy ending, the story was based on truth.

William Cobbett

Even more down-to-earth was William Cobbett (1763-1835), a farmer-writer whose *Weekly Political Register* (1802-35) had a great influence upon the working class whom he wished to help and educate. He travelled the southern part of England, and left a lively record thereof in his *Rural Rides* — for he was, in truth, a blunt, straight-telling man, who pitied the peasants and cursed those who oppressed them — the Jews, the tax collectors, the grasping landlords. No journalist has ever attained such influence upon the working class, as William Cobbett, and since his 'Register' did not contain any news, it did not have to pay the newspaper tax, thus bringing it within the purchasing power of the poorest.

So Cobbett recorded his travels:

'At Marlborough . . . a group of women labourers . . . presented such an assemblage of rags as I had never seen before, even amongst the hoppers at Farnham, many of whom are common beggars. I never before saw country people — and reapers, too, observe — so miserable in appearance as these. There were some very pretty girls, but ragged as colts, and as pale as ashes. The day was cold, too, and frost hardly off the ground; and their blue arms and lips would have made any heart ache.'

At Cirencester

'The labourers seem miserably poor. Their dwellings are little better than pig beds, and their looks indicated that their food is not nearly equal to that of a pig. Their wretched hovels are stuck upon little bits of ground on the roadside, where the space has been wider than the road demanded. In many places they have not two rods to a hovel.'

'At Upstreet I was struck with the words written upon a board which was fastened upon a pole, which pole was standing in a garden near a neat little box of a house. The words were these, "Paradise Place. Spring guns and steel traps are set here".'

'A family of five people have just as much, and eightpence over, as goes down the throat of one single footsoldier.'

'These fine oxen, this primest of human food, was, aye, every mouthful of it, destined to be devoured in the Wen (London) and that, too for the greater part, by the Jews, loan-jobbers, tax-eaters and their base and prostituted followers, dependents, purveyors, parasites and pimps, literary as well as other wretches, who, if suffered to live at all, ought to partake of nothing but the offal, and ought to come but one cut before the dogs and cats.'

So violent and abusive was his language, that, at one time, from 1817-19 he thought it desirable to seek the safety of America in order to avoid arrest. Even so, he still continued to send his articles to England for publication!

When he was at last arrested in 1831, on a charge of inciting people to revolt, his stinging criticism of the Government in the public law courts made the authorities wisely refrain from further prosecution. The following year, Cobbett became the Member of Parliament for Oldham.

Robert Owen

But the man who actually practised what the others only preached was the energetic Robert Owen (1771-1858). At the early age of 28, he had, by sheer hard work, become a managing partner in the New Lanark Mills in Scotland. The mills horrified him — grim, gaunt buildings whose workpeople were the scum of the gutters and the dregs of the slums — drunk, dirty and dishonest.

Amid these conditions, Robert Owen gradually developed his belief — a belief which was far in advance of his time, for only now has it been generally accepted. It seemed to him that a person's character was formed by the surroundings in which that person lived; for example, if a child was reared amid the filth and vileness of the slums, he would very likely become a wastrel or a criminal, but if he dwelt amid clean and decent surroundings, he would be more likely to grow up into a good citizen.

To prove this belief, Owen built good houses for his workpeople, and insisted on a high standard of sanitation. He paid higher wages than other factory owners . . . and for shorter hours — while the money thus earned could be spent in the very low-price shops which he opened. Nor would he allow child labour to brutalise his factories. No child under ten was employed in the New Lanark Mills; instead, they were sent to a school which must surely have been one of the happiest of its kind.

These activities staggered the industrial world. To men in authority, who regarded the labourer as a kind of lower animal, utterly incapable of reaching any higher level, these new ideas were a sheer waste of effort, time and money. Lunacy run riot, indeed.

But the fact that saved Robert Owen from the full blast of mockery, sneers and condemnation from his fellow factory owners was that the New Lanark Mills showed a great profit. (Naturally — since men who were contented and happy worked better and harder.) This, of course, altered the situation completely. In days when profit was very highly worshipped, other mill-owners could hardly be too disapproving of the new ideas. Indeed, some of these owners were sufficiently attracted to study them, but in the end very few could be persuaded to follow them. So the book Owen wrote in 1814, *A New View of Society*, did not have the success he had hoped.

He then tried to improve the conditions of the working class by means of Parliamentary laws. As a result of his efforts, a Factory Act was passed in 1819 which limited the work of children aged from nine to sixteen in cotton mills to 12 hours a day. But the employer of child labour merely laughed at the Act, for there was no proper inspection to see that these rules were carried out. In fact, the Justices of the Peace who were responsible for enforcing the law were often the mill-owners themselves. So the children continued to toil their 14 to 15 hour day.

Nor was Owen any more successful with his idea of 'Co-operation' (or 'Socialism' as it is now called). His aim here, indeed, was no less than a complete re-organisation of society — a re-organisation which did away with employers, the use of money, and the idea of making a profit at someone else's expense. Instead, every man would be a worker on the same social level. Every man would produce whatever he was able, and then exchange with others who had produced what he wanted. So money was not necessary, since business was conducted by exchange. In any event, money was not required, for no one made anything for his own profit; everything produced was handed over for the general benefit of the community.

But though Owen went to America in 1824, and at a place called New Harmony in Indiana, tried to found a 'Village of Co-operation' for 900 people, where everyone worked for the common good instead of personal benefit, this venture failed too. After all, human nature has always been greedy and selfish; few people want to work other than for their own benefit.

Nevertheless, on his return to England in 1829, he continued his efforts in a different form, and his ideas had such effect that by 1830, there were 300 Co-operative Societies in existence; by 1832, there were 500. Each member of these early Co-operatives paid a small amount every week to form a fund. With the money, the Societies then provided education for the workers; or they enabled the workers to set up their own general stores for buying and selling cheaply; while in some cases they set up their own small factories to produce cheap goods for the workers. It was a magnificent effort on the part of Owen's ideas, but by 1834, the movement had failed, due, among other reasons, to a lack of knowledge to overcome the difficulties involved.

Owen then turned his attention to the Trade Union movement, and for that you must read pages 178-179 of this book. There you will learn how the Grand National Consolidated Trades Union of half a million members collapsed within a year, as a result of financing a number of unsuccessful strikes, and through the opposition of employers and Government.

So Robert Owen died amid his disappointments — the man who founded Socialism, but at a time unsuitable for it to succeed. Yet, though his life was one of failure, the beliefs that he held were sound . . . and later ages have proved them for him.

Jeremy Bentham

The influence which William Cobbett had upon the working class was equalled by that of Jeremy Bentham (1748-1832) on the upper class of society.

Jeremy Bentham was a child genius. At the age of five, he could speak four languages, and he obtained his degree at Oxford University when he was 15. Being rich, he had the leisure to consider, to write and to travel abroad, and so could express and extend his influence.

In his view, to find the value of any organisation, institution or idea, it was only necessary to ask 'What use is it?' It was this use (i.e. the utility) which mattered, hence his views were called Utilitarianism.

The best answer to the question was that the use gave 'the greatest happiness of the greatest number'.

So with this question and answer, Bentham examined the Government of the country. Quite clearly, a Government was of use; it was needed in order to organise the nation. To provide 'the greatest happiness of the greatest number', Bentham advised that M.P.s should be elected by giving every man the vote, and Parliament should then increase the flow of trade, help the poor and oppressed, and promote education, hospitals and other social services.

The influence of his ideas was to last for over a century and a half. Nearly every aspect of Government was affected by it — the Reform

Bills, Free Trade, Trade Unions, Factory Acts, Poor Law, education, public health, law reform and prison reform.

But Jeremy Bentham intended to be remembered for even longer and more effectively than that. In his will, he left his fortune to University College, London, on condition that his body was preserved, and exhibited at the College meetings. Faithfully the University obeyed his wishes, and there he has remained ever since, sitting upright in the hall of the College. His broad-brimmed beaver hat rests on the death mask of his face, a gloved hand holds his cane, the embalmed body is neatly dressed in one of his suits, while his skull rests in a glass-domed case between his feet. There he presides to this day at a Council meeting — present, but not voting.

Chapter XVIII

Trade Unions

Early Unions
'Unity is strength'.

The Agricultural and Industrial Revolutions had reduced the working class to desperation and a determination to improve their conditions. The question was . . . how? The employers were against them, and the employers controlled Parliament; Parliament made the laws and controlled the army. Against such powerful opposition — employers, Parliament, law courts and army — what chance had the working class? Certainly, one man on his own could not hope to succeed. He would merely lose his job, and never obtain another. He might even lose his life. But . . . there was one faint hope . . . yes . . . one faint hope . . . 'unity is strength' . . . 'unity is strength'.

So the working men began to unite. They started by trying to develop the local trade clubs and organisations which had appeared from the late 17th century onwards. These organisations had provided sickness and unemployment benefits to their members, as well as negotiating for higher wages and better conditions of work. Now, in the later 18th century, the workers tried to make them even more powerful.

They had, however, chosen a very unfortunate moment to do so, for it was then the period of the French Revolution. On the far side of the Channel, the French peasantry, infuriated by years of grievances, had resolved on desperate measures. They swept into the capital city, captured the great prison-fortress of the Bastille, and paraded triumphantly through the streets with the heads of their enemies born aloft on the ends of pikes.

After that, their vengeance became even worse. The gutters of Paris were swilled with human blood; in the Place de la Concorde, the guillotine never ceased its gory task, and cartloads of human bodies were flung into the fields outside the city walls. In such a frenzy and fury of mob rule, not even the highest in the land could hope for mercy, and in January, 1793, Louis XVI, King of France, was guillotined, to be followed nine months later by an old, haggard, grey-haired woman — the once gay, lively, beautiful Marie Antoinette, his Queen. To show the citizens of Paris how well they were doing their work, the authorities compelled a brilliant wax-modeller, Madame Tussaud, to take death masks from the freshly-severed heads of the nobility so that casts could be made and exhibited. In 1802, this Madame Tussaud brought her best work to England.

The British Government at the time was in a state of alarm lest the influence of the French Revolution should not be halted by the waters of the English Channel. The leading Ministers and nobility had no wish to become further candidates for Madame Tussaud's skill, and accordingly any attempt on the part of the English working class to unite was treated as a threat of revolt.

In 1799 and 1800, therefore, the Combination Acts were passed to prevent any union meetings. It was now illegal for the workers to combine to raise wages. It was also illegal for the employers to combine to lower wages, but the laws were not enforced against the employers who, in any case, could easily evade them. For a quarter of a century, these Acts remained in force, not being repealed until 1824.

The repeal, indeed, when it came, was due to 15 years untiring effort by one man . . . Francis Place, a London tailor, the backroom of whose shop became the centre of the campaign. From here, he arranged for Trade Unions to continue by calling themselves Friendly Societies — organisations which, commencing about 1650, provided sickness, unemployment and old age benefits from their members' subscriptions, but, unlike the trade unions, were not so concerned about working conditions. Place then wrote letters and Press articles, interviewed witnesses, obtained evidence, spoke to M.P.s, tradespeople and workmen, and not least gained the help of Joseph Hume, a Member of Parliament, who put forward the Union views to a Commission.

Fifteen years of such careful, thorough and untiring work, had its success — in 1824, the Combination Acts were repealed, and though an outburst of strikes caused them to be partly re-enacted in 1825, nevertheless Trade Unions were now at least legal, even if limited in power. They could bargain for better conditions of work, but in the event of a strike, they were not allowed to 'obstruct', 'molest' or 'intimidate' non-strikers or others . . . and the three words in apostrophes could be very widely interpreted by the law.

In due course, the fears caused by the French Revolution lessened, and so the idea of the union of the workers was revived. Five early efforts were made. From 1829-30, John Doherty founded a Spinners Union, while from 1830-1 he established a more ambitious organisation called the National Association for the Protection of Labour, which included cotton workers, potters, coalminers, blacksmiths and many more. In 1832-4, the Builders' Union of joiners, masons and similar trades was formed. Then, in 1834, Robert Owen founded the Grand National Consolidated Trades Union (G.N.C.T.U.) of half a million members, to unite workers from all trades, and to take over control from the employers. His G.N.C.T.U. even included in its organisation such branches as 'The Female Tailors', 'Miscellaneous Females' and 'The Ancient Virgins'. It had, however, a shorter life than its title, for it lasted less than a year as a result of financing a number of unsuccessful strikes. For the same reason — a disastrous strike in 1844 — the Miners' Association founded in 1840, had gradually faded away by 1850.

It was not really surprising that these early unions failed: the difficulties they faced were by no means few or slight.

Even at the outset, their own organisation was weak. The workers, uneducated and unintelligent, had not enough money to form funds; the leaders had no experience of organising. In many cases, local groups were formed, which made their own decisions — often with fatal results.

Then, ready to emphasize any weakness was the fact that everyone else was against them. The alarm of the Government, and hence its opposition was well shown in the case of the 'Tolpuddle Martyrs' in 1834. In the little village of Tolpuddle, in Dorset, six poor labourers had their wages reduced. They held a meeting to consider the calamity, and resolved to form a union — a branch of the G.N.C.T.U. Worse still, they took an oath in front of a painted figure of Death, whereupon they were later arrested, and sentenced to seven years' transportation on the excuse they had taken an illegal secret oath. This sentence, however, though in accordance with the law, had carried the powers of the Government beyond the limit which even the early 19th century was prepared to admit as justice. The unions organised demonstrations, public sympathy was aroused, and 250,000 people signed a petition for the release of the unfortunate labourers. But the Government still contrived to delay the matter, and it was not until four years had passed that all the six men were brought back from Australia.

The law, too, was against the unions. Their funds were not protected by the laws and, as a later case showed, when Mr. Hornby,

Treasurer of the Boilermakers Union, stole some of his Union money in 1867, the union could not take any effective legal action about it. Also, when a strike was ordered, and the employer obtained other workers from elsewhere, any attempt at picketing (when strikers stood around the factory, and tried to discourage other employees from going to work) was a crime.

Thirdly, public opinion was against the unions . . . and it must be admitted that whenever there was a strike, it was often the public who suffered. Another reason for public objection, however, was the violence of the smaller unions, particularly when, for example, the Saw Grinders Union of Sheffield in 1867 compelled non-members to join by breaking their tools, maiming them and even by murder.

The employers were naturally against the unions, and tried to make all employees sign a statement that they did not belong to a Trade Union. The chief weapon of the employers was the 'lock-out' — if the workers of one factory went on strike, the other employers in the district would threaten to lock out (i.e. suspend from work) all the workers in their factories. Or the employers refused to take back the men when the strike was over.

Economic ideas were against the Unions, too. At this time, there was a belief in a fixed total wage fund, i.e. there was a definite fixed amount of money available to pay all the wages of the nation. Thus if one group of workers obtained an increase in pay, other workers would have to receive less. Though the idea was wrong, people believed it.

New Model Unions

It was only gradually that the Unions began to overcome such opposition. The first step towards victory occurred when the earlier and unsuccessful type of Union began to fade, and in its place came the 'New Model Union' — as for example, the Amalgamated Society of Engineers, founded in 1851.

This Society of Engineers was obviously a far better organisation altogether. In the first instance, only the skilled workers (i.e. the higher paid) were allowed to join, and thus the union, having built up a large reserve of funds from their subscriptions, could employ paid officials, and could afford good publicity. It also engaged lawyers to fight its legal battles, for even when cases were lost, they still served to show any injustice of the law.

In any event, however, the most important feature of the New Model Union was its desire for peace rather than war, its desire to negotiate rather than to strike. And the men who led the negotiations were skilled, courteous and moderate in their requirements, thus creating a favourable impression on employers and Government officials alike. Of course, the money saved by avoiding strikes and the giving out of strike pay, enabled much higher unemployment, sickness, accident and funeral benefits to be paid to members.

Further to improve union organisation, a 'junta' as it was called (from the Spanish word for a council), consisting of the Secretaries of the five leading unions, met in London 1860-71, to decide matters of common policy. Then, in 1868, the Trade Union Congress was established to hold a general conference of labour organisations every year. So not only were the workers getting together to form unions, but also the unions themselves were getting together.

Unskilled Unions

After the New Model Unions for skilled workers, there came the next stage . . . an energetic effort to help the unskilled workers to form unions. As a result, in 1888-89, three outstanding successes were achieved when Bryant and May's match girls led by Annie Besant, the gas workers led by Will Thorne, and the London dockers all secured better wages.

Of these three examples, the most effective was undoubtedly the Dockers' Strike, which was organised in 1889 by three men — Thomas Mann, Ben Tillett and John Burns. The dockers demanded an increase in wages so that they could earn a total of 2½p. an hour—'the dockers' tanner' — and also that they should be given regular employment, instead of having to trample each other underfoot in a desperate bid to be selected for work whenever a ship entered the port.

The dock-owners refused these demands, and the strike began. It was to be an amazing and a unique effort. As the long processions of gaunt, ragged and starving men, carrying, for all to see, the docker's usual meal of fish heads and stale bread, made their peaceful way through the streets of London, they aroused a sympathy that extended over the entire nation. For four weeks, the strike continued. The public contributed generously to the dockers' cause; money came even from Australia. The Roman Catholic Archbishop of Westminster, Cardinal Manning, himself negotiated on the dockers' behalf with their employers, and after four weeks, the dockers won their 'tanner' and better conditions of work.

Of course, nothing succeeds like success, and more and more men began to apply for union membership, until by 1890, 20 per cent of the male working population were in the Trade Unions.

Government help

At the same time, the Government also began to help the workers by making Trade Unions legal bodies and protecting their funds 1871, by allowing *peaceful* picketing in 1875, while no act committed by two or more persons in a trade dispute was to be punishable unless also punishable if committed by one man.

Also, in 1867, a very important Master and Servant Act was passed. Previously a worker who left his work could be arrested, convicted and imprisoned for breaking his agreement or contract. In the course of his trial, he was not allowed to give evidence against his employer. On the other hand, if an employer broke a contract, he could only be sued for damages, and could give evidence. Now, from 1867, more or less the same conditions were applied to the worker as to the employer, and in 1875, complete equality was given.

Then in 1896, after many previous attempts, the Truck Acts abolished the payment of wages in kind (i.e. in goods), for some employers had established their own shops, and compelled their workers to purchase goods there at high prices in part payment of their wages.

The following year, the Workmen's Compensation Act was passed by which employers in certain occupations had to compensate employees for any injuries which happened in the course of their work, whether the injuries were the fault of the employer or not. In 1906, this compensation was extended to all accidents in all trades.

Chapter XIX

Trade Unions in
the 20th Century

New Unions

The 20th century saw the tremendous triumph of the Trade Union movement.

The success was based on the 'New Unions', as they were called — unions of the less skilled men, with little money, who were willing to strike against the hated class of employers, and who wanted to have their own representatives in Parliament to help the cause of the workers. (Do not confuse this 'New Unionism' with the 'New Model Unionism' of 50 years before. There were at least four main differences. The New Model Unions, remember, (i) were composed of skilled men, (ii) with large funds, (iii) and they wished to work with the employers by negotiation rather than strikes. (iv) Nor did they have their own representatives in Parliament, but usually relied on help from the existing Liberal Party.)

Influence in Parliament

For a long time, many of the working class had realised that since Parliament made the laws, they should seek to have power and influence in that Parliament. If only a number of people willing to help the lower classes could become Members of Parliament, then laws could be passed to make life freer and fairer for the poorer ranks of labour.

The first steps began when the Reform Act of 1867 gave the vote to artisans (town workers) — about one million persons altogether. As a result, in 1874, Alexander McDonald (Stafford) and Thomas Burt (Morpeth), both coalminers, were sent to Parliament by the working class votes. Then followed the Reform Act of 1884, giving the vote to agricultural workers also — another two million, and accordingly, in 1885, Joseph Arch rode in triumph through King's Lynn as the newly elected Member of Parliament for Norfolk, given that honour by the agricultural labourers' votes.

The next stage was to establish some form of Parliamentary organisation, so in 1893, the Independent Labour Party was founded. Its founder was Keir Hardie, a Scottish miner of humble birth, and a man who, when he was elected to the top-hatted, striped-suit brotherhood of the House of Commons in 1892, arrived in a cloth cap, red tie and a workman's clothes.

It was Keir Hardie, too, who tried to obtain the support of the Trade Unions, while he also received help from the Fabian Society. This society, beginning in 1894, was a middle class movement, and included the brilliant minds of George Bernard Shaw, H. G. Wells, and Mr. and Mrs. Sidney Webb. The group provided the brains and a policy of tremendous value for the future. There was nothing violent or vicious about the Fabians; they wished peacefully and slowly to influence public opinion so that the country could be organised for the good of everyone, and not for the benefit of a few individuals only. The Society took its name from the Roman general, Fabius Cunctator, who succeeded in his campaign by patiently waiting for the best moment to advance.

So the Independent Labour Party, the Trade Unions and the Fabian Society joined to form the Labour Representation Committee in 1900*, and by the time the Committee changed its name to the Labour Party in 1906, it already had 29 Members of Parliament. The value of this Parliamentary force was soon to be shown.

First, there was the celebrated Taff Vale case. In 1901, there was a strike on the Taff Vale Railway in South Wales. During the strike, naturally, the Company lost a lot of money, and therefore sued the Union for compensation; the Union had called the strike, and so why should not the Union pay for any damage that resulted? The highest court of law, the House of Lords, agreed, and the Union was fined £23,000. Immediately, the whole Trade Union movement rose up in alarm, for if they had to pay for any damage caused every time there was a strike, they would soon be bankrupt. So the Labour M.P.s used their influence, and the 1906 Trades Disputes Act said that Unions would not have to pay for strike damage.

A second challenge was the Osborne Case. At the beginning of the

---

*The Social Democratic Federation also joined, but withdrew 1901. The S.D.F. founded by Henry Hyndman in 1881, wanted Parliamentary reform, State help for the poor, nationalisation of land, railways and mines. In 1911, it formed the British Socialist Party.

20th century, Members of Parliament received no salary, and therefore had to have a private income of their own. In order to pay the Labour M.P.s (who came from a class of people who were not likely to have a private income) the Trade Unions required their members to contribute to a fund. But in 1908-9, W. V. Osborne, a railway union secretary and a Liberal in politics, successfully objected to the political use of his money to benefit the Labour Party, and the practice was declared illegal. Many Labour M.P.s thus lost their income from the Unions, and therefore went into action with an even greater determination. As a result, in 1911, Members of Parliament received a salary, while in 1913, the Trade Union Act allowed political funds to be collected by Trade Unions, but members could 'contract out' (i.e. not pay) if they wished.

From then onwards, the unions developed in strength, especially in 1914 when the Miners', the Railwaymen's and the Transport Workers' Unions all combined to form the 'Triple Alliance'. Here indeed, was a vast and united labour force, $1\frac{1}{2}$ million strong, greater and more powerful than had ever before been known in union history — men, money and organisation — all ready to act in its own interests. Thus it is not surprising that after the First World War, when prices rose, wages fell and unemployment increased, some trade unionists believed they might challenge the Government itself. The contest was not long delayed, and the battleground was the coal mines.

General Strike

After the Great War, the coal industry suffered from foreign competition, particularly from the U.S.A., Germany and France, and also from the use of petroleum, oil, and hydro-electric power. Amid the changing conditions of the 20th century, indeed, the demand for coal declined rapidly — for example: the petrol-engined motor car was replacing the steam locomotive, the motor vessel replaced the steamship; while in furnaces, boilers and home fire grates, a more efficient construction enabled the same heat to be obtained from less fuel.

Our most profitable coalfields were the Northumberland and Durham, Yorkshire, South Staffordshire, Derby, Nottinghamshire and South Wales, but even in these, many of the best seams were already finished, and the machinery we used was out of date. As a matter of fact, only one-seventh of the coal we produced was cut by machines; the rest — about 240 million tons — was hacked out by human muscle power. This was a less expensive method in small mines with thin seams, but very costly in terms of human effort, disease and death.

So by 1925, the miners were facing a very serious situation indeed.

Two Commissions of Enquiry had been set up to find out what help could be given. In 1919, the Sankey Commission, under Judge Sir John Sankey recommended that the Government should take over the mines (i.e. nationalise them), and in 1926 a Commission under Sir Herbert Samuel opposed such nationalisation. In any event, the Government took no action at all to improve the conditions in the mines except to provide a State subsidy (a grant of money).

Then, in 1926, this subsidy was withdrawn, and in order to sell more coal by lowering the price, the employers proposed to reduce the men's wages and extend the hours of work. The miners' reply was prompt and definite, 'Not a penny off the pay; not a minute on the day'. They went on strike, and the battle against the employers began.

But the real seriousness of the situation then occurred, for the Trade Union Congress supported the miners, and a General Strike of all workers was called in sympathy with them. Thus no longer was this merely a battle of the coal miners against the coal mine owners; it was now seen as a threat by the T.U.C. against the Government itself, for the whole nation was involved.

It was no mean threat either. The railways, road transport, the docks, the iron and steel works, the builders, the electric, gas and printing industries, all closed down. Three million men went out on strike, and for a brief while it seemed that the life of the nation would be halted and crippled.

But the Government was ready to act. Troops and voluntary workers were employed to keep the essential services going — the troops manned the docks and the power stations, while trains and buses had volunteer drivers and surprisingly few accidents. The Government also managed to print a broadsheet called the *British Gazette,* and above all, controlled the radio, so the only means of giving news, instructions and propaganda to the nation were under the control of Parliament.

The strike itself varied in emotion. There was trouble in some areas, but that was inevitable. Workers going to their work received rough treatment from the pickets. Buses manned by volunteers travelled along with boarded windows and barbed wire across the radiators. Convoys of food lorries were escorted by armoured cars. The *Flying Scotsman,* the fast express train from London to Edinburgh, was derailed by removing part of the track. But in other areas, police and strikers played football; the county cricket matches and the city ceremonies continued as usual.

In face of such determination by the Government and, to be quite honest, by the lack of desire by many T.U.C. leaders to be engaged in such a conflict, the General Strike ended after nine days (4th to 12th of May, 1926), and though the miners struggled on for some months more, lack of funds finally compelled them to submit, and they had to return to work under conditions worse even than before.

The Government, however, was determined that there should be no repetition of such a national struggle, and accordingly in 1927, the Trades Dispute Act was passed: (i) a strike was illegal if it was used for any purpose other than the trade dispute by which it was caused, and a strike must not coerce the Government. (ii) general and sympathetic strikes were also illegal — one union must not go on strike merely in order to support another union strike. (iii) protection would be given to non-strikers in illegal strikes; (iv) Union funds must not be used for illegal strikes.

Unions 1927-60

For a while, therefore, until the Second World War in 1939, the trade union movement became quieter, but the trade unions were not defeated. They continued their previous policy of gaining influence in Parliament, and they reaped their reward when the Labour Party (which they supported) came into power, and repealed the 1927 Act in 1946.

Then, once again, the trade union movement increased its strength. By 1951 it was obvious that the trade unions had become so strong that they could afford to ignore altogether the Parliamentary means by which they had climbed to power. Some $9\frac{1}{2}$ million workers were now trade union members, and giant organisations such as the National Union of Mineworkers, the National Union of General and Municipal Workers, and the Transport and General Workers Union, looked after their interests.

Mention of the Transport and General Workers Union (T.G.W.U.) naturally leads to the mention of Ernest Bevin (1881-1951), the greatest trade union leader of the century, and a man with the most remarkable of careers.

He was born a labourer's son in Somerset; he was left an orphan at the age of seven, and he finished his schooling four years later. After a short time as a farm boy, he moved to Bristol at the age of 13, and became a carter, van-lad and van-driver. From such a start in life, he attained a height rarely equalled by any others.

Joining the dockers' union as an official, he gained a nationwide fame in 1920 by his skill in handling the claims of his union against even a learned barrister. The occasion earned him the title of 'the dockers K.C.' (King's Counsel — the highest distinction for a lawyer), and he certainly deserved it. For three days, he conducted the case for the dockers with a brilliance that no one could deny. He showed beyond doubt that an average dock labourer heaved a heavier load in a day than a dockside dray horse in a week. And the horse was better fed. When the employers argued that a man and his family could live on a wage of just over £3 per week at the time, Ernest Bevin promptly purchased the essential foods to that sum, and in front of the entire court silenced his opponents by presenting the food to them and inviting them to live off it. When he sat down at the end of his speech, the whole court joined in the applause.

He also had brawn to support his brain. At one dockers' meeting, his speech was constantly interrupted by the vulgar abuse of an Irish navvy. Finally, Ernest Bevin paused, climbed slowly down from the lorry platform, took a firm grasp of his opponent, and hurled him into the dock.

His success continued when, out of 32 separate unions, he created the single Transport and General Workers Union — a mammoth organisation with over $1\frac{1}{4}$ million members by 1960 — and became its general secretary from 1921-40.

Parliamentary fame followed. In the Second World War (1939-45), he was appointed Minister of Labour, and through the respect in which he was held by the working class, he prevented industrial unrest during the critical years when England fought for her life. In the Labour Government of 1945-51, he was Secretary of State for Foreign Affairs — an incredible status for the Somerset labourer's son who left school at the age of eleven. He was, without doubt, the most skilful of negotiators, straight-forward and straight-talking, but above all he was a realist — a man who knew the difference between the desirable and the possible. His services to the working class of this nation will long be remembered in history.

Unions today

So the mighty trade union movement continued on its way. Success in any dispute was almost certain, for the unions possessed ample funds, and were armed with a terrible weapon — the strike — and the strike could paralyse any industry at any moment. No longer need the worker fear, as in years gone by, the threat of sweated labour, of working long boring hours in unhealthy factories, where he was the slave of a machine. Instead, the union was there to help and protect him, and in this respect the benefit of the trade unions to the working class cannot be denied.

In this respect also, however, the trade unions must be further considered. For they existed solely for the benefit of the working class. In order to prevent unemployment, it has been suggested that the unions tended to resist any new and labour-saving methods of production. In order to prevent unemployment, the unions forbade overtime, and would not allow redundant workers (those for whom there is no work when trade for some reason becomes less) to be dismissed. In order to prevent unemployment, the unions compelled employers to have two men where there was work for only one. So the English public had to suffer from high prices, and English trade suffered when it had to compete against cheaper foreign goods.

Admittedly, no longer need the worker fear, as in days gone by, the threat of sweated labour or of unjust dismissal. But indeed, it has been argued that the pendulum has swung so far in the other direction that he need not even fear dismissal for any reason whatsoever, whether just or unjust. No employer could withstand his union, so the situation in fact became so farcical that in some cases if an employer attempted to run his own business, the men immediately protested, and if even a naughty word was used, there was a strike.

And when a strike occurred, an employer was helpless. He could find no other labour to carry on, for it took a very brave man to try to enter the factory, even with police protection, against the howling, jeering, threatening mob of pickets outside, and a non-union man who continued to work in a strike factory might not be murdered, no doubt — but could certainly be driven to commit suicide by the hostility of the other union workers afterwards.

To make matters worse, many of the strikes were unofficial. So vast had the trade union organisations become that the leaders were out of touch with the rank and file; thus the shop stewards (local leaders elected in the factory) had too great a power, which encouraged them to take unofficial action. But whether a strike was unofficial or not, the English public still had to suffer, and England's trade also had to suffer when competing against unhampered foreign firms.

In such a situation as this, the Government slowly commenced to act. In 1896, the Board of Trade offered to settle disputes if asked to do so, and in 1912, a special Industrial Council was established for the same purpose.

Then in 1917, a Committee under Mr. J. H. Whitley, (M.P. for Halifax, and later Speaker of the House of Commons), suggested that the prevention of disputes was better than trying to cure them after they had started. Thus a National Council, District Councils and Factory Committees was set up, so that both employers and employed could discuss matters with a view to avoiding trouble. Though this idea did not succeed, it marked a stage of progress.

Steadily, the Government continued its efforts to prevent strikes, and by 1960, the Minister of Labour could offer to settle any dispute. Moreover, he could arrange for Special Courts of Inquiry into a dispute and publish the reports, so the whole country could judge if one side was being unreasonable.

Very truly, indeed, the maintaining of good relationships between employer and employed is one of the most difficult problems that face this country today.

Chapter XX

The Chartists

Reasons for Chartism

The workers were dissatisfied.

The 1832 Reform Bill, they well knew, had given the vote to the manufacturers and the middle class, but not to them. So the lower classes could not expect any help from Parliament to improve their lives.

When the workers tried to form unions, John Doherty's Spinners' Union (1829-30) and his National Association for the Protection of Labour (1830-1) which included cotton workers, potters, coalminers, blacksmiths and many more . . . each lasted only about twelve months. The Builders Union of joiners, masons and similar trades managed to exist from 1832-4. Then in 1834, Robert Owen founded the Grand National Consolidated Trades Union of half a million members, and this had a shorter life than its title, for it lasted less than a year as a result of financing a number of unsuccessful strikes, and of facing the overwhelming opposition of employers and Government.

It is not surprising these early unions failed. Even at the outset, their own organisation was weak. The workers, uneducated and un-intelligent, had not enough money to form funds; the leaders had no experience of organising. The Government, fearing revolution, opposed the unions, particularly in the case of the Tolpuddle Martyrs of 1834, when six poor Dorset labourers who formed a union, were arrested on the excuse they had taken an illegal secret oath, and sentenced to seven years transportation. The law was against the unions, and did not protect their funds, while when a strike was in progress, picketing was a crime. Public opinion disliked the unions, for when there was a strike, it was often the public who suffered. The employers were naturally against the unions, and made all those who wanted work sign a statement (the 'Document', as it was called), to the effect they did not belong to a trade union. In addition, the employers locked out men, or refused to re-employ them when a strike was over. Finally, the belief in a fixed total wage fund meant that if some workers gained more pay, other workers would have less.

So the trade union movement, overwhelmed by all this opposition, was unable to improve conditions for the working class.

And if a worker became poor, remember, the Poor Law Act 1834 (see page 203) sent him to the workhouse. This was a place of bare brick walls, wooden tables, wooden benches and rough straw beds. The conditions were deliberately made as grim as possible for the healthy, while the aged and sick were neglected to die. The sexes were separated to prevent the breeding of pauper children, and of those babies who did enter the workhouse, one-third of them died. In any event, the aged, infirm, sick, the very young and lunatics were all herded together. The food they received was generally sufficient but monotonous, and on that grim diet they toiled at oakum picking (separating the strands of old rope for re-use) or stone breaking, for wages lower than could be earned outside. Small wonder they called the workhouses the 'New Bastilles' (from the Bastille — the grim prison-fortress in Paris).

Meanwhile, amid all this dissatisfaction, the ideas of Robert Owen were spreading. He wrote *A New View of Society* in 1814, urging better conditions in the factories and in workers' homes. It was he who founded 'Socialism' — a faith that required no less than a complete re-organisation of society. This new world of Owen's would do away with employers, the use of money and the idea of making a profit at someone else's expense. Instead, every man would be a worker on the same social level. He would labour in happy co-operation with his fellows rather than in grim soul-destroying competition, and would obtain his wants by exchanging his own work for the different goods produced by others. Ideas such as these began to reach and to rouse the hopes of the lower classes

The Chartist Movement

So yet another effort was made by the workers to try to improve their conditions.

There were three leaders of this effort, each operating in a different area. In London, there was William Lovett, Secretary of the London Working Men's Association founded in 1836 — a man of real determination and utter sincerity, a great believer in the value of education. Meanwhile, in Birmingham was Thomas Attwood, another very capable organiser. Both these men believed in moral force — the peaceful means of obtaining their desire. But it was in the north that the real leadership of the movement lay, and here was the fiery Feargus

O'Connor, editor of the newspaper *The Northern Star*. O'Connor, of course, was an Irishman, and believed in physical force and violence to gain his ends.

The aims of the three leaders were written down in a document called *The People's Charter* which was published in 1838, and the followers of the movement were thus called Chartists.

The People's Charter had six demands: (i) every adult man to have a vote; (ii) no need for a Member of Parliament to have to own property. At that time, a county M.P. had to have an income of at least £600 a year from his land, and a borough M.P. at least £300 a year from his property, so only the wealthy could enter Parliament. (iii) Annual Parliaments. (iv) Members of Parliament to be paid, so a poor working man could be an M.P. (v) Equal electoral districts, i.e. the same numbers of voters in each area; (vi) voting by secret ballot.

At first sight, you will say all these aims were political . . . and that is quite true, they were . . . but if these six demands were accepted — (so study them carefully again) — it would mean that the workers would have a vote, and could even become Members of Parliament. Once the workers had thus obtained power in Parliament, they could pass laws to improve the economic and social conditions in which they had to live.

First petition

So when the Charter had been drawn up, its demands were presented to the House of Commons in 1839 . . . and rejected.

The consequences might have been foreseen, for many had placed great hopes on the Charter. There were riots at the meeting place called the Bull Ring, in Birmingham, and there was talk of a national general strike.

The chief reaction, however, came from South Wales, and here the leader was the gallant John Frost. A draper by trade, he was so respected by his fellow citizens, that he became mayor, magistrate and Justice of the Peace. When the Chartist movement came to Wales, he was one of its leaders, for well he knew the sufferings of the coal-miners and the iron workers in the area.

The rejection of the Charter saw the revolt in South Wales. On the night of November 3rd, 1839, over 1,000 men gathered on the hinterland mountains above Newport. Their intention was to march upon the city, and then journey to Monmouth to release any Chartists imprisoned there. John Frost moved amid the gathering, and therein

John Wesley

Oil painting of 1766 by Nathaniel Hone, R.A.

Elizabeth Fry

Painting after Charles Robert Leslie, R.A.

(both reproduced by courtesy of The National Portrait Gallery)

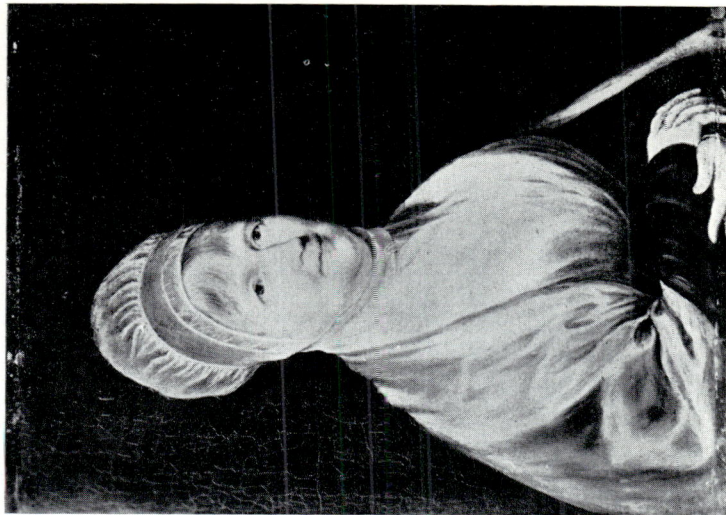

The Seventh Earl of Shaftesbury

Painting by George Frederick Watts

Robert Owen

Drawing attributed to Sam Bough

(both reproduced by courtesy of The National Portrait Gallery)

Chartist procession at Blackfriars, 1848

(from an engraving in the Mansell Collection)

Sir Thomas Spencer Wells operating with use of the Lister Carbolic Spray and Junker's Chloroform Inhaler

lay the tragedy. Mayor and magistrate John Frost was; military leader he was not. To move 1,000 untrained men over the mountains in the darkness was a task too difficult, and, worse still, a torrential downpour of rain occurred. Thus it was ten hours before the ragged formations even entered Newport, by which time the alarm had been given and the troops alerted. As the columns moved across the square, the soldiers opened fire, and all was over in 20 minutes. Twenty-four died, some 40 were wounded, and Frost and other leaders transported to Botany Bay in Australia whence they did not return for 17 years. It was a tragic end to a hopeless effort.

Second petition

As soon as the news of the rejection of the presentation was announced in England, however, Feargus O'Connor came to the fore. Another presentation, with $3\frac{1}{4}$ million signatures, was made in 1842 . . . and again rejected. The chief riots that followed this time were the 'Plug Plots' in the Midlands, where the plugs of steam boilers were pulled out to prevent the machinery working. More important, Feargus O'Connor went into action. Unfortunately, he was no real leader, and his anger and activities were turned first upon his own colleagues, and then to support other matters outside the main interests of Chartism. For some years, therefore, the Chartist programme itself remained inactive.

Third petition

Not until 1847 did the movement commence to revive, and then, once again, its thoughts turned towards another petition to Parliament. But this time it was to be O'Connor's idea of a petition — a mammoth endeavour with millions of signatures, borne through the streets of London by enthusiastic thousands of Chartists. The magnitude of such an effort would overwhelm the Government, and ensure the triumph of the working class. A new Republic of Britain would then be established. Its President, not surprisingly, was to be Feargus O'Connor.

It was a favourable opportunity, too. The year 1848 was to be recorded in history as the Year of Revolutions. In that year, Louis Philippe, King of France, fled for his life to the shores of England. Meanwhile, in Sicily, a revolt compelled the King to grant a constitution, and the fever of rebellion then spread onwards to Austria, Hungary, Italy, and the German States, as each of these areas strove

G

to rid itself of harsh and tyrannical rulers. Thus in Austria, Prince Metternich, virtual dictator for 40 years, gathered his belongings and fled swiftly over the border en route to England. In Hungary, the riotous mobs compelled the Austrians to withdraw, and leave them free to govern themselves; the peoples of Italy also rose up to expel their hated Austrian rulers; and at the same time, the princes and other powers in the various German States were only too glad to give way to the demands for better government. The whole of Europe was in ferment.

Then, amid such an atmosphere as this, the British Government received the news of the Chartist Petition, and the planning of a giant parade by its supporters. It is not surprising, therefore, that the Government of England rose up in a justifiable alarm and panic. The great Duke of Wellington, breaker of the Maratta power in India in 1803, hero of the Peninsular War against France (1808-14), conqueror of the genius of Napoleon at the battle of Waterloo in 1815, the most respected and revered figure of the time, was consulted, and agreed to take charge of counter-measures.

Accordingly, the great old Duke prepared.

The Queen left London for the safety of the Isle of Wight. Eight thousand soldiers paraded along the Embankment of the river, with the knowledge that twelve heavy cannon were all ready for action at the Royal Mews. Four thousand police constables guarded the bridges over the River Thames, and the area round Trafalgar Square; 1,500 Chelsea Pensioners were assembled for the defence of Battersea and Vauxhall. Should the roads be blocked, three steamboats on the Thames were prepared to move the troops to any threatened area immediately. The Government offices in Whitehall were organised as for a siege, and rifles were issued to the clerks in the General Post Office. An even more likely target for assault, the Bank of England, had its walls barricaded with sandbags and cannon mounted on the roof. Finally, in the rear of all these preparations was a force of 170,000 special constables.

The Chartist meeting passed off peacefully. The great procession made its way through the streets without incident, and the petition, with its 5,700,000 signatures, according to O'Connor, and weighing five tons according to O'Connor, was duly presented to Parliament.

Here it was carefully investigated . . . and a gale of ever-increasing laughter began to sweep through Whitehall. It was indeed quite obvious that O'Connor's enthusiasm had affected his mathematical capacity. The members attending the mass meeting of the Chartists was found to be somewhat less than O'Connor's estimate of 500,000 . . . instead, about 20,000. The weight of the petition was realised not at five tons, but five hundred-weight.

From then onwards, the farce developed more rapidly. A careful survey of the petition reduced its claim of 5,700,000 signatures, to a mere two million, and among these occurred such doubtful ones as 'Queen Victoria', 'The Duke of Wellington', 'Sir Robert Peel', 'Pugnose', 'Flatnose', 'Punch', 'No cheese' as well as other names which no self-respecting human being would ever have dared to possess. The reason for these fantastic forgeries was only too clear. The various sheets of the petition had been left lying about anywhere for signature, and schoolchildren and other wits had not been slow to seize the opportunity.

The Chartist Movement thus died from ridicule.

Reasons for failure

But there were also other reasons for its failure. The leadership of the movement was very poor, and very badly organised; many of the leading Chartists were more concerned with quarrelling among themselves. The upper class opposed them; the middle class did not join them. Most important, however, was the fact that by 1848, better conditions for the working class were already coming into force, especially when the Repeal of the Corn Laws in 1846 gave cheaper bread, and the Ten Hours Act of 1847 meant less work. Furthermore, for those who were still dissatisfied, the Trade Unions and Co-operative Societies provided far more attractive organisations to help them.

Nevertheless, it is interesting to note that all but one of the Chartist six demands (i.e. annual Parliaments) were later granted. The movement was before its time, and an inspiration for further effort.

Chapter XXI

Factory Laws

Early Laws

It was a pitiful procession that passed daily through the slum streets on its way to the factories. Ragged children, half-starved and filthy, bent, stunted in growth, hopelessness written deeply upon their faces, — children old before they had even had time to be young — stumbled wearily and wretchedly over the rough cobbled stones. Ahead of them lay 15 hours of grim and brutal toil in the sweating atmosphere of the factory. And somewhere in the public conscience, something stirred. We call that something 'humanitarianism' — the love of human beings, and it was this force which began to compel the Government to take action against those responsible for such conditions of work.

Yet to the employers of child labour, there was every justification for their policy. If England was to maintain her low-cost production against foreign competition, then long hours of work were necessary for all employees, while child labour was needed on account of its cheapness. Furthermore, an increase in leisure for the working class would automatically mean an increase in crime; the Devil found work for idle hands. It was far better that children should be working in the factories than become juvenile delinquents roaming the streets.

Neither the humanitarians in Parliament nor the owners of the factories would give way. So the result, when it came, was a battle of wits between the Government and the employers of child labour.

The Government opened the attack. In 1802, an Act was passed for pauper children in cotton mills; they were not to work more than 12 hours a day, and no night work. Then, in 1819, these regulations were extended to all 9-16 year-olds.

And before we learn any more, let us stop for a moment. Let us pause, if only for a few minutes, to consider again the terms of this 1819 Act, and to see what they *really* mean. Here are the terms: the regulations for 12 hours work per day were extended to 9-16 years old. In other words — and here is the full horror of it — a child of nine . . . *only nine* . . . was not to work . . . *more than* . . . 12 hours per day . . .

every day . . . in a factory. Have you ever appreciated anything more grim? What, in all truth, must it have been like to work even only 12 hours a day in a factory, at the age of nine? Nevertheless the employers of child labour merely laughed at the Act, for there was no proper inspection to see that these rules were carried out. In fact, the Justices of the Peace who were responsible for enforcing the law were often the mill owners themselves. So the children continued to toil their 14-15 hour day.

Lord Shaftesbury

But the battle against the employers was then continued by Anthony Ashley Cooper (1801-85), Lord Ashley, later Earl of Shaftesbury. Although a rich Dorset landowner, he was nevertheless well aware of the pitiful procession that passed daily through the slum streets, and out of sheer human kindness he resolved to do his best to end it all.

His influence lay in his personality. It was impossible to accuse him of being a mere rabble-rouser, a gutter-bred revolutionary, or a starry-eyed idealist. On the contrary, he was a deeply religious person, a peer of the realm, and a man of acknowledged commonsense.

Furthermore, he possessed the wonderful gift of oratory; he was a truly wonderful speaker. On one occasion, he spoke for two hours on the conditions of children condemned by the hell of their employment. Carefully he marshalled his facts into a truth which no-one could deny, and for two hours the Members of the House of Commons listened to him . . . and they wept. When he had finished, one of his greatest opponents, a person who believed that the commercial prosperity of England would be ruined without the help of child labour, walked across the floor of the House to shake his hand in open congratulation. With a terrible brilliance of descriptive power, it was Shaftesbury who, when they appeared before him, sadly referred to the workers in the factories as 'like a mass of crooked alphabets', so bent and twisted were they by their deformities.

Such was the man who now entered the fight against the employers of young children in the textile mills.

To help him, there was the great Yorkshireman, Richard Oastler (1789-1861), whose letters to the *Leeds Mercury* voiced his indignation at the 'Yorkshire slavery' in the factories of the area.

Nor must we forget Michael Sadler (1780-1835), M.P. for Aldborough, whose untiring efficiency amassed and recorded the conditions of factory purgatory with a skill that made the account one of the greatest of the documents of history — 'Report of Select Committee on Factory Children's Labour 1831-2. Chairman: Michael Sadler'. His report was a simple, unvarnished truth — the sorrow and suffering of the industrial poor, whose wretched toiling lives could only welcome death. It told of the unending hours they slaved, of the body-crippling conditions they faced, of the cruelty they had no choice but to suffer. And not even the grimmest statements did any factory owner ever disprove.

So the fight for child welfare in the factories continued.

By an Act of 1833 (known as Althorp's Act from the then Home Secretary), inspectors were appointed in all textile factories (except silk) to ensure that: those under the age of nine, no work; age nine to 13, a 48 hour week (with, in addition, two hours education per day); age 13 to 18, a 69 hour week.

This Factory Act was a good attempt, but the employers of child labour merely laughed again. Ages nine to 13? 13 to 18? How could anyone discover the age of a child in days when there were no birth certificates — (compulsory registration of births was not established till 1837) — and as the children were starved and stunted in growth, appearance was no guide. As for education — the factory owners merely converted the stoke-hole into a classroom, and when the stoker had a few spare moments, he became a school teacher.

Undeterred, however, Lord Shaftesbury continued his efforts by three further Acts of Parliament:

1842: the Mining Act prohibited female or child labour underground.

1844: Peel's Factory Act. In textile factories, children from eight to 13 had to work $6\frac{1}{2}$ hours per day; those from 13 to 18 and all women, 12 hours per day. The eight to 13 year olds had also to have three hours education per day, or they could work a 10 hour day in the factory, and then attend for a day at school, and so on alternately. In some areas, the children worked half a day in school, and the other half-day in the mill. This was called the 'half-time system'.

A further requirement of the 1844 Act was for factory machinery to be fenced.

1847: Ten Hours Act. Boys under 18 and all women, 10 hours per day.

But the employers were still at least smiling. Since the number of hours of work were laid down, they evaded the regulations by shift work, which made it difficult for the inspectors to discover when any particular person actually began and finished work.

Accordingly by the 1850 Act, the actual times of work were laid down: 6.00 a.m. to 6.00 p.m. in summer, 7.00 a.m. to 7.00 p.m. in winter, including 1½ hours for meals. Saturday was half-day. As this Act applied to women and young persons, and was extended to children in 1853, it also, in practice, applied to men, for it was of no use to work the factory when perhaps half the staff, i.e. all the women and children, had left. Similar conditions were applied 1845-61 to allied trades such as bleaching, dyeing and lace-making.

Dangerous trades

Then in 1864, regulations were made for non-textile industries — pottery, match-making, cartridge manufacture, etc. These latter industries, indeed, were by no means as pleasant as many people imagined . . .

Even in pottery making there was danger, and a danger none the less deadly because it was slow. Once the potter had finished his articles, young lads from the ages of six to sixteen were employed to carry them across the yard to the heating rooms. Thus the boys ran backwards and forwards from the cold open-air of winter into a room heated to 130 degrees . . . and in due course they died of asthma and tuberculosis.

After the pottery had been heated, it was dipped into a solution containing carbonate of lead. The clothes of the dippers became wet with the solution and as they rarely changed their clothes or washed their hands before meals, they were easy victims of lead poisoning.

The last fatal process in the manufacture was the scouring to remove particles of very finely ground flint from the surface of the ware. This task was usually done by women and girls using sandpaper and brushes, so that the room was soon filled with flint dust. Every breath swept the particles into the workers' lungs, until death from bronchitis followed.

Match making was no less dangerous a trade, for the heads of the matches had to be dipped into heated phosphorus, whose vapour reeked through the building, and which splashed on the faces of the workers who had to lean over it. The result was usually what the men termed 'Phossy Jaw', a disease which attacked the bone, and even if a person survived, he might lose the whole of his lower jaw. In the expressive words of a witness before a Royal Commission in 1863, describing one of those afflicted, 'You could take his chin and shove it all into his mouth'.

Thus the Acts of 1864 which compelled better conditions in these and other non-textile industries were a step in the right direction.

Later Laws

But the employers still had at least a faint smile, for the factory regulations only applied to places where either there were over 50 employed or where women and young persons were employed. So the employers reduced the numbers of employed to below 50, and when the inspectors came round, the women and young children were carefully hidden in the lumber room, toilet or outhouse. The building was then classified as a 'workshop', not a factory. The Government tried to overcome this evasion by the inspection of workshops from 1871, and in 1878 by defining a factory not according to the number of workers employed, but by the fact that it used mechanical power.

By the end of the 19th century, there was no doubt that Government action had succeeded, especially when all the numerous laws which had been passed to improve factory conditions 'bit by bit' were replaced by the single great Act of 1901, applying to all classes and covering all aspects of work. By this time, too, the age of child employment had been raised in stages from eight years in the 1844 Act to 12 years old. Children had now to be sent to school instead of to a factory.

The only lingering smile on the face of the employers was in such industries as tailoring, shirt-making, boot making, etc., which were outside the Factory Act of 1901, since the workers toiled in hidden backrooms or in their own garrets, and where the conditions were as grim as they could possibly be. But by the 1909 Trade Boards Act, this 'sweated labour' was lessened by imposing minimum wages. (The Trade Boards were replaced by Wages Councils in 1945.)

Then in 1937, a Factories Act put all the previous laws together; employees aged 14-16, 44 hours a week; 16-18 and all women, 48 hours a week. A 'factory' included almost anywhere where manual labour was employed for gain, e.g. garages, laundries, docks, wharves, quays, film studios, open-air premises, and the laws covered almost every aspect of work — health, welfare, safety, wages, etc.

By the 1944 Education Act, the school leaving age, and thus the age for entering employment, was raised to 15.

The employers could have no smile at all now, but it is only fair to say that by this time their attitude had undergone a very great change.

It was now realised that long hours do not necessarily mean good work. It was also realised that contented workers do more and better work than those unhappy and dissatisfied.

So instead of slave-driving their workers under the grimmest possible conditions, the factory owners provided model villages such as Fry's at Bournville ('the factory in a garden') or Lever Brothers at Port Sunlight, as well as 'music while you work', welfare clubs, canteens, playing-fields, staff outings, shares in the firm's profits, etc.

If there was any reason why the employers were no longer smiling, and in fact, had a more than usually serious headache, it was not due to the Factory Laws. It was due to the power of the trade unions, which we have just considered in another chapter. The days when the workers could be too harshly treated or victimised were over.

Chapter XXII

The Poor Laws

Early Poor Relief

How did the Government try to help the poverty which resulted from the Industrial and Agricultural Revolutions?

'The poor ye always have with you', said Jesus, and the efforts of the 18th century had done little to alter the truth of that statement. Nevertheless, let us have a look at some of the attempts which were made.

It had long been established that every landowner in a parish was required to pay a tax called the 'poor rate', and the money thus collected was given to help (relieve) the poor — hence 'poor relief'. Those who received this poor relief were called paupers.

In 1722, the Workhouse Act allowed parishes, if they wished, to establish a workhouse, where all poor relief was to be given — that is, there need be no outside relief whereby people received money from the parish while still in their own homes. If you were poor and wanted help, you had to enter the workhouse.

But this new system failed, because the workhouses were often farmed out — that is, offered to the highest bidder, who then naturally tried to recover the cost of the deal and to make a profit. So if the workhouse owner was paid a lump sum by the parish to cover all the costs of organising the workhouse, he admitted as few as possible, and made life as unpleasant as possible. If he was paid for the work the inmates did, then they toiled until exhausted. In any case, the unlucky poor (poor through no fault of their own) were mixed with the regulars (poor because they were too lazy to work), so there was a general decline of standards.

In 1782, Gilbert's Act was passed, and made compulsory in 1795. By its terms, the parish had to establish workhouses for the infirm, and encourage the able-bodied to find work even to the extent of supplementing their wages if necessary.

But it was in 1795, at the little parish of Speenhamland in Berkshire, that a meeting of the magistrates there achieved a nationwide fame. For at this meeting, the magistrates decided (i) to grant money to the poor according to the price of bread, estimating an average of 26 lb. of bread per week for a man, and 13 lb. for a woman or child; (ii) to increase low wages by a grant from the poor rate, so that every man would get a decent living wage.

The intentions of the magistrates were undoubtedly excellent; the results were undoubtedly appalling. The employers, of course, at once lowered the wages, because the amount would now be made up out of the poor relief. At the same time, the labourer reached almost the lowest state of his existence, for since only paupers had their wages made up, a farmer would only employ such people, so a man was compelled to become a pauper in order to get work. Furthermore, since children now became a good investment for poor relief, illegitimacy was encouraged — the more children, the more money.

Apart from this degrading method of relief, other systems were also employed in this country. Under the Gang System, groups of paupers were employed on the roads or on the farms, often working 14 hours a day. Under the Roundsman System, paupers were hired to the farmers at weekly auctions for low wages, the rest of the wages being paid by the poor rate. Sometimes agreements were made that each farmer should employ a percentage of paupers instead of paying rates. Then in some areas even, the poor were subjected to the humiliation of being harnessed to a cart and being sent round to beg for relief.

Such was the wretchedness of poverty right to the beginning of the 19th century.

But it was not just the wretchedness that counted; there was another consideration far more important than that. The increase in the number of poor, the high cost of the Speenhamland system, the dishonesty of the Poor Law officials, and most serious, the rise in prices of food and other essentials to provide for the paupers, had all combined to cause a tremendous increase in the poor rate . . . and, therefore, an equally tremendous outcry from those who had to pay that rate. By 1834, remember, one out of every ten people in the entire nation was a pauper, and the poor rate had quadrupled in 37 years.

Poor Law Amendment Act 1834

Quite clearly, indeed, action had to be taken not merely to help the poor, but also to lessen the cost of poor relief, and it was with these thoughts in mind that the Poor Law Amendment Act of 1834 was passed. As the beliefs and regulations of this Act were to last for over a century, we must study it very carefully.

In charge of the new organisation were three Poor Law Commissioners in London, together with a Secretary, Edwin Chadwick — the man mainly responsible for the Act. Edwin Chadwick (1801-90) indeed, was one of the most energetic, hard-working, thorough and capable organisers of his day. His record of work, both for poor relief and for public health, was impressive by any standards. Unfortunately, he was certainly not a person who could suffer fools gladly. His manner was overbearing and dictatorial, so that although he was extremely efficient, he was also very unpopular, even hated.

According to the new Act, outdoor relief (i.e. money given to people in their own homes) could be paid in the case of the aged, infirm and sick, if need be. In industrial areas, where a sudden depression caused a temporary mass unemployment, outdoor relief had also to be given because the workhouse could not cope with the sudden mass entry.

Apart from these instances, however, for all able-bodied people (and in some places, for the aged, infirm and sick also), the Act imposed what was called the 'Workhouse test'. The test that you were genuinely poor was that you were willing to enter a workhouse. That also meant that conditions in the workhouse were to be such that only those who *were* in really desperate need would ever consider entering.

The Commissioners then set to work to organise the building of a workhouse either in each parish or for a union of parishes. In charge of each workhouse was a local Board of Guardians, but it was the Commissioners who established the rules for discipline, for diet and for work.

As far as the building was concerned, everything possible was done to cut down the cost — brick walls, wooden tables, wooden benches and rough straw beds. The conditions were made as grim as possible for the healthy, while the sick and aged were neglected to die. The sexes were separated to prevent the breeding of pauper children, and of such babies who did enter the workhouse, ⅓rd of them died. In any event, the aged, infirm, sick, the very young and lunatics were all herded together.

As far as diet was concerned, the food was sufficient, but it was monotonous — mainly oatmeal, very little meat, and no tea or sugar. Cocoa was the chief drink. There were exceptions to this general standard of meals, nevertheless. At one workhouse, near Leeds, the inmates fed from a trough like pigs. In Andover, in Hampshire, they fought for the marrow of the bones and over pieces of gristle in an effort to avoid starving to death.

Idleness was certainly not encouraged. The wretched poor toiled at oakum-picking (separating the strands of old rope for re-use) or stone-breaking, and moreover, it was carefully calculated that any payment that they were given for their work was far less than they would have received for wages if they had been in normal employment outside the workhouse.

All these grim conditions followed what was called the 'principle of less eligibility', i.e. less desirability. The conditions of those inside the workhouse were to be made far worse than of the meanest labourer outside.

So the workhouses succeeded in their aim. Only as a last resort did a person enter them. The 'New Bastilles' they were named (from the Bastille — the grim French prison-fortress in Paris). Admittedly, the poor rate fell; admittedly, the idle poor were now compelled to find work. But the cost of those benefits was the suffering of the inmates inside the workhouse, and out of the dissatisfaction of the poor arose the Chartist movement (see Chapter XX).

We know that, as time went on, a few improvements were made. For children, foster parents were provided, while nurseries and schools for those in the workhouse were also established. For the old people, workhouse infirmaries were built. But in the main, the workhouse test and its conditions continued into the 20th century.

And the result was still failure. It was a terrible shock to realise that despite all attempts to help the poor, at the end of the 19th century the great cities of this country still had 30 per cent of their population (that is, three out of every ten inhabitants) living 'below the poverty line', i.e. their income was not enough to keep them in the minimum of good health. The proof of this statement lay in the investigations made by Charles Booth from 1887-1902 in London, and of Seebohm Rowntree in 1889 in York. Both these men . . . industrialists who had devoted their lives to social reform . . . showed beyond doubt that too high a percentage of our population were scarcely able to live, and the poorest class of society was doomed to die in squalid hopelessness. It was this urgent problem which was passed on from the 19th century to its successor.

20th Century Poor Relief

By the 20th century, however, a different attitude to poverty had developed.

In the 18th century, poverty had been regarded as the fault of the poor — the result of idleness, dishonesty, thriftlessness and any other vices. Therefore relief was given either as an act of charity, or to prevent the poor being driven by desperation into a revolt, but in either case it was distributed as sparingly as possible. In the 19th century, poverty was still regarded as the fault of the poor, and every effort was made to frighten a man into not becoming a pauper — the workhouses made pauperism very unattractive.

But by the 20th century, a new attitude had arisen. It was now realised that poverty might not be the fault of the poor; it could be the result of misfortune rather than vice; it could occur through circumstances over which the worker had no control, such as a trade depression, accidental injury or ill-health. Therefore the poor must be helped — not scorned or tolerated — and it was the duty of the Government to be responsible. For a country to have a large number of paupers was a reflection, not upon the paupers, but upon the way the Government organised the State.

So in the 20th century, another effort was made. First of all, the poor were classified into those who had no work, and those who could not work (e.g. the cripples, etc.), and then the Government tried to help both.

For those who had no work, the Unemployed Workmen's Act of 1905 established local distress committees to give relief aided by a Government grant. Labour Exchanges were set up in 1909, to which those who wanted work, and those who had work to offer, could both apply, and so be put in touch with each other.

Equally so, it was expected that a worker himself should try to provide against unemployment, as well as having Government assistance. So in 1911, by the National Insurance Act, workmen had 2p. a week deducted from their pay for when they were ill or unemployed, while the employer had also to contribute 1½p., and the Government 1p. The money went into a central fund which paid for a sick worker to have free medical attention, reduced price medicine, and a weekly illness allowance for a limited period. Also by the same Act, a similar scheme of contributions by employer, workman and State enabled those in certain trades only (building, ship-building, engineering, etc.) to receive a weekly allowance for up to 15 weeks if they were unemployed.

After 1918, however, there occurred a depression which became greater and graver, until by 1933, the number of unemployed in this country reached the almost unbelievable total of three million. Desperately the Government took action. Training schemes were arranged so that workers could learn new jobs; transfers of workers were arranged from one job or area to another where there were better prospects of employment. Government grants were given to promote public works (road building, etc.), to establish new factories, to enable the completion of the world's greatest liner, the *Queen Mary* on Clydebank, and more particularly to help 'special areas' such as Durham and South Wales, where the unemployment problem was worst.

During this depression, the money provided by the National Insurance scheme — which lasted for 15 weeks unemployment — was hopelessly inadequate. Men were out of work for years, let alone a few weeks. So the period of benefit had to be extended, the extra money being known as the 'dole'. The 'dole', however, proved expensive, and in an effort to reduce the cost, the Government in 1931 introduced the 'means test'. In future, the amount of the Government grant was dependent upon the total income which a family received. This, no doubt, seemed a fair and sensible decision, but unfortunately it involved a full enquiry into the financial circumstances of the family which applied for the dole, and the poor bitterly resented this intrusion into their private lives. It was, too, a deep humiliation for many an out-of-work father to have to reveal that the family was being supported by the earnings of his children.

The next stage to provide against possible unemployment occurred after the Second World War. Then, in 1946, came the National Insurance Act by which every employee had so much a week deducted from his wages, every employer had to pay so much a week for each workman, whilst local rates and the State also paid certain amounts. The money thus obtained provided (among other benefits) for unemployment relief.

For those who could not work, the Old Age Pension for the over 70's on low incomes was introduced in 1908 (later reduced to age 65), and in 1948 the National Assistance Board was created to help the blind, the tubercular, vagrants and old people. Unmarried or deserted mothers, and the families of those in prison, also received National Assistance.

So, in the 20th century, the old workhouse system, with its Commissioners, its Boards of Guardians and its grim inhumanity, was ended. By 1935, the workhouses were in the charge of the County Councils and County Borough Councils. Within them were the aged and the infirm poor only, for local authorities looked after orphans, and the able-bodied poor were the concern of the Unemployment Board.

This does not mean that poverty itself had ended. Perhaps it never will, but at least, it had become more endurable.

Chapter XXIII

Public Health

Early History

'Cleanliness is next to Godliness' . . . but in the early 19th century slums, it was next to impossible. So amid the dirt and filth of the slum areas, there was a Paradise for germs, and to prove that the bacteria were making the most of their opportunities, outbreaks of cholera occurred in the most devastating waves of epidemic. In 1831, 22,000 people died of this one disease alone, and there seemed every prospect of even greater casualties in the future. The illness itself had originated in India, and then spread westward into Europe. Here it struck its victims with lightning-like suddenness, crippled them with vomiting and torturing pains, and killed them within a few hours. The doctors knew very little about the causes of the disease, and had no idea at all about how to cure it. A wave of helpless terror swept over England, together, however, with the realisation that the plague flourished mainly in the vile areas of the slums.

Without doubt, some action had to be taken. Accordingly, the Municipal Corporation Act of 1835 said that local authorities could pave, light and cleanse the streets . . . if they wished. Even then, a special local Act of Parliament was required, thus adding to the delay and the cost. So not surprisingly, the outbreaks of typhus and cholera continued unchecked.

It was 13 years before the next development occurred. It was then that the writings of Charles Dickens, the description of London slums by Dr. Southwood Smith, the brilliant report by Edwin Chadwick (secretary to the Poor Law Commissioners) on 'The sanitary conditions of the labouring population of Britain in 1842', and the efforts of Lord Shaftesbury, together with an almost nationwide fear after a cholera epidemic in 1847 . . . all combined to result in the passing of the Public Health Act of 1848.

This Act of 1848 established a Central Board of Health in London, and local Boards of Health in the provinces who could improve sanitation in their areas . . . if they wished. One might feel it was about time, too, for there were over 200,000 undrained cesspools in London alone.

For six years, under the magnificent energy and efficiency of Edwin Chadwick (1801-90), now a Public Health Commissioner, the Central Board issued its excellent reports and recommendations. For six years, it suggested and urged (but had practically no power to order) improvements in every aspect of public health ... and it met with an equal degree of hatred and opposition. The ratepayers feared there might be an increase in the rates to pay for the cost of slum clearance and other health measures; landlords of slum property did not want to lose their income ... nor did the owners of the cemeteries, either. Local authorities strongly objected to the dictatorship of the Board; and the idea of *laissez-faire* (leave it alone) still existed in the mind of the Government. Thus the Board was ended in 1854, and with it, the selfless work of its Commissioner, Edwin Chadwick. A new Board was set up without him ... and ended in 1858.

So the cholera continued, its outbreaks becoming more and more serious — not to mention, of course, the eruptions of scarlet fever, smallpox, whooping cough, measles, diphtheria, enteric fever, dysentery tuberculosis and typhus ... all of which attacked the population as well. The Old Stone Age man who roamed this country in the year 500,000 B.C. had an average life expectation of 20 years. By 1870 — over half a million years later — civilisation had so improved upon human prospects that the life expectation had been increased only by another twenty-two years — to 42.

It was, of course, realised that longevity depended upon the circumstances and place of your residence. If you were born of a fairly well-to-do family, in country surroundings, you might not die until you reached the ripe old age of 70. On the other hand, if you were born in the slum areas of some of the great industrial cities, the average age at death was 15. Thus the slums, the places of filth, were recognised as the places of disease, and one way to check the plagues, therefore, would be to clean and clear the filth of the slums.

Public Health Act 1875

At long last, the Government passed the Public Health Act of 1875. By this Act, all local authorities were compelled to pave, light and cleanse the streets, and they had also to appoint a Medical Officer of Health, a Surveyor and a Sanitary Inspector to attend to sewerage, water supplies, infectious diseases, unsound food and unfit housing.

This was a tremendous advance in the history of public health, and so important that we must now consider some of these undertakings more carefully.

In the first instance, the supply of water to the large towns was appalling. In 1845, eight out of ten houses in Birmingham, and nine out of ten in Newcastle, had no water; the water supplies of London, were drawn from the Thames just *below the exit of the sewerage.* Such a state of affairs most certainly required attention, and gradually the situation improved.

The most important development was when town water supplies were piped from the surrounding country. Thus in 1856, Glasgow obtained water from Lake Katrine; in 1876, Manchester from Lake Thirlmere; in 1877, Liverpool from Lake Vrynwy. Other towns sunk artesian wells. At the same time effective methods of filtering were found, and as people drank the purified supplies, the epidemics of cholera declined. Indeed, this disease had almost entirely gone by 1895.

Also in the 19th century, there came a rather unexpected development in the story of public health. Whilst a cholera epidemic was raging in Liverpool in 1832, a poor Irish woman, Kitty Wilkinson, by name, offered to let her even less fortunate neighbours use her kitchen to wash themselves and their clothes. Gladly they accepted the offer, and the news spread rapidly and widely. Thus what had commenced as a simple act of private charity later developed into a city organisation for everyone's benefit. The council of Liverpool heard of Kitty Wilkinson's generosity, and realising its value on a larger scale, became the first town authority to provide public baths and wash-houses for its citizens. But even then, the story was not finished, for fourteen years later, in 1846, Parliament passed an act for other towns to establish public wash-houses as well. Which may all explain why, in the vast structure of the new Cathedral in Liverpool today, you will find, amid the stained glass images of saints and of angels, of great men and women of our land . . . you will find a window to the memory of a poor Irishwoman, Kitty Wilkinson by name.

It was to be a long time before the next major improvement in Public Health occurred — a century in fact.

The symbol of the Industrial Revolution was smoke. The factory chimneys and the workers' homes belched forth a filthy blackness into the air, a blackness which loaded countless tons of grime upon city buildings until the stonework began to crumble, and also deposited untold masses of residue on to human lungs until the tissues ceased to function. By the 20th century, this combination of smoke and fog produced a pollution appropriately called smog, and its effect upon human life became serious. Indeed, in 1952, some 4,000 people died of smog in London in a week, and several thousand more died in the following few months.

Accordingly, in 1956, the Clean Air Act was passed. The great industrial cities were divided into smokeless fuel zones, and in that way the preservation of public buildings and the safeguarding of human life was assisted.

But it was not only the air that required cleansing. The waterways also became polluted as factories poured their waste liquids into the rivers and canals, thus poisoning the fish and plant life. Local authorities and river boards tried to persuade firms to make their waste harmless before it was discharged.

Another modern form of pollution was noise. A sudden loud noise, such as the take-off of a jet aircraft, caused physical pain, while continuous loud noise — in factories, for example — caused deafness. In extreme cases, an exceptional volume of sound could be fatal. A person's health also suffered when noise interfered with sleep.

Thus the Noise Abatement Act of 1960, enabled local authorities to investigate complaints of harmful sounds.

MEDICAL CARE AND PUBLIC HEALTH
Disease

After this, let is consider the medical control of health, a task in which seven names found their greatness, and however briefly, we must know something about each of them. You can always find books which will give you more detailed accounts of their lives.

In Gloucester today, there is the statue of a man standing on a pedestal. Inscribed on that pedestal is one word — nothing more . . . no dates, no record of glory or fame, no praise or false flattery. Just one word . . . and nothing more. That single word is 'Jenner'.

For hundreds of years, smallpox had ravaged this country, afflicting many thousands of people a year. It was as accepted as the common cold; most of the sufferers died, and the remainder bore the pock-marks for the rest of their lives. Not until 1796 did the Gloucestershire doctor, Edward Jenner (1749-1823) vaccinate an eight year old boy, James Phipps, by injecting him with a small dose of cow-pox (a similar, but weaker, disease), and later giving him a dose of smallpox from which he duly recovered. It was thus proved that in certain illnesses — smallpox, rabies, typhoid, diphtheria, etc. — the overcoming of one weak attack prevented the success of a further full assault.

That is why only one word was needed on the pedestal. When the statue was erected, everyone knew all the rest about Edward Jenner, who, by the discovery of vaccination, saved more lives than any other sole person in history.

Operations

But this major advance in medical knowledge applied only to diseases. There still remained the heavy death roll which resulted from attempts to operate. Indeed, three main causes of death in the operating theatre had to be faced.

First, there was the inexperience of the doctors, many of whom had very little opportunity to practise. They knew what to do in theory, but when it came to the actual operation, that was a very different matter. Though they had learnt the correct procedure from textbooks and by watching others, when they themselves actually had to perform, that was when the mishaps occurred. Admittedly, a great deal of practice was required before a doctor could be expected to succeed in his operations, but why should patients have to die while and until each surgeon gained the necessary experience and ability to ensure success?

To solve this problem, therefore, appeals were made for people to agree that after death their bodies should be handed over to the medical schools. Students would thus be able to practise on corpses before they operated on a live human being later.

This was an excellent suggestion, but unfortunately most persons in those days disliked the idea of their bodies being mutilated after death. They wanted a normal Christian burial, and anything else appeared very distasteful and, indeed, irreligious. Only very few people, therefore, would consent to their dead bodies being used for surgical practice.

In consequence, the outstanding result of these appeals was to create a new career — body snatching. Those who took up this novel occupation paid hurried nightly visits to the local graveyards, dug up any recent burials, and sold the corpses to the students' colleges. These colleges were so full of gratitude that it prevented them asking any questions, and a very profitable business could thus be established.

So popular did this new career become that many people began to have tombs in the form of a strong metal cage, stoutly padlocked, together with spring guns, trip wires and other devices carefully concealed amid the surrounding wreaths. In reply, body-snatching developed into a skilled occupation, and with the help of assistant labourers, informers, and bribes to undertakers, sextons and churchyard watchers, one London professional raised and sold as many as 300 or more bodies a year, the usual selling price at the time being four guineas each. But the demand still exceeded the local supply, so the body snatchers — or, to give them their professional title, the 'Resurrectionists' — had to move further and still further afield . . . and still further. Thus, for example, Liverpool was finally receiving its surgical supplies from Exeter.

But still more corpses were required, until it was obvious that the burials from the normal death rate were quite insufficient to meet the demand. Thereupon two gentlemen in particular, Messrs. William Burke and William Hare of Edinburgh, decided to improve upon the general slowness of nature by their own man-made, but swifter, efforts. Their usual method was to make their victims drunk, and then suffocate them, after which the bodies were sold to the surgical colleges. Thus in the course of twelve months, they were responsible for at least 16 murders, before being brought to justice. Hare turned 'King's Evidence' (i.e. he 'sneaked' on his friend), and received a pardon. Burke was naturally found guilty, and sentenced to be hung. But the law, in its wisdom, decided that the cause of science which he had served so well in his lifetime, he should continue to serve after his death. Therefore, as soon as Burke had been hung in 1829, his corpse was sent to the college of surgeons to be used there by the students.

But the position had now become so serious that Parliament was compelled to intervene. The urgent and genuine needs of would-be surgeons, must not be satisfied at the price of murder. So in 1832, the Anatomy Act ensured that medical colleges would receive an adequate supply of bodies of paupers, executed criminals, etc., and as a result the illegal trade in corpses ceased, while ample surgical practice could still be undertaken.

The second cause of operational deaths was shock — a very difficult matter to prevent. The knowledge of drugs to check pain was not far advanced in the days before the 19th century, so that most operations had to be performed upon fully conscious patients. It was a ghastly business . . . The pain that those patients endured from the knife, as strong men, or stout ropes, held them down on the operating table, can never be expressed in writing. Let us only say that the victims' agony was often such that it made the greatest surgeons of the day turn pale, or even vomit after the task had been completed. Not even they could become used to the hell they had no choice but to inflict.

The first relief from the torture came in 1800, when Sir Humphrey Davy discovered that nitrous oxide (the 'laughing gas' now used by dentists) could render a patient unconscious while an operation took place, but only for such a short time as was needed, for example, to extract teeth.

In 1847, however, Dr. James Simpson, a Professor at Edinburgh University, used chloroform to enable a longer painless operation which, therefore, did not result in shock. This discovery regarding chloroform was certainly fortunate. Dr. Simpson and two of his friends had inhaled some one day in the course of an experiment, and duly collapsed unconscious under the table. When he recovered, Dr. Simpson realised that here at last was something which could deaden the senses against pain — that is, an anaesthetic — and thereupon resolved to use it.

The real test of the new drug first came when it was administered to a woman in childbirth. The baby girl was born without causing any pain to her mother, and subsequently went on her way in life rejoicing in good health. The discovery about chloroform now made possible operations which could never have been attempted before. It was not, for example, until 1888, that the removal of an appendix was first achieved.

Yet even when an operation had been successfully completed, the surgeons were still horrified to observe that the area concerned gradually became septic, and the patient died. It was the great French doctor, Louis Pasteur (1822-85) who showed that infection was caused by germs in the air. (From his name, we have the word 'pasteurised' meaning 'germ-destroyed'). To kill these germs, Dr. Joseph Lister (1827-1912), Professor of Surgery at Glasgow University, in 1867 introduced the method of dressing wounds with carbolic acid, and so ensuring that they healed. Also, during an operation, the surgeon's hands and instruments were washed in carbolic acid, and the same antiseptic was sprayed into the air of the operating theatre. The carbolic acid was later diluted to avoid burning the patient and to lessen the fumes in the theatre. It was a great pity that Lister's methods were not put into practice more swiftly, for by 1869, two out of every five patients operated on in the main hospitals still died.

Next came a really tremendous aid to the surgeon — the German,

Wilhelm Rontgen's discovery of x-rays, in 1895, for now it became possible to see what would need to be done before the actual operation commenced.

So remember, then, the great services to health given by Edward Jenner, Sir Humphrey Davy, James Simpson, Louis Pasteur, Joseph Lister and Wilhelm Rontgen.

20th Century medical developments

But it required the horrors of 20th century war to rouse medical skill to achieve its greatest triumphs, for it had then to face what seemed the utter hopelessness of battle-wrecked bodies. Determinedly, the doctors and the scientists set about the task, which appeared far beyond the power of human ability. Consequently, the results achieved were almost unbelievable. Men with both legs shattered, men with parts of their bodies torn out, men with the lower jaw blasted away . . . were sent from the hospitals, able to walk, with bodies rebuilt, capable of speech and mastication. Such was the power of the new sulpha drugs (e.g. M. and B. 693 for pneumonia); Dr. Alexander Fleming's discovery of the healing agent, penicillin, in 1928; of blood transfusions made possible by the discovery of the different human blood groups in 1900; of plastic surgery; and of organ transplants, such as the first kidney transplant in 1951, when the kidney of one human being was transferred to another person.

Of all these new medical discoveries, we might, perhaps, mention penicillin in particular. Dr. Alexander Fleming (1881-1955) was cultivating some bacteria in a dish in 1928. By sheer chance, a fungus entered the open window nearby, settled on the dish, and destroyed the bacteria. It was unfortunate that Dr. Fleming, who noted the power of this new discovery, was unheeded by his colleagues. Not for eleven years, and then only with the aid of American scientists, was penicillin produced in large quantities . . . but still in time to save the lives of thousands of men wounded in the Second World War. This drug was the first of the anti-biotics, i.e. substances produced by fungus and which kill bacteria.

Also, now that insulin has been discovered (1922) against diabetes, and the knowledge of vitamins has increased, the three chief diseases yet to be conquered are tuberculosis, cancer, and strangely enough, the common cold.

At the same time as the cure of disease and the skill of surgery improved, so also did the hospitals. Hospitals, which had once been built by private charity, were now established by local councils. Within them, the name of Florence Nightingale reminded everyone of the high standard required to be a nurse . . . indeed, in 1860, St. Thomas's Hospital, London had been founded to train nurses for this great profession, and to be the forerunner of similar institutions elsewhere.

But all these new cures, and the accommodation in the new better hospitals, were costly, so in peacetime it seemed that only the rich could hope to enjoy them. Already, however, in 1911, under the National Insurance Act, workmen had 2p. a week deducted from their pay for when they were ill or unemployed, while the employer also had to contribute $1\frac{1}{2}$p, and the Government 1p. The money went into a central Fund which paid for a sick worker to have free medical attention, reduced price medicine and a weekly sickness allowance for a limited period. Doctors and chemists wishing to enter the scheme, arranged to play their parts, so that the working class could receive the benefits of medical assistance at a price they could afford. Then in 1946, to enable even the poorest to take advantage of all the most recent medical discoveries, the National Insurance Act was passed. Henceforth, medical services were to be free to all, and the cost was to be met by payments from the employees' wages, from employers, from local rates, and from the Treasury.

At the same time as the improvements in public health and in medical care, there came a third factor to make life happier — the improvement in living conditions.

After the first shock and misery which the Industrial Revolution caused, there came, later on . . . much later on — more and cheaper clothes, more and cheaper soap, more and cheaper houses; while the railways brought more and cheaper food (particularly meat, milk, butter and sugar), as well as providing work or transport to work and enabling holidays in the country or by the sea.

As working hours were gradually reduced by the Factory Acts (see Chapter XXI) people had more leisure. Schoolchildren, too, benefited from the school medical service, free meals in needy cases (1906), P.T. and organised games in school hours, and school camps. It is not difficult to realise how all these developments made a healthier and happier population.

Not least among the new benefits was better housing, and to this we have devoted a separate chapter — the next one.

Chapter XXIV

Housing

Conditions

It was a very usual type of Victorian house — a house that bore some of the characteristics of its owners — solid, prosperous-looking, self-satisfied. It was three storeys high, together with attics and a basement to accommodate large numbers of servants. The doorway was palatial with two magnificent oak portals. Its windows were large and rectangular, set amid tall decorated columns of 15th century style.

Inside the house, ornamental stairways led to the various large and lofty rooms, all of them so crammed with furniture that it was difficult to move about. Amid all this furniture indeed, you did have an occasional glimpse of the gaudy-coloured carpet, in the same way as you had a glimpse of the equally gaudy wallpaper amid the host of heavy gilt-framed pictures on the walls. There were heavy velvet window curtains, thick dark-crimson door curtains, a plush valance round the mantelpiece, velvet tablecloths, antimacassars, ribbons, bows, tassels, fringes — all in reds, greens, yellows, and purples, until the eyes ached. And on every available space was the delight of the Victorian houses — oddments, curios and bric-a-brac in unnumbered confusion. The house was thus filled to capacity.

But these were the homes of the wealthy and of the respectable middle class, whose riches had been created by the Industrial Revolution. There was, however, another aspect of England, also created by the Industrial Revolution — the unplanned, over-crowded slums in the factory areas.

In these areas, land was in great demand, and therefore costly, while the builder and the landlord both realised that the worker could not afford high rents. The result was a grim density of cheaply constructed buildings, crammed to capacity with human beings.

In the vast vileness of the industrial cities, indeed, the conditions were almost unbelievable . . .

Here were large houses which, as late as the 1880's, rose out of a sea of stench in dense, dirty masses. From cellar to three-storey height, the aged, ramshackle buildings extended . . . structures so rotten that entry was through any of the numerous holes in the brickwork. The rain streamed direct into the rooms, yet the downpour scarcely affected the thick layer of grime that covered the walls, nor the myriads of vermin that crawled from ceiling to floor. All was dark and gloom, for every window was a glassless square covered with boards or stuffed with rags.

It seemed scarcely possible that these places could provide a habitation for human beings, yet from cellar to attic, in rooms not more than ten foot square, from four to as many as eight people lived per room. They dwelt there amid a heap of boards, bricks and rubble — the only furniture — and with the droppings of rats to form a kind of carpet. In conditions such as these, there existed 66,000 people per square mile.

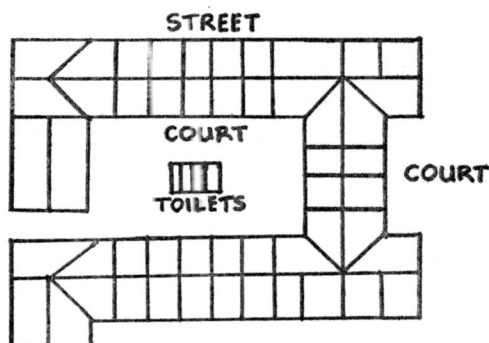

"Back-to-back" houses.

More residential areas comprised what were called 'back-to-back houses'. Here, a building had another house on each of three sides. Each home measured about 11 foot in width by $11\frac{1}{2}$ foot from front to rear, and contained two rooms, stairs from the lower room leading to the upper. In this way, one could build 130 houses on an acre of land.

Conditions such as these created an urgent and terrible problem for society.

Housing improvements
To point a way to cleaner industrial conditions, to show what could be done, from 1887-1910, Lord Leverhulme, founder of the great soap manufacturing firm, built Port Sunlight, near Birkenhead, for

his employees. To avoid the grim, distressing sight of hundreds upon hundreds of dull brick-and-tile homes, all exactly the same size and style, arranged in row after monotonous row for acre after hideous acre, Port Sunlight had each pair of houses a different design, as well as bright green lawns and open spaces between.

At Bournville, in 1895, Cadbury's chocolate works had a 'Factory in a Garden' — lawns, flowers, shady trees and neat houses for the employees, all surrounding large, light, airy work buildings. Then at Letchworth in Hertfordshire, a Garden City was designed by Ebenezer Howard in 1903, a city for healthy living and industry, large enough for a good social life but no larger, and surrounded by a green belt of country. These were but three examples of the practical answer to the slums.

But it was not enough merely to build the new; it was also necessary to destroy the old. During the 19th century, two important housing acts were passed — the Artisans Dwelling Act in 1868, and the Housing Act introduced by the Home Secretary, Richard Cross, in 1875. Both these Acts enabled local authorities to find, and then either to improve or else close, unfit houses.

So under these orders, the great cities of London, Liverpool, Manchester, and Birmingham in particular, began a programme of slum clearance. In many cases, the houses had to be disinfected before the workmen would enter to demolish them. The programme was none too soon. Almost faster than the authorities could destroy the old slums, more people were crowding into the towns to create new ones. In 1851 half the population of England lived in towns, by 1901 three-quarters, and by 1921 four-fifths. The Government, however, urged on the good work. The Town Planning Act of 1909 insisted again on slum clearance, and forbade the building of any more 'Back-to-back' houses.

The Government also assisted in other ways. After the 1914-18 War, money was given to help private builders, while local authorities were authorised to build council houses and let them at a cheap rent, the rest of the cost being paid out of the rates. By this means, about 4½ million houses were built between the two World Wars.

Then came the Second World War of 1939-45. From the airfields of the Continent, the legions of German bombers roared their way across the skies, sending death and destruction upon the great factory cities of England. The bombs of the 'Luftwaffe' (German Air Force) were far more effective than Acts of Parliament or Town Bye-Laws.

Vast acreages of slums, which would have taken years of talk and reams of paper to remove, disappeared in a few moments. The way was open to rebuild, to establish new, better and cleaner factory cities, with pleasant flats, and green belts of gardens and parks.

Every effort was made to achieve all this. At first, the Government controlled rents to prevent landlords taking advantage of the shortage of houses caused by bombing, and charging what they liked.

Then, to provide accommodation, large old houses were converted into flats, new high blocks of flats were constructed, and new estates created. As a temporary measure, prefabricated houses were produced. These were constructed in sections at the factory, the sections were then carried to the site and bolted together on a concrete foundation by semi-skilled workmen. Ugly, and later damp, such erections were, but they nevertheless provided swift homes for thousands of otherwise homeless people.

After this, from 1950 onwards, the house-building programme proceeded in earnest, particularly in the period 1950-4 when over one million houses were completed by local authorities and private builders, both of whom received Government help.

Finally, to prevent new slum properties being created in the towns to add to the one million that still existed by 1955, the Government planned and controlled all building development.

This control of building was essential, for the increase of population made the towns larger and larger. Eighty per cent of the population lived in towns, remember, and as the great industrial cities expanded they had to develop into each other, thus forming one vast unit, or 'conurbation' as it was called. By 1960, there were seven of these conurbations — in order of size: Greater London with a population of eight million, south-east Lancashire (around Manchester), the West Midlands (Birmingham and Wolverhampton), central Clydeside (around Glasgow), West Yorkshire (Leeds and Bradford), Merseyside (around Liverpool), and Newcastle upon Tyne.

To overcome this vast expansion of city development, the Government in 1946 passed the New Towns Act. As a first stage, twelve new towns were created to take the 'overspill' population from the large cities. Eight of these were to cope with London alone, and the others were in the counties of Durham (two), Northamptonshire and Monmouthshire. Planned and pleasant, these new centres had parks, entertainments and factories to form a community of suitable size and organisation.

Nevertheless, this great development of the towns could only be accomplished at the expense of the country. Gradually, the green fields, the rolling dales and the open places began to disappear beneath brick and tile houses, concrete factories, motorways and aerodromes. The works of man commenced to scar the landscape as the first Industrial Revolution had done.

Many people, however, were not prepared to accept so grave a loss, for once the natural beauty of a country has been destroyed — its fields, forests, flowers and wild life—it has gone for ever. As a result of the untiring efforts of such people, National Parks were created. By 1970, these occupied no less than 1/11th of the total area of England and Wales. In Northumberland, by the mountains and waters of the Peak District, the open moors and beautiful unspoilt dales of Yorkshire, the white-clad peaks of Snowdonia, the stormy coast of Pembroke, the Brecon Beacons, the heath and heather of Dartmoor and Exmoor — all these had to be preserved, and no activity could be concerned with them that would destroy their own individual beauty.

Furthermore, other areas of outstanding natural beauty, including Gower, the Quantock Hills, the Surrey Hills and the Malverns, were to be kept unspoiled. National forest parks and numerous nature reserves completed the saving of the beauty from the industrial development of this country. Thus the city dweller and the factory worker could leave the noise and the smoke-filled crowded industries, and know and breathe the peace of the countryside before a refreshed return to work.

Chapter XXV

Education

This chapter is divided into the following sections:

Education in the 18th century, (elementary; secondary; universities).

Education in the 19th century, (elementary; secondary; university; adult education).

Education in the 20th century, (secondary; health service; Education Act 1944).

EDUCATION IN THE 18th CENTURY

Elementary Education

If you had been born in the 18th, or early 19th centuries, what kind of an education would you have had?

The answer is that you might not have had any at all. Poverty was the chief reason why working class children did not attend school... they often lacked enough clothing. Many of them, also, had to go out to work, earning the money the family so desperately needed. In such cases they toiled in mills or mines; or sometimes they were sent on to the streets because they could beg more effectively than their parents. For the poor, therefore, there was little schooling.

If any education was received, it came from one or more of eight sources.

Elementary education (that is for younger children) was provided firstly by the 'dame schools' for infants. If an old lady, widowed and poor, wished to rescue herself from poverty, she became a schoolmistress. Similarly, there were the 'common day schools' for older children, which were usually organised by males. If a man was unable to work due to accident or constant ill-health... he opened a school. If a man was too ignorant to succeed in any business or career... well ... he became a schoolmaster.

All that was necessary in such cases was to put in the window a torn and dirty piece of paper with the word 'SKOOL' scrawled on it, and the establishment was duly open. The classroom was an attic, a cellar, or a barn. The solitary text-book was a torn and dilapidated New Testament, and the exercise books were heaps of sand on the floor where the pupils formed the letters with sticks. The more de-luxe establishments however, provided rickety benches, primitive desks and horn books. A horn book was a small sheet of paper, generally about eight inches by five inches, and with the alphabet, the figures one to nine and the Lord's Prayer printed thereon. This piece of paper was pasted on to a thin piece of wood, with a transparent sheet of horn placed over it and tacked down.

Both Dame and Common Day Schools charged a small fee for their educational services.

For the poorer children, there were the Charity Schools, maintained by subscriptions from the upper classes, shopkeepers, artisans and non-conformists. Here, reading, writing, religion and morals were taught; the children were clothed and apprenticed. Unfortunately, by the end of the 18th century, these useful schools had faded out.

Some of these charity schools were organised by the S.P.C.K. (Society for the Promotion of Christian Knowledge) founded in 1699, which naturally introduced religious information in the teaching of reading and writing.

Also at this point, we should mention Robert Raikes (1735-1811), who, at Gloucester in 1780, commenced his Sunday School to relieve the misery and ignorance of the poor children of that city. He lived to see such schools extend over the whole of England.

Secondary education

Secondary education (that is for the older children, from about 13-17) was only for the richer people. There were the Grammar schools — local, town day schools — and there were the Public Schools — boarding schools, attracting pupils from all over the country, some examples being Winchester, founded by William of Wykeham in 1387, with its famous motto 'Manners Makyth Man'; Eton, founded by Henry VI in 1440; Westminster founded by Queen Elizabeth I in 1560; Rugby 1567, Harrow 1571, Charterhouse 1611.

It was unfortunate that both these types of schools — the Grammar and the Public—were old-established, and having failed to proceed with the times, had therefore become old-fashioned as well. They had been founded in the days when education consisted of a knowledge of Latin and Greek, so these two subjects occupied nearly all of the teaching. However as the centuries passed, Latin and Greek became

Slums

**A School under Joseph Lancaster's Monitorial System
in the East End of London, 1839**

(reproduced by courtesy of Radio Times Hulton Picture Library)

The Shop in Toad Lane
by Thomas Wakeman

(reproduced by courtesy of Rochdale Art Gallery Committee)

The Great Eastern

(reproduced by courtesy of Radio Times Hulton Picture Library)

of less value; they were no longer required — especially in the age of the Industrial Revolution, but the masters appointed to teach those subjects could not legally be removed from their posts. Hence there occurred the well-known instance where two teachers had the almost ideal existence of a salary of £700 per year between them, and only one pupil to instruct. The schoolmasters' Paradise on earth did actually occur, however — a master who drew his salary for 40 years — and never had a pupil to teach.

Not only was the education by the Grammar and Public Schools valueless, but also discipline was grim. The cane was both teacher and text-book, and the greatest schoolmasters of their time were likewise those of the most splendid physique. John Keate, Headmaster of Eton 1809-34, at the age of 60 could, and did, flog 80 boys in the course of a single day. Perhaps there may have been some excuse for such severity, for forms in those days were larger than they are now — Keate taught a class of over 170.

But violence bred violence, and the answer to the brutal discipline was revolt. The results could scarcely be imagined at the present time. In a riot at Rugby in 1797, the door of the Headmaster's study was blown open with gunpowder. At Winchester, a riot in 1818 had to be put down by two companies of soldiers with bayonets fixed. There were riots at Eton in 1768, 1783, 1798 and 1818; and again in 1832. There was, indeed, never a dull moment.

Universities

From the secondary schools, the pupils proceeded to the Universities, those centres of knowledge, Oxford and Cambridge. Centres of knowledge they certainly were in the 18th century. Professors were noted not only for a lack of interest in their work, but also for a lack of knowledge of their subject. Undergraduates attended lectures only if they wished to do so, and frequently left their college for days at a time, for hunting or gambling trips, and were not discovered. Tutor and pupil often never knew each other.

Such intensive education was expected to prepare these undergraduates for a degree, and strange as it may seem, it succeeded. Perhaps one of the reasons for success lay in the number and type of question that was asked at the examination. It is on record that one candidate was examined in Hebrew and History. There were only two questions, and he had to answer them orally. "What", asked the examiner, "is the Hebrew for 'Place of the skull'?" He replied, "Golgotha". "Who founded University College?" "King Alfred", he replied. "Very well, sir", said the examiner. "You are competent for your degree".

It will thus be realised that the students of the University were unbelievably idle, and that the examination was a farce.

It was equally obvious, too, that by the end of the 18th century there was considerable room for improvement in the whole educational system of this country. The only places of real educational value, indeed, were the Nonconformist Academies where those who, because of their religion, were not allowed to enter the Anglican Universities, received a better education that the Universities provided, and not only in Greek, Latin and religious study, but also in mathematics, science and medicine.

EDUCATION IN THE 19th CENTURY
Elementary education

The 19th century, fortunately, saw the improvement that was so urgently required. Let us, therefore, trace this improvement, and see how it affected the teachers, the teaching, the schools and the pupils respectively.

First of all, the *teachers*:

In elementary education, a new idea was introduced in the form of Voluntary Schools:

  (i) the National Schools for Anglicans founded in 1811 by Dr. Andrew Bell;

  (ii) the British and Foreign Schools Society for Nonconformists set up in 1814 from the earlier efforts of the Quaker, Joseph Lancaster.

Both of these received a Government grant of £20,000 in 1833. (That same year, the upkeep of the Royal horses and dogs at Windsor received a grant of £70,000.) The schools were responsible for teaching the 'three Rs' (Reading, wRiting and aRithmetic or Reckoning), and the pupils were admitted at any age between six and fourteen, for a period of about three years education, in classes from 60 to 80 in number.

Under such conditions, discipline created a problem, to solve which both rewards and punishments were given. Rewards were provided in money, or by toys suspended from the classroom ceiling until awarded. The usual punishment was the cane, but other methods were not despised. One teacher, indeed, gained a reputation for his skill at banging pupils' heads together. Unfortunately, he had at last to give up teaching, because his right arm became paralysed.

The chief difficulty in education at this time was certainly that of obtaining teachers, for the schools were ill-lit and ill-ventilated, and the salaries of the staff were low.

To solve this problem, the Voluntary Schools introduced the 'Monitor system'. The teacher taught a group of elder or more able children (called 'monitors'), and each of these then repeated the lesson to a class of other children. There were no text books — the children assembled round printed sheets affixed to the walls. While the other children were learning this lesson, or outside school hours, the teacher then taught the monitors the next lesson, and so on. In this way, one teacher could instruct hundreds of children (even up to a thousand) by means of the monitors.

It was a brilliant way to overcome the shortage of teachers, but the education given was merely a mechanical drill — the children repeated and recited spellings, mathematical tables and lists of facts until they knew them off by heart. They had no real understanding of what they learnt.

From the idea of the monitors, however, there came the idea of a proper training for teachers. The person responsible was Dr. J. P. Kay Shuttleworth (1804-77), who, in 1840, founded as his own private undertaking, the Battersea Training College for teachers, where those who intended to enter that profession served a seven year apprenticeship. In 1846, when Secretary to a Government Committee for education, he began the idea of pupil teaching. From the ages of 13 to 18, selected children taught in schools, and by passing an examination after that, could then attend a training centre. This was certainly a better system, but even so, the pupil teachers were too young, they had not sufficient education, and at best could only became class teachers able to teach a few subjects to a not very high standard.

Having thus produced the teachers, the 19th century now tried to improve the *teaching*, and in 1862, there began the very famous and well-known system of 'Payment by results'. This idea, indeed, had the appearance of being the finest scheme ever devised. From then onwards, the amount of money received by a school every year from the Government was to depend on an annual test given to the pupils by Her Majesty's Inspectors (H.M.I.s). The test was based upon attendance and on the three R's.

The theory seemed excellent. The schools with the best attendance, and the best teachers, would get the best results, and therefore the more money. The poorly-attended schools, where the teaching was inefficient, would suffer.

The theory, as we have said, seemed excellent, but the actual practice was shocking. Since the money depended on the attendance, the teachers carefully falsified the registers. Since the money depended on the three R's, the teachers spared no effort, particularly physical effort, to drill the three R's into their classes. It was all mechanical teaching — the children learnt by memorising the facts and passages, aided by repetition and the cane. In many cases, the children did not 'read' the selected passage; they knew it off by heart. They could have 'read' it even if the book had been held upside down, or even if they had never had the book at all. The older and brighter children never developed their ability to the full. They were neglected while the teacher strove to teach the younger or duller to the standard required for the exam (and so obtain the money).

Having thus organised the registers and the teaching, each school awaited the success of its efforts. The day of the examination itself was a battle — a battle waged bitterly and relentlessly between the teacher and the H.M.I. Any child likely to pass the exam had to be present on that particular day — even if it had to be fetched from a sick bed, and sit in the classroom wrapped in blankets, while suffering from chicken-pox, measles or any other infectious disease (who knows, the H.M.I. might catch the disease too!). As the Inspector asked the questions, the teacher would have a secret code which enabled the children to give the correct answer — a wink meant 'yes', scratching the head 'no', rubbing the nose meant 'multiply', hands in pocket 'divide', and so on.

In face of such circumstances, the 'payment by results' system had gradually to be modified until it ended, unregretted, in 1897.

Having thus produced the teachers and the teaching, the 19th century then tried to produce the *schools*.

The 1870 Education Act, devised by the Liberal statesman, William Forster, said that where there were not enough Voluntary Schools, the district could establish State schools under School Boards for elementary education. The cost would be paid from the rates, parents' fees and a Government grant. The Voluntary Schools, of course, were religious — (the National Schools for Anglicans, and the British and Foreign Schools Society for Nonconformists) — but in the new State schools, religious instruction was to be undenominational (i.e. a general religious instruction not belonging to any particular faith). Children whose parents so wished, however, need not attend scripture lessons.

Forster's Education Act was an important development, but the Schools Boards were often inefficient, particularly as they were not compelled to do anything. They could establish schools, they could compel attendance, they could pay the fees of those too poor to do so . . . if they wished. Many of them, therefore, did very little.

So in 1902, by the Balfour Act, Local Education Authorities (L.E.A.s) were established instead. These took over State Schools, and in the case of the Voluntary Schools, the L.E.A.s were responsible for books, equipment, salaries and secular (i.e. non-religious) matters, while the School Governors were responsible for the upkeep of the building and religious affairs.

Having thus produced the teachers, the teaching and the schools, the *pupils* were now required. Already by the 1833 Factory Act (Althorp's Act), 9-13 year-olds who worked in factories had to have two hours education per day.

Next, in 1844, the 8-13 year-olds had to have three hours education per day, or they could work one day in the factory and then attend school for one day, and so on, alternately — this was called the 'half-time system'. In some areas, the children worked half-a-day in school, and the other half day in the mill. The results, of course, were unsatisfactory. It could hardly be expected that arrangements such as these would be effective, and to quote but one example of the consequences, about half the male population and two-thirds of the women in Manchester were illiterate.

Improvement did not follow swiftly, either. Under Forster's Education Act of 1870, the School Boards could compel attendance . . . if they wished — so in practice, they took no action. It saved a lot of trouble.

It was not until 1880, indeed, that education was at last made compulsory — and then for all children from the ages of five to ten; while in 1900, all children had to remain at school till the age of 12. Parents were expected to pay a small amount each week until 1918, when elementary school fees were abolished entirely, and from that year onwards, all children had to receive a free, full-time education to the age of 14.

So much, then, for the improvements in elementary education in the

19th century — monitors and pupil teachers, payment by results, Voluntary and State schools, the raising of the school leaving age.

Secondary education

But also in the 19th century, secondary education (for older children) was being improved, so let us now turn to consider this. There were five aspects: *technical schools, girls' schools, private schools, Grammar Schools* and *Public Schools*, and we will say a few words about each.

Firstly, a new type of education began to develop — technical education. It had become increasingly clear from 1850 onwards that the skill of other manufacturing nations was overtaking ours. If we wished to maintain our lead, then we had to train our apprentices more thoroughly.

Accordingly, technical education really commenced in 1889, when local councils were made responsible, and a rate could be levied for the purpose. It was further assisted the following year when money obtained by the Government from a tax on spirits was used to help. This use of 'whiskey money', whereby every drunkard benefited the educational system of the country, provided ample opportunity for varying degrees of wit in the press. Nevertheless, the improvement that resulted (to the technical education!) encouraged the Government to give a grant in 1902 for the setting up of junior technical schools. These filled the educational gap for those who had left school at the age of 13 to 14, and were waiting to start their apprenticeship at 16.

It was during the 19th century, too, that the higher education of girls developed. Before this, the richer parents had their daughters taught at home by a governess (herself often ill-paid and ill-educated), or sent the girls to a boarding school. In any event, their education was concerned only with the 'social graces' — music, dancing, sewing, embroidery, cookery, the correct way to speak and walk — so that even if they were able to write, it is quite likely that they could not spell. It was, of course, realised that the aim of their studies was to secure a husband, and that success in their educational examinations was in the form of a marriage certificate.

But music, sewing, embroidery, etc. were hardly an 'education', and gradually girls began to be taught other subjects, and to a higher standard. It was an important event when in 1848, Queen's College, London, was founded in order to train women teachers. From this college came two star students — Mary Buss, later Headmistress of London Collegiate School in 1850, and Dorothea Beale, later Principal of Cheltenham Ladies' College in 1858.

Gradually, education for girls developed further, until in 1869, Girton College, and in 1871, Newnham College, at Cambridge University were founded for women students. The first women's college at Oxford University was Somerville, 1879.

Now let us consider similar educational developments for boys.

For the sons of less wealthy middle classes, who could not afford the fees of the Grammar and Public Schools, secondary education in the 19th century was provided by Private Schools of which there is little record. Some of them were indeed very good, teaching more 'useful' subjects such as arithmetic, history, geography and art. Most others, however, were of the appalling type described so vigorously in Charles Dickens' famous story, *Nicholas Nickleby*:

'Where's the second boy?' asked Mr. Whackford Squeers, Headmaster of Dotheboys Hall in Yorkshire.

'Please Sir, he is weeding the gardens', replied a small voice.

'To be sure', said Squeers, by no means disconcerted. 'So he is. B. O. T. bot, t-i-n tin, bottin, n-e-y ney, bottiney, noun substantive, a knowledge of plants. When he has learnt that bottiney means a knowledge of plants, he goes and knows 'em. That's our system!'

For those, however, who could afford the fees of the Grammar and Public Schools, there was good news.

By the Municipal Reform Act of 1835, the Grammar Schools came under the control of local energetic citizens. Their curriculum was extended to teach not only Greek and Latin but also mathematics, modern languages, history and science.

At the same time, the Public Schools reached the peak of their fame. The reason, it was clear, was due to their teachers — men of a quality and calibre which we do not seem to breed now, men of a tremendous personality who had a real influence upon boys.

Of these, four supreme Headmasters must be mentioned. There was Samuel Butler, Headmaster of Shrewsbury, 1798-1836. Even more famous was Thomas Arnold of Rugby, 1828-42, a dynamic and dominating personality, who aimed at making boys into Christian gentlemen, with a sense of responsibility, and who, in the process, developed the now well-known prefect system in schools. The teachers he selected to serve under him were required to be Christian gentlemen, active, possessing common sense, an interest in their work and an understanding of boys. Is it surprising that teachers with such qualities had a real and lifelong influence upon the pupils whom they taught? Also, it may be mentioned, it was at Rugby in 1823 that William Webb Ellis 'picked up the ball and ran with it' during a game of football, and thus commenced Rugby football.

Another outstanding Headmaster was Edward Thring of Uppingham, 1853-87, who established the then new ideas of organised games, a gymnasium, swimming baths, music rooms and an old boys' organisation. Finally came F. W. Sanderson of Oundle, 1892-1922, who taught boys to live, not merely earn a living, and tried to help every child who came to him. 'We must not cast out or send our weak ones away'.

It was these men, and these ideals, which have influenced not only the Public Schools, but also the State-organised Grammar Schools, and have extended their standards far beyond even these.

The influence of the Public Schools, indeed, was tremendous. Their scholars were few, and limited to the sons of the wealthy, but for a period of over 100 years to the middle of the 20th century, they trained the leaders of the nation, a small but distinguished band in every aspect of life. From the Public Schools came the men who occupied the highest positions in the church or became the leading statesmen of their time; the men who managed the high responsibilities of the Civil Service both at home and abroad; who maintained England's prestige in the conduct of battle; who developed England's influence in the spheres of art and sciences. The influence of the Public Schools was thus out of all proportion to the fewness of their numbers; it was a supreme example of quality not quantity.

Beyond the secondary education which we have just discussed — (technical, girls, Private, Grammar and Public Schools), lay the universities and a number of other different organisations.

Universities

The history of the 19th century improvement reached the Universities. At Oxford and Cambridge, Nonconformists were admitted in 1871; the women's colleges of Girton, 1869, and Newnham, 1870, were founded at Cambridge, and Somerville Hall (later College) in 1879, at Oxford; while the educational standards of the Universities were also improved.

New universities, too, were being founded:- Durham in 1832,

Wales 1893, and after these Manchester, Liverpool, and Leeds 1903-4, Sheffield 1905, Bristol 1909, Reading 1926, Nottingham 1938, and Southampton 1952, Hull 1954, Exeter 1956, up to Salford 1967. All these differed from Oxford and Cambridge in that they were local universities — their students came from the neighbourhood, which also meant they came from the Grammar and Secondary Schools, rather than the Public Schools; they were non-resident; and their studies were influenced by local industry and local requirements. London University, founded in 1836, is the only one to grant external degrees, i.e. you have no need to belong to the University in order to take its examinations.

Adult education

But education is not a part of life limited to the first few years thereof, or even to the end of a University course. There were many, indeed, who still desired to be taught, long after they had left school, both for pleasure and for profit. So the 19th century began to develop adult education.

In 1823, Dr. George Birkbeck (1776-1841), at one time a Glasgow Professor and later a London doctor, founded the London Mechanics' Institute where working men could learn mathematics, English, French, Latin and science, and could borrow books from the library there. The idea spread to other industrial areas such as Leeds, Huddersfield, Manchester and Birmingham.

Unfortunately, however, the lectures were of a standard too high for the ordinary working man to understand, so that gradually only the more skilled workers and middle class clerks remained as members. By 1850, lack of funds was another weakening factor, so that the Institutes gradually faded away, becoming technical schools or social clubs. The London Mechanics' Institute itself became part of London University, to provide evening classes where those who worked during the day could study at night for a degree.

Of more lasting fame were the evening institutes founded by Quintin Hogg in 1880, to educate apprentices and working men in their trades, and to promote social gatherings. This, and similar organisations which developed from it all over the country, were called Polytechnics.

In 1899, a more ambitious effort was made when Ruskin College was set up at Oxford to give working men the opportunity to study at a University.

For those adults who wanted to achieve some recognised standard in their studies, the Royal Society of Arts commenced its examinations in 1854, while in 1880 the City and Guilds Institute was founded to encourage the teaching of science in schools, to organise evening classes and to hold examinations.

EDUCATION IN THE 20th CENTURY
Secondary education

The 20th century came, and from 1902-44, there were rapid developments, more particularly in secondary education. Previous efforts had been concentrated mostly upon the younger children in elementary schools . . . and indeed, before 1902, only five or six boys out of every thousand (and fewer still girls) went from the elementary to the secondary stage of education. Now, however, it was to be the turn of the older children in the secondary schools.

The value of the secondary education was at last being generally realised. Parents wanted to obtain for their children a better education for greater opportunities in life, than they themselves had had. Public libraries, films and the B.B.C. had widened people's interests, and they wanted to be educated in order to make the most of these new interests. Business and industry realised that England must have well-taught minds if she was to withstand competition from abroad. The Government realised that the working class had now received the vote, and must, therefore, be educated to use it; no one wanted the danger of uneducated mob rule.

These powerful reasons for the development of secondary education reacted upon teachers, pupils and parents alike.

Teachers received better training, smaller classes and higher salaries. The schools themselves became much more pleasant — there was less class teaching and more individual or group tuition; the subjects were less academic and more realistic; lessons were made more interesting by better books and equipment, the use of films, B.B.C. broadcasts and educational visits, and the discipline was not so strict.

For pupils, there developed the idea of a national system of education for all. In 1918, by Fisher's Act, named after Dr. H. A. L. Fisher, the historian and head of the Board of Education, elementary school fees were abolished entirely, and also the 'half-time' system introduced in 1844, so that from 1918 onwards, all children had a free, full-time education to the age of 14.

If a child worked hard and had the ability, he could go from the elementary to the secondary school. Under the Balfour Act, 1902,

L.E.A.s could provide fee-paying secondary schools, and these became the new grammar schools. Clever pupils, however, could be given free places in such schools, and to encourage this, in 1907 the Government gave a grant to fee-paying grammar schools who allowed 25 per cent of their admissions free. In 1932, this 'free place' system was altered to the 'special place' system, whereby the parents of successful pupils paid for the grammar school education at a fee based on their income. From the grammar school, the child could win a scholarship or other grant, and go to a University free of charge.

There was thus a complete 'ladder of education', and any clever boy or girl, however poor, could climb from the elementary classroom to a University degree.

Parents also began to take an interest in their children's schooling as a result of Open Days, exhibitions and parent-teacher associations.

School Health Service

It is a sobering thought that as the schoolmaster of 1902 gazed at what we will call a 'typical form' sitting in front of him, he knew that nine out of every 10 of those children could be classified as 'dirty', that is, filthy and verminous. Not only so, but eight out of 10 of them suffered from dental decay; six out of 10 were infested with nits (the eggs of lice); two out of 10 had eye, nose and throat trouble; and one out of 10 was terribly underfed. It is an even more sobering thought that within the course of their school career from the ages of five to 12, the schoolmaster knew that one out of every three hundred in front of him would die of disease.

There is no doubt at all that the school medical service which began in 1907 — doctors, dentists, nurses, school clinics — has been one of the finest assets to the nation ever devised. Its efforts were helped by free meals for needy cases (in 1906), P.T. and organised games in school hours, and school camps, while to assist those children for whom no cure was possible, the State provided Blind and Deaf Schools, as well as schools for mental defectives, epileptics, cripples and tubercular cases.

R. A. Butler's Education Act 1944

Then in 1944, when the Second World War was drawing to its close, and the minds of men were turning to thoughts of rebuilding, a national universal scheme of education became law. This scheme was placed under the control of Local Education Authorities, though the voluntary schools were allowed to remain if they paid 50 per cent of the cost of the improvements required, otherwise the L.E.A. took over.

The stages of education were to be as follows: Nursery (under five), primary five to seven, junior seven to 11. At the age of 11 +, every child had to take an exam to decide whether he should go to a Secondary Modern School for less academic pupils, or to a Grammar School for the more academic, from either of which there might be a transfer to a Technical School. The school leaving age was raised to 15, and during the whole of a pupil's school career, the L.E.A. had to provide free of charge, a medical service, milk and meals and clothing for the needy, and recreational facilities. This, of course, was together with free education.

For those who distrusted state education, however — whatever, its apparent benefits — and who could afford to do so — there was a wide variety of private schools, including Public Schools, Roman Catholic Schools, A. S. Neill's 'Dreadful School' at Summerhill in Suffolk, 1921, where the children decided what they should do in school, and also private tutors.

Then after leaving school, boys and girls could attend evening classes to increase their knowledge of their career, and later on, they could attend such forms of non-vocational (i.e. not concerned with their careers) education as were provided by University Extension courses, Adult Residential Colleges, Workers' Educational Association founded in 1903, Women's Institutes, Y.M.C.A. (Young Men's Christian Association), Y.W.C.A. (Young Women's Christian Association), Mothers Unions, Girls Friendly Societies, etc.

For those who desired to obtain a recognised standard of ability, in 1951, the General Certificate of Education (G.C.E.) Ordinary and Advanced Level Examinations were introduced, while in 1965, the Certificate of Secondary Education (C.S.E.) was introduced for less able pupils.

All this did not mean that the new educational system was faultless. However excellent the plan might be, it still depended on having the necessary teachers to make it work. Here was a great difficulty, for teaching is an exacting occupation, and the prospects and conditions in industry and other professions were far better than in schools.

Considerable criticism was made of the division at the age of 11 + into grammar, secondary modern and technical schools. To avoid this, some educational authorities set up comprehensive schools: these provided education of a grammar, secondary modern and technical nature all within the same school. Such schools, however with their 1,000 to 2,000 pupils were felt to be too large and unwieldy.

Also the new aids to learning — the television, radio and film shows — instead of inspiring the children, tended to make them idle. Instead of learning, it has been said they just sat, listened and watched, passively accepting the programme.

The history of education, indeed, entered a difficult period.

Chapter XXVI

Agriculture 1815 — 1914

Agriculture in the 19th century was a see-saw story — bad times, good times, bad times, good times — and may be divided into the following periods: 1815-53, 1853-73; 1873-93; 1893-1913.

1815-53

This period saw the continuing change from the small to the large farmers, and therefore the disappearance of the yeoman (the small farmer).

When the Napoleonic Wars were over, an avalanche of difficulties hit English farming. Taxation was high, while the parish levies of the poor rate (to help the poor) and the highway rate (to repair the roads) were paid mainly by the farmers. Trade was bad, so prices rose and fell. Wet seasons ruined the crops, and disease killed the cattle. Under conditions such as these, it was impossible to pay the high farm rents required, or to repay wartime loans obtained when farming was prosperous, so the farmers went bankrupt.

Government attempts to help the distress failed. Though the Corn Laws from 1815-46 limited the import of foreign corn, they did not give British agriculture the benefit that was expected. Equally contrary to expectation, the Repeal of the Corn Laws in 1846 did not ruin British farmers; prices remained steady for the next 20 years.

One fact, however, was quite evident. Only the large farmer could cope with all these difficulties, and do so by means of better production. Only the large farmer could afford better drainage with clay drain pipes, the cost of chemical manures (sodium nitrate, ammonium sulphate, and guano from Peru), and the renewal of old buildings. Thus the old three-field (or 'open-field') system was practically ended by 1850; England had become a land of large and enclosed farms.

Meanwhile, the labourer was in desperation. Enclosure had deprived him of the common land and waste land for grazing and fuel; he had lost his regular employment, and faced increased rents or eviction. When he poached for food in order to live, he faced the risks of mantraps and of the death penalty under the Game Acts. Finally, when, desolate and desperate, he turned to violence, the Labourers Revolt of 1830 in Kent, the Home Counties, the West Country and East Anglia, was crushed by troops, imprisonment, execution and transportation. After 1834, if he was starving, he faced the grim misery of the workhouse.

1853-73

Good times. There was no foreign competition. Russia had no railways; America also lacked railways and was engaged in the Civil struggle of the North against the South (1861-5); while Germany was occupied with her national pastime — war — against Denmark 1864, Austria 1866 and France 1870.

So the English farmer made the most of the opportunity, particularly with the aid of labour-saving machinery. Instead of the six-oxen

Fowler's Steam Cable Plough, 19th century (Pictorial Education).

plough, he employed a steam cable-plough whereby steam engines at either end of the field dragged the plough across by means of cables. Instead of the sower and his basket scattering here and there, a horse-drawn drill planted seeds at regular intervals in straight furrows. Instead of scythes and sickles, the reaping machine was used; the flail was replaced by a threshing machine, after which came the winnowing machine and the chaff-cutter: while other mechanical devices crushed oats, split beans and pulped turnips.

Not only the machines, but also the weather of this period enabled fine harvests, and after that the railways provided cheap and rapid transport to wider markets so that the farmer could supply the increasing food demands of an increasing population. The same railways, of course, brought seeds and fertilisers to the farms.

Small wonder that, by 1870, there were no less than 13 million acres under the plough.

The stock farmer likewise prospered. Skilful breeding and the care of cattle improved existing herds, particularly the Sussex and Jersey. Romney Marsh sheep were famous; the Cheviots and Southdowns were outstanding for both meat and fleece. Animals were now housed in clean, dry farm buildings; they were fed on imported foodstuffs during the winter, and had the care of qualified veterinary surgeons when required.

If a farmer wanted advice, the Royal Agricultural Society was established in 1838; if he wished to learn the results of new ideas, the Rothamsted Experimental Station in 1843 began its careful research into the scientific farming of the soil.

Finally, in this period of 1853-73, trade was good, prices were high and taxes were low. Even the most complaining of farmers had to admit that this was 'the Golden Age of British Agriculture'.

But what of the poor agricultural labourer at this time? Alas, his situation was still a most unhappy one, despite some improvement on the previous period. His home was a hovel, he and his family were desperate for food, there was little work, with low wages, and how honest can a man be when he must either starve or steal?

True, the Government tried to help him by the grant of allotments so he could grow his own food, but the farmers feared the labourer might become too independent, or spend too much time on his own land, the shopkeepers feared loss of trade if the labourer grew his own fruit and vegetables, and the innkeepers realised that men might be digging instead of drinking. So in view of all this opposition, the idea of allotments did not succeed.

Then the labourers of Warwickshire tried to help themselves, and appealed for assistance to Joseph Arch, a fairly wealthy hedge-cutter and lay-preacher, who was well-known for his interest in the lower class. One February night in 1872, a thousand of these poor working men assembled under a chestnut tree, and as he gazed at the gaunt and hungry faces in front of him, Joseph Arch resolved to help them if he could. As a result, he formed the National Agricultural Labourers' Union, with sick benefits and help for those who wished to emigrate. Naturally, this aroused the opposition of the farmers, and when the labourers tried to strike, the farmers replied by lock-outs, (i.e. wholesale dismissals in the area) and by obtaining help from the military at harvest time. Thus the Union declined, as its money was spent on unsuccessful strikes.

1873-93

Bad times. There was now a flood of foreign imports, especially from Russia, from the hitherto uncultivated prairies of America, and from Canada where a 16 foot depth of rich virgin soil grew splendid crops. Also, railways and steamships could now carry this vast tonnage of grain to the English markets. At the same time, cold storage (refrigeration) enabled mutton and dairy produce to be sent from Australia, as well as chilled beef from the Argentine. Because England was a Free Trade country, there was nothing to stop the inrush of all this cheaper foreign food.

Even under the best possible circumstances, British farmers could not cope with these cheap imports. To make it worse, the circumstances were not the best possible. Year after year of appalling weather meant year after year of appalling harvests. The year 1879, indeed, was so wet that it was called the 'Black Year'. Five million sheep died of liver rot, pigs were killed by swine fever, and cattle perished from foot-and-mouth disease and pleuro-pneumonia. The expenses of farming increased, too, for the 1870 Education Act meant that the cheap child labour was now in school.

Is it to be wondered, therefore, that broken fences and gates enclosed fields choked with weeds and thistles?

The labourer naturally continued to suffer, but he did have one ray of hope. In 1884, the agricultural worker received the vote (i.e. he could vote to elect Members of Parliament), and in 1885, Joseph Arch rode in triumph through King's Lynn, as the newly-elected Member of Parliament for Norfolk, given that honour by the agricultural labourers' votes.

1893-1913

The motto that faced the British farmer was now quite clear; 'Adapt or Perish'. So he began to produce goods that were not imported — milk instead of meat, fruit and vegetables rather than cereals — and began to keep cattle for breeding purposes. Mixed farming (i.e. both crops and cattle) increased.

To help him, the Board of Agriculture was established in 1889 to give advice and instruction, to undertake research, and to try to check cattle diseases. Later, rates on agricultural land were reduced and the Government gave grants for rural industry, forestry, etc.

But the position of the agricultural labourer was still unsatisfactory. It was so bad, indeed, that it became a matter of national concern, for workers were leaving the land to go into industry or to go abroad, and in such numbers, that a serious shortage of farm labour was threatened. In 1887, therefore, the Government compelled local authorities to provide allotments, and in 1908 to buy, and then to sell, or let, small-holdings (one to 50 acres). But these efforts still failed to stop the agricultural workers seeking the better prospects offered in industry or abroad. Indeed, between 1870-1900, some 300,000 left the farms.

Moreover, the First World War was threatening, and what of England's food if supplies from overseas were stopped? Before 1914, 2/5ths of our meat and 4/5ths of our wheat were imported.

Chapter XXVII

'Co-ops'

In the normal stages of business, there is the person who makes the goods, and the person who sells the goods — or as we call them, the manufacturer and the shopkeeper. In between the two comes a 'middleman', who buys the goods from the manufacturer and then sells them to the shopkeeper at a higher price.

Admittedly, the middleman may serve a useful purpose. He takes large quantities of goods at a time from the manufacturer who can thus keep his factory space clear for further production. Secondly, he 'breaks bulk', dividing the masses of goods into numerous small quantities for individual shops — a task which otherwise the manufacturer himself would have the expense and delay of doing. On the other hand, some manufacturers prefer to market and sell their goods themselves.

But whether the middleman serves a useful purpose or not, he sells the goods to the shopkeeper at a higher price than he paid for them in order to make his own profit. So the shopkeeper in turn has to charge more to the customer, and this increase in prices is a particular hardship to the poorer buyer.

One man who tried to make goods cheaper, and the life of the working classes happier in consequence, was the energetic Robert Owen (whom we have already met on page 172).

His aim, indeed, was no less than a complete reorganisation of society — a reorganisation which did away with employers, the use of money, and the idea of making a profit at someone else's expense. Instead, every man would be a worker, and he would produce whatever he was able in order to exchange with others who produced what he wanted. So money was not required, since trade was conducted by exchange. In any event, money was unnecessary for no-one made anything for his own profit; everything produced was handed over for the common good.

But although Owen went to America in 1824, and at a place called New Harmony in Indiana, tried to found a 'Village of Co-operation' for 900 people, where everyone worked for the common good instead of personal benefit, his venture failed. After all, human nature has always been greedy and selfish; few people want to work other than for their own benefit.

Nevertheless, on his return to England in 1829, he continued his efforts in a different form, and his ideas had such effect that by 1830, there were 300 Co-operative Societies in existence; by 1832, there were 500. Each member of these early Co-operatives paid a small amount every week to form a fund. With the money, the Societies then provided education for the workers; or they enabled the workers to set up their own general stores for buying and selling cheaply; while in some cases they set up their own small factories to produce cheap goods for the workers. It was a magnificent effort on the part of Owen's ideas, but by 1834, the movement had failed, due, among other reasons, to a lack of knowledge to overcome the difficulties involved.

But although Robert Owen failed, the beliefs that he held were sound . . . and later years were to prove them for him.

Thus it was, that in a shop in Toad Lane (The Old Lane — T'Owd Lane), in Rochdale, in 1844, 28 working men started an idea that was to extend over the whole nation. They bought their goods direct from the manufacturer, and sold them among themselves at normal prices. As there was no middleman involved, all the profit made was their own. They used that profit first of all to build up the business, and once that had been achieved, the money was then distributed back among the members.

The success of the movement spread. Originally, there were just 28 working men who paid £1 each to start what was to be known as the Co-operative Society. More shareholders joined, and by 1845, they had £180. As the idea spread to other areas, similar shops were established all over the country. By 1851, there were 130 Co-operative Societies, by 1862, 450 Societies, while by 1959, indeed, the movement had over 12 million members.

The story of success developed particularly from 1864, when the Co-operative Wholesale Society was formed. This bought supplies on a large scale (and hence more cheaply), and distributed them to the smaller Co-operative shops. Next, instead of buying goods from others, the C.W.S. began to produce its own goods, building its own factories, and even extending abroad to possess its own farms in English colonies, and tea plantations in Ceylon. It became sufficiently wealthy to act as a bank, a Building Society and as an insurance agency.

The method of organisation was simple. Each Co-operative store sold its goods at market prices, and at the end of every year the amount of money received was carefully checked. Rents, wages, interest to shareholders and other expenses were paid out, and part set aside for education and charity. The rest of the money was called the profit, and was divided (hence called a 'dividend') among the members in proportion to their purchase. Thus if at the end of a year, the Co-operative Society had made a profit of 3/- on every £1 of goods sold, each member received back a dividend of 3/- for every £1 spent.

The advantages of this system were obvious. The customers said what they wanted, the co-operative factories produced it, and sold it to them. Thus there was no expense of unwanted wasted stock, no cost of advertising, no middleman's profit, and since all profits were returned to the purchaser, no shopkeeper's profit. Thus poorer people obtained more for their money, and since the Co-operative Societies insisted upon cash payment, the evils of bad debts were avoided.

Equally important was the fact that in an age when shopkeepers sold bags of sugar consisting mainly of sand, mixed generous quantities of chalk with the flour they traded, poured brown sawdust in the coffee, and red lead or brick dust in the pepper, as well as adding sulphuric acid to the vinegar — in such an age as this, the Co-operative Societies guaranteed the purity of their foodstuffs.

The members, too, had the right to vote on the affairs of the company, and could thus gain experience in business.

So good indeed, seemed the idea of the Co-operative movement that its principles were applied to industry and agriculture. The workers in the factories and on the farms had each to pay so much, and in return received wages, interest on their money, and dividends. This failed, however, because the workmen could not pay enough to provide sufficient capital, the management was often inefficient and there was competition between the different co-operatives.

Then, as the 20th century proceeded, some of the weaknesses of the co-ops began to develop. Though the membership numbered millions, that did not mean there were millions of eager and enthusiastic co-operative supporters. Many joined not because they believed in the principles of the co-operative movement, but simply because the co-operative shop was conveniently near their home, and even then they probably purchased only one commodity such as milk or coal. The amount of interest in the co-operative movement as such is shown by the fact that only about two out of every 100 members take part in the voting for the management and administration of their societies.

Furthermore, there is now a very serious competition from the great departmental stores such as Woolworths and Marks and Spencer. These have a central control over buying to enable bulk purchases at a very cheap rate, whereas each local co-operative is independent in respect of buying, and so makes smaller, dearer purchases.

Most successful in the following of co-operative principles, however, have been the Building Societies, whose members lend money to form the capital. From this capital, various amounts are lent at interest to anyone wishing to buy a house, such interest (less expenses) forming the profits of the Societies.

Chapter XXVIII

Banks and Banking

Early banking

As the Industrial Revolution progressed and trade developed, the manufacturers and merchants began to acquire more money, and this meant that they had to find some safe place in which to keep it. The one-time private places of storage — the hole in the back garden visited at dead of night, the mattress, even the strong oak chest or locked safe — were no longer suitable. Some far better sanctuary had to be found. The rich merchants of London, of course, were particularly concerned, and many of them had originally chosen to store their wealth in the Tower. This was undoubtedly the safest place in the city, and remained so for many years until the Stuart kings came to the throne.

Then, in 1640, Charles I of England, in desperate need of money seized £130,000 of silver which had been deposited by these merchants in the Tower. The merchants at once sought security elsewhere, and so the goldsmiths entered the scene. For they already had strong rooms to keep the metal upon which they worked; they were already accustomed to dealing with gold and silver; and they also acted as money-changers for foreign currency.

So the merchant deposited his money with the goldsmiths, and received a receipt for it. As these receipts could be exchanged for money on demand, they were the fore-runners of bank-notes. Also, if a merchant wanted to pay a debt without having the trouble of going to the goldsmiths, he would write to the goldsmith asking him to pay the sum owed. This note, therefore, was the forerunner of the cheque.

So profitable did the storage of money become, that one leading goldsmith Sir Francis Child (1642-1713) abandoned that profession altogether, and became a banker only. Others followed his example.

No doubt the goldsmiths would have continued to act as bankers, but another Stuart king prevented this. The goldsmiths had soon realised that all the money deposited with them would not be withdrawn at the same time, so they kept some of it ready for withdrawals, and lent the rest at interest to the Government. In 1672, however, Charles II, wanting money for the Dutch War, stopped all Government repayment of loans for 12 months, and thus ruined the goldsmith lenders. So once again, the merchants had to find somewhere else to store their money.

Bank of England

It was a Scotsman who solved the problem. Under the leadership of William Paterson, a number of rich men subscribed £1,200,000 and lent it to the Government in return for £100,000 per annum and permission to found the Bank of England in 1694.

According to the regulations laid down, the Bank (i) could not borrow or lend more than its capital; (ii) could make loans, but not to the Government without Parliament's consent; (iii) could provide credit. This last was the most important, for credit is the life-blood of trade and war. Thus the Bank lent money to the East India Company, the Hudson Bay Company, the Russia Company and the Africa Company; it lent money to the Government in the Seven Years' War (1756-63) and in the War of American Independence (1775-83).

But above all, the Bank of England enabled the Industrial Revolution to take place by lending money to manufacturers, mine owners, canal builders and railway companies. All these undertakings required money to pay for buildings, equipment, materials and wages before they could even commence to operate, let alone show a profit. This money could be borrowed from the Bank of England.

The story of banknotes

Apart from these very important activities, the remaining history of the Bank of England is chiefly concerned with the issue of bank notes. We must consider this section very carefully indeed, because it will explain why we can use pieces of paper to buy food and goods nowadays.

By the terms of its charter, the Bank could also issue notes, and in 1708 became in practice the only large organisation allowed to do so (otherwise only banks with six or less partners were allowed such power).

The right to issue notes was indeed a valuable privilege, for they were far more convenient to carry than coins, and if stolen could more easily be traced, since they were all numbered. Hence merchants would be attracted to deal with any bank which issued such a form of currency.

Of course, the notes could always be exchanged for gold coins if desired, and that is why from now on we must remember one very important fact. A banknote was only valuable because it represented, and could be exchanged for, a piece of gold. A banknote which could not be exchanged for gold was only a worthless piece of paper. Obviously, therefore, a bank must not have more notes in circulation than it had gold to exchange for them if necessary. This is quite simple to understand . . . but it proved far easier said than done.

First of all, during the period of the French Revolution and the Napoleonic Wars (1792-1815), the Government borrowed gold, and when the Bank had very little gold left, cash payment (i.e. in exchange for notes) was suspended 1797-1821 and more notes were issued. The number of notes in circulation was then further increased by forgeries, and not even the severe penalty of the law which hung over 300 people for forgery between 1797-1817, could prevent 31,000 false notes being produced in that period alone.

The situation, then, became worse.

Previously, the Bank of England had been the main bank, while others of six or less partners opened in London, and were known as 'private banks'. Then, in 1716, James Wood, a soap and tallow dealer, opened a 'country bank' in Bristol, to begin a widespread and rapidly increasing number of such organisations, each of which produced its own notes.

These new banks, the 'private' and the 'country', had two grave weaknesses. Firstly, there was no restriction on quantity, so by 1793, there were already 300 of them, and by 1815, there were 900. Local shopkeepers, corn merchants, wool merchants and Welsh cattle drovers, all commenced the business. Secondly, the number of partners was limited to six or less by the Act of 1708, thus restricting the amount of capital they possessed. But there was nothing to prevent them issuing notes to any total value they wished, irrespective of the amount of gold they held. It is not surprising, therefore, that these banks failed, either through the dishonesty or incompetence of the founders, when people demanded gold in exchange for the notes. Indeed, no fewer than 200 country banks failed between 1815-30 alone. In 1825, 70 banks failed in six weeks.

So as a result of the shortage of gold caused by the Napoleonic Wars, as a result of forgeries, and of the note issues of private and country banks, there were far more notes in circulation than there was gold available in exchange. And a note which could not be exchanged for gold, was, as we have said, only a worthless piece of paper.

Three Acts of Parliament had to put matters right.

In 1826, joint stock banks were allowed to be established and could issue notes, but only beyond a 65-mile radius of London. Their notes, too, were of high amount, for no note issued was to be of value less than £5 — a law that lasted till 1928.

Next, the Bank Charter Act of 1833 allowed stock banks to be established in the London area, but not to issue notes. This Act marked the beginning of what are now regarded as the 'Big Five' among the Banks — Barclay's, Lloyd's, the Midland, National Provincial and Westminster. These banks, since they could not issue notes, became purely deposit banks where money was kept and the customers used cheques instead of banknotes. (In the case of a banknote, the bank promises to pay, so anyone who hands a banknote to the bank will receive an equivalent value in currency. In the case of a cheque, the person who makes it out promises to pay, and the bank will only hand over the money if that person has the necessary amount of money in the bank.)

The use of cheques increased, as it was far more convenient to handle one slip of paper than wads of banknotes. Now when a person sent a cheque, the receiver handed it into his own bank, so the sender's bank had later to take the sum involved to the receiver's bank. Clerks from various banks, therefore, met daily to settle the amounts each bank owed the others, and in 1775, an organisation called a Clearing House was set up to make such settlements easier.

Thirdly, by the Bank Charter Act of 1844 (i) no new banks were allowed to issue notes, and banks already in existence had their issue limited; (ii) the Bank of England could only issue notes to the value of the gold it held plus the amount of money owed to it by the Government; (iii) the note issuing department of the Bank of England was to be separated from the ordinary banking department; (iv) the Bank had to publish weekly accounts.

As a result, by 1921, only the Bank of England issued notes, all the other note-issuing banks having ceased to exist. (In 1914, there was a shortage of gold currency, as gold was needed to pay for the Great War, so as a substitute for gold coins, the Treasury issued 10/-and £1 notes. These notes were called 'Bradbury's', from the signature on them of the Secretary of the Treasury, Sir John Bradbury, and they lasted till 1928, when the Bank of England became responsible for exchanging them for coins.)

So it would have seemed that at last all was well. Only the Bank of

England could issue notes, and such notes were backed by gold.

Unfortunately, this happy state of affairs had only just been reached when the times began to change again, and once more, indeed, there arose the question of the value of banknotes. True, until 1914, a banknote could still be exchanged for gold coin, but as we have said, when the First World War broke out, gold was needed to pay the cost of fighting, so exchange was no longer permitted. For some years, therefore, it was not possible to convert paper money into gold currency.

Even when the war was over, a long argument then began as to what was to be done. Should you be able to have gold coins for paper money, or not? Finally, in 1925, it was decided that all notes were once more to be made 'as good as gold' . . . but for export purposes only. That is to say, in exchange for notes, the Bank would give you a definite amount of gold, but in the form of gold bars which were only of value abroad, and not in the form of gold coins, which were no longer to be used in England.

In 1931, however, England left the gold standard, so notes could no longer be exchanged even for gold bars, and gradually the Bank was allowed to issue more notes until now they are not really backed by gold at all. Instead, the Government has ordered that all such paper money can be used in business in England in the same way as gold coins were previously used. So long as paper money can be used to buy what is desired, people are quite satisfied to use it.

But we must return to finish our story of the Bank of England. By this time — that is, the period of the 20th century — the Bank of England had become a very powerful organisation indeed. It was adviser to the Government in financial matters; it looked after the money collected by the Government (e.g. taxes, etc.), and it acted as the agent of the Royal Mint. Other banks kept their accounts there, thus making it a 'national bank', and because of its vast wealth, it provided the entire credit system of the country.

So it was not surprising that in 1946 it was nationalised, i.e. placed under Government control instead of being in the hands of private individuals.

COINAGE

The coinage of this country from 1700-1970, has an interesting history.

In 1700, the chief currency was in the form of gold and silver coins, and it was no easy task to find adequate supplies of the precious metals required. Coins, of course, had to be the correct weight and fineness, otherwise they would lose their value for trade, so it was no solution to lessen the gold or silver content in each piece. Nor could the currency be too small in size — particularly when George I required all his titles to be inscribed. This involved a massive array of lettering — 'BRUN. ET.L.DUX.S.R.I.A.TH.ET.EL' (the Latin initials for 'Duke of Brunswick and Luneburg, Arch-Treasurer of the Holy Roman Empire and Elector') on one side of the coin, not to mention 'D.G.M.BR.FR. ET.HIB.REX.F.D.' ('By the Grace of God, King of Great Britain, France and Ireland, Defender of the Faith') on the other side.

Silver was the more difficult commodity to obtain. Fortunately, the period 1700-1800 commenced well. On October 21st, 1702, Admiral Sir George Rooke struck at the Spanish treasure fleet in Vigo harbour in the Azores. With 150 ships, 3,115 cannon and 30,000 troops, the assault cleared the harbour defences, and though the Spaniards in desperation set fire to their galleons, the English withdrew with a treasure including bullion, plate and 11 million coins of silver. The precious metals were melted down at the Royal Mint in London, and the word 'Vigo' was triumphantly inscribed on the English coins then made.

From 1740-44, Admiral George Anson journeyed round the world, sustaining his long voyage by attacking Spanish bullion ports and Spanish treasure galleons en route. He returned in triumph, his ship ballasted with Spanish gold, and the English coins made from the melted-down plunder bore the name of one of the chief Spanish New World ports, 'Lima' (in Peru).

Lesser supplies of silver were imported by the South Sea Company — the coins being marked with the letters 'S.S.C.' Coins with a design of plumes came from the silver mines of Wales.

Even so, all these sources were far from sufficient to supply the amount of silver required, and by the end of the century, the Mint were desperately counter-marking $2\frac{1}{4}$ million Spanish dollars, and issuing Bank of England tokens, in an attempt to solve the shortage of silver money.

To complicate matters still further, there was a serious shortage of small change altogether. From 1754-70, and again from 1775-97, no pennies, halfpennies or farthings were minted. So a vast quantity of imitation halfpennies and farthings were produced — and the adjective 'vast' is correct, for about 60 per cent of the small coins in circulation in the 18th century were false.

These false coins were crudely struck, and to avoid the grim penalties for forgery, they were issued with deliberately blundered legends. For example, instead of the correct wording 'Georgius III Rex' (Latin for 'King George III'), the counterfeiter would inscribe 'Grimruis iti nex', and instead of 'Britannia' on the obverse, there would be written 'Bonny Girl'. In any event, forgeries were easy to produce; many of the genuine coins in circulation had worn smooth, so the counterfeiters used blanks, or smoothed down cheap French francs.

But in the 1790s, the issue of a token coinage was undertaken by leading tradespeople and local authorities, whose business affairs had been seriously handicapped by the lack of small change. Among such were the ironmaster John Wilkinson, the Low Hall Colliery in Cumberland, Birmingham Workhouse, and several town councils. The coins now produced were mainly of good weight and material, well-struck, and accepted within the business or the locality. They bore the name of the issuer, who promised to redeem them for genuine coins whenever possible. The designs they bore — of factories, furnaces, looms, canals, ships, ale flagons, teapots, hats, and many more — provided a fascinating pictorial history of the economic and social life of the time.

Then, at long last, the Government took action to remedy the shortage of small change. At the Birmingham Mint, one of James Watt's steam engines was installed and in 1797 produced the largest British coin ever made — the famous 'Cartwheel Two-pence' — $1\frac{1}{2}$ inches in diameter and two ounces in weight. It was also the first coin to be made by steam-powered machinery. Later, more . . . and smaller! . . . copper coins were minted.

The 19th century opened with an important decision regarding our coinage.

In 1816, it was decided that English currency should be based on gold only. From then onwards, silver coins would be merely tokens, with the value of the metal content less than the face value of the coin — although, of course, they were still legal tender. As if to honour this decision to rely on gold, the Mint had appointed a brilliant Italian designer, Benedetto Pistrucci, whose skill was to remain upon English coins to the present day. On the reverse of the 1817 sovereign, there appeared the 'St. George and the Dragon', and the grace, strength and vigour of that design have not yet been surpassed.

The next important change occurred in 1860, when copper coinage ceased, and was replaced by bronze (copper, tin and zinc).

It was to be half a century before the silver coinage was similarly

affected. To obtain much-needed supplies of silver after the First
World War, the silver content of our coins was reduced from 92½ per
cent to 50 per cent in 1920. Worse was to follow after the Second World
War, however, when, to repay in silver the money lent to us by America
during the fighting, the silver coinage was withdrawn in 1947, and
replaced by pieces consisting of 75 per cent copper and 25 per cent
nickel. Thus there is no silver in 'silver' coins today.

In the year 1937, a new shape for British coinage was introduced —
a threepenny bit with twelve sides.

In 1971, decimal coinage was introduced to bring us into line with
Europe.

THE GOLD STANDARD

A note about the Gold Standard might be useful.

In 1821, England was on the Gold Standard, and the only country
in the world to be so. This meant that the gold sovereign was to be of
a definite weight, viz. 123.27447 grains, or approximately ¼ ounce.
The coin was eleven-twelfths pure gold, and one-twelfth alloy. (The
quality of gold is measured in carats; pure gold is 24 carats, so a coin
eleven-twelfths pure is said to be 22 carats.)

From 1821-1914, the price of gold was fixed at £3 17s 10½d (approx.
£3.89) per ounce, i.e. £1 could purchase approximately ¼ ounce of gold.

Other major countries also adopted the Gold Standard later, each
declaring its currency to be equal to a particular weight of gold.

As a result, in 1914, the United States dollar could be exchanged for
.053 ounces of gold, and the British pound could be exchanged for
.257 ounces of gold. Thus there were 4.86 times as much gold in the
British pound as in the American dollar, so the exchange rate, as it
was called, was 4.86 dollars to the pound ($4.86 to the £).

From 1914-25, England virtually left the Gold Standard. The
exchange rate fell to about $4.40.

Then in 1925, England returned to the Gold Standard, but fixed
the rate as it had been pre-war, i.e. $4.86 to the £. This meant that
British goods became dearer, because America and other countries
had to pay more dollars or other currency for the pound. For example,
to buy £10 of British exports, Americans who had previously paid
44 dollars, now had to pay 48.6 dollars. Britain, therefore, lost trade.

In 1931, we left the Gold Standard. The value of the pound dropped
to 3.4 U.S. dollars, so our goods became very much cheaper, thus
helping our export trade. To buy £10 of British goods, the Americans

who had previously paid 48.5 dollars, now had to pay only 34 dollars. Though the value of the pound dropped to 12s. (60p.), public confidence in the currency was not, however, shaken.

Chapter XXIX

More About Money

The most expensive single item in any country's history is war. Wars have to paid for, not only in the form of human lives and human suffering, but also in money. To obtain this money, the Government must either borrow or tax.

Before 1694, the Government borrowed money to pay for wars, but such loans had been swiftly repaid.

Then, in 1694, the Bank of England was founded, and under its terms, the Bank lent the Government £1,200,000 at eight per cent interest. This, however, was to be a long-term debt — that is, a debt not paid back immediately, but to be handed on from generation to generation. This long-term debt which the Government owed to the people of this country was called the National Debt, and as Government after Government continued to borrow money, so the Debt increased as the following table shows:

1693	£1.2 million	Lent by the Bank of England
1697	£14½ million	
1714	£56 million	War of Spanish Succession 1701-13
1748	£75 million	War of Austrian Succession 1740-8
1757	£77 million	
1763	£132 million	Seven Years' War 1756-63
1783	£241 million	War of American Independence 1775-83
1793	£245 million	
1802	£523 million	French Revolutionary War 1793-1802
1815	£834 million	Napoleonic Wars 1803-15

Then a steady decrease until:

1900	£610 million	
1903	£798 million	Boer War of 1899-1902
1914	£650 million	
1920	£7,829 million	First World War 1914-18
1940	£9,083 million	
1945	£21,366 million	Second World War 1939-45
1950	£25,291 million	
1960	£27,735 million	

To pay off the Debt, Income Tax was introduced from 1798-1816, and again from 1842. There was also a land tax on the value of land. Other taxes levied between 1500-75 included those on goods coming in and out of the country, taxes on servants, windows, racehorses, carriages, hats, hairpowder, drinks, medicines, building materials, and many more items.

Apart from the cost of wars, however, the Government faced more and more expenses once it began to have an interest in Health, Education and Factory Acts. The cost of looking after the welfare of the public became higher and higher, until borrowing could not provide enough to pay.

So the old taxes increased, and new taxes were introduced. Thus in 1894 came Death Duties — a tax on everything a person owned at the time of his death. This tax was graded so that the richer paid more than the poorer, and as a result, the great families of England perished. To meet the tax required when the head of the family died, the great estates had to be broken up and sold, while the beautiful houses that showed so wonderfully the glory of the Victorian age, were demolished, or cracked and crumbled through lack of repair. Those that remained could only do so by sale to a Government department or for a college, or by opening for the public to pay to look round.

But the Government still needed money, especially to pay for Old Age Pensions which were introduced in 1908, and to cover the cost of building a more powerful navy. Thus it was that the fearless Welsh Chancellor of the Exchequer, David Lloyd George, produced in 1909 his Budget — a budget aimed to 'soak the rich'. Income Tax was increased, and on very high incomes a new Super Tax had to be paid, while death duties were also increased. Tobacco, spirits and stamp duties cost more. There was to be a new tax on petrol, and motor car licences had to be bought, the money thus obtained being put into a Road Fund to improve the roads. Then finally to 'soak the rich', a duty was placed on land values, particularly when a profit was made on the sale of land.

Despite the powerful opposition of the wealthy, the Budget was passed. It proved to be, however, but a beginning ... for two World Wars followed, and this has meant still heavier and still heavier taxation. To make the process easier, the system of 'Pay as you earn' (P.A.Y.E.) was introduced in 1940. The tax due from employees' earnings was worked out; employers deducted the amount in monthly instalments from wages, and paid the money to the Government.

Chapter XXX

Commercial Policy

Companies

During the Industrial Revolution, many of the new ideas and schemes — especially the railways, shipping, gas and water undertakings — needed vast sums of money in order to pay for the materials, the buildings and all the other costs of putting them into action. One way to obtain this money was to form a company, and to invite anyone who so wished to purchase shares therein. Then as soon as the money had been obtained, the undertaking was set up, and the profits (if any) distributed among those who had purchased the shares (the shareholders).

The usual type of company was known as a 'joint stock company'. The members subscribed so much each, the business was conducted by paid officials, and the members shared the total profit or loss in proportion to the amount they had subscribed.

There was, however, one fact which did not encourage people to buy shares in these companies. If the company failed and was in debt, the shareholder not only lost the money he had paid to purchase the shares, but also had to help pay off the debt — indeed, his own private property could be seized and sold so that the company's debt could be paid off.

It was not until 1855, that the idea of the Limited Liability Company was made legal for all trades and producers. People who bought shares therein would, if the company failed, lose only the amount they had paid for the shares; they would not be liable to pay any more. That is why you now see the abbreviation 'Ltd.' after the name of a company.

So after 1900, businesses ceased to be controlled by outstanding individuals, family concerns or partnerships. Instead, the Limited Liability Companies developed.

Sometimes people who have bought shares in a company wish to sell their shares; other people want to buy them. Those whose business it is to arrange such buying and selling of shares are called stockbrokers (who act on behalf of a client who wishes to buy or sell) and jobbers (who do the actual buying and selling). These businessmen used to meet at Jonathan's Coffee House in London, and in 1773 this Coffee House was re-named the 'Stock Exchange'. Twenty-six years later, the organisation moved to the site of an old boxing hall in Capel Court, where it still remains.

Having now understood the general principles of companies, let us have a closer look at some of them.

Insurance Companies

First of all, we must mention the Insurance Companies, a very old established line of business. Even by the 17th century, it was possible to insure against most calamities ranging from accidental death to marriage.

Life insurance, indeed, was already in existence as far back as Elizabeth I's reign. The policies had to be renewed every year, and the premium (the payment for the insurance) increased as you grew older. Not until 1756 was the Equitable Society founded — the first Life Insurance Company based on scientific lines, i.e. on a scientifically worked-out expectation of life, so that you paid a fixed annual premium according to your age when you entered the insurance, and not a premium which increased as you grew older.

Insurance against bodily injury began about the middle of the 19th century, and originally concerned railways. The idea gradually developed, however, until such insurance now covers almost any type of injury under almost any circumstances.

After the Great Fire of London, 1666, the Fire Office Insurance companies began. Other companies were formed later, e.g. the Sun Fire Company 1710, and developed particularly during the Industrial Revolution, when manufacturers wanted their factories, machines, etc. insured.

The most famous among insurance companies has been Lloyd's. Marine Insurance was by no means a new idea, for as long ago as the 15th century (the time of the great and dangerous voyages of Bartholomew Diaz to the Cape of Good Hope in 1486, of Vasco da Gama to India via the Cape of Good Hope in 1497; and of Christopher Columbus to the West Indies in 1492), merchants had been able to insure against the loss of their ships, and by the 17th century, these insurers, or underwriters as they were called since they wrote their signatures under the terms of the insurance policy, used to meet at Lloyd's Coffee House in London.

Edward Lloyd, however, was not only interested in running a coffee house, but in 1696 he published a newspaper giving commercial news. So in 1707, when a number of underwriters decided to form a club, they naturally took the name of Lloyd's, and in 1726 the first Lloyd's List, giving shipping news, was published. Even though, in 1774, the marine insurers moved to the Royal Exchange, and later on to Leadenhall Street, the old name was still kept, and remains so to this day. It is also interesting to know that in assessing a ship, the quality of the hull was indicated by a letter, and the quality of the equipment by a figure. Hence 'A.1' indicated a ship whose hull and equipment were both in excellent condition, and the term has passed into common use.

So useful did insurance become, that in certain cases, it was made compulsory. Mine owners (before the coal mines were nationalised, i.e. run by the State instead of private owners, in 1946) had to insure against accidents to the miners; owners of aircraft had to insure in respect of their passengers; motor vehicle owners had to insure in case of accidents involving injury or death to anyone else.

Even more important was the National Health Insurance Act of 1911. Workmen had 2p. a week deducted from their pay for when they were ill, while the employer had also to contribute $1\frac{1}{2}$p, and the Government 1p. The money went into a central fund which enabled a sick worker to have free medical attention, reduced price medicine, and a weekly illness allowance for a limited period. Also by the same Act, a similar scheme of contributions by employer, workman and State enabled those in certain trades only (building, ship-building, engineering, etc.) to receive a weekly allowance for up to 15 weeks if they were unemployed.

Then in 1946 came the greatest National Insurance Act of all. Every employee had so much a week deducted from his wage, every employer had to pay so much a week for each workman, and local rates and the State also paid a certain amount. These contributions affected nearly all persons from 16-65 years of age, and so the National Health Service (see page 303), widows' and Old Age Pensions, death grants, unemployment benefits, etc. were all paid for.

Chapter XXXI

The Reform of National
and Local Government

The Situation

In the late 18th or early 19th centuries, let us suppose you had decided
to become a Member of Parliament. Not, perhaps, that you felt capable
of guiding the vital destinies of the nation, but more likely you considered the additional letters 'M.P.' after your name would add to
your personal pride and general prestige. Furthermore, once in Parliament, you might be able to obtain a post in some Government department where you received a considerable salary for doing no work.
Even at the worst, you should make a reasonable income, for if the
Government, or the Opposition, in Parliament wanted your vote in
any debate, then, of course, they would have to pay for it. Your political
conscience was at the disposal of the highest bidder. As Sir Robert
Walpole, Chief Minister of England 1721-42, once remarked, 'All
these men have their price'.

Accordingly, you decided to become a Member of Parliament. You
were, of course, a wealthy person ... that was essential — the York
election in 1807 cost the candidates £200,000. Indeed, to qualify at
all as an M.P., you had to own land worth either £600 per annum in a
county or £300 per annum in a borough.

The area you chose in which to be elected was, quite naturally, the
South of England ... and the reason for this explains the entire
pantomime which follows:

Voters and Voting

The Industrial Revolution had affected the whole of the nation ...
except Parliament. For over a century and more, the population had
declined in the once-prosperous southern half of the country. The
once great agricultural towns there had dwindled into unimportance,
or even out of existence altogether. Instead, there developed a great
mass of people working in the industrial north, and new cities arose in
that area in order to accommodate them.

But Parliament remained completely unperturbed, unchanging amid the change. It made no difference to the seat of Government that the north of England was now far more important than the south. Seventy per cent of the Members of Parliament still came from the south as in the days of its former prosperity. Every county in England continued to return two Members, just the same as before . . . which meant that the small county of Rutland with 800 electors, had, until 1821, exactly the same number of M.P.s as the giant county of Yorkshire with 20,000 electors. (In 1821, Yorkshire received four M.P.s.)

Not only the counties, but every borough in England continued to return its members to Parliament as it had always done. Thus Old Sarum, near Salisbury, which had once been an important township, was now derelict and deserted to the extent of justifying its description as 'a green mound and a wall with two niches in it'. Yet it nobly continued to send two members to Parliament. Dunwich in Suffolk was partly beneath the North Sea — but it was still represented in Parliament. At the same time, the small villages of the north which had now swollen into great cities — places like Manchester, Leeds, Birmingham and Sheffield — had no representation at all.

Nor did it make any difference to Parliament that industry was now the chief aspect of England's economy; Members of Parliament were still the once-prosperous agricultural land-owners.

So you decided to choose the south to seek election — preferably the county of Cornwall, from which came 42 M.P.s (three less than for the entire realm of Scotland, and 18 more than from the principality of Wales!)

You had a choice of three types of boroughs. There was the 'rotten borough' where the lord of the manor sold the right to represent the area to a candidate, who then bribed the few voters to vote for him. There were also the 'pocket' or 'nomination boroughs', where the lord of the manor was the owner, and named ('nominated') whom he wished to be the Member of Parliament. So if you were in the favour of the local lord, you could become a Member of Parliament without any difficulty.

The third type of borough was where you had to seek the electors and secure their votes. This, however, was still not as difficult as you might have imagined. The franchise (the right to vote for a Member of Parliament) was truly somewhat limited. There were three million adult males in the whole of England and Wales . . . but only 435,000 had the right to vote — one in seven. Thus in the south of England, for example, Rye in Sussex had six voters; Winchelsea, also in Sussex, had three voters; and Gatton, on the North Downs, had only one voter.

Not only was the franchise limited, but also it was very varied.

In a county, the £2 freeholders (those who held land in their own right and equal to the value of at least £2 rent a year) had the vote.

In the boroughs, however, variety reached much better proportions. There were the 'scot and lot' boroughs, where six months' residence, and differing other conditions (such as paying the poor rate, or never having been a charge on the poor rate) gave a person the right to vote. There were the delightfully named 'pot-walloper' boroughs, where it was necessary to prove you were a house-holder, i.e. you boiled a pot there on your own hearth. Other boroughs were the 'burgage' boroughs, where the person who rented a certain piece of land or property had the right to vote — but the holding could be a ploughed field, a dove-cot, or even a particular pig stye. In 'corporation boroughs', the corporation had the right to vote; in 'freeman boroughs', the freemen could vote, though the status was often sold to non-residents; in a borough like Preston, all the inhabitants could vote.

Having discovered the voters, you had now to secure their votes. Bribery was often a very successful method, although a cheaper way was by intimidation (particularly if you employed the voters, or owned the houses they rented). Finally, for those who could be neither bribed nor bullied, there was but one alternative. On the days of the election, they would be 'missing'.

The days of the election were equally significant. For 15 days (until 1785, it had been 40 days), the voting took place — and in an atmosphere overwhelmed by beer, bribes and bullying. Each elector, in the presence of a large and noisy crowd, had to mount the steps to a platform (the hustings), and openly declare for whom he was voting. After that, he either swilled down the ale, or ran the gauntlet.

Such were the Parliamentary elections before 1832 — a farce so grave that Parliament no longer represented the nation. From such a Parliament, it was hopeless to expect any improvements in corrupt local government, or any remedies for the grim factory, the squalid housing and appalling health conditions in the new industrial cities. Neither the workers, nor even the middle class, had any power in the Government of the country.

Reform Act 1832

By 1832, therefore, the demand for reform had become too great to be ignored. The First Reform Bill of 1831 was rejected by the Commons, and the Second Reform Bill by the Lords. The Third Bill, after King William IV had promised to create, if necessary, enough peers to overcome the opposition in the Lords, was passed in 1832 amid national rejoicing.

Rotten boroughs and small boroughs lost their representation, their members being distributed among the counties and the new large towns.

The franchise was extended. In boroughs, householders with property worth at least £10 a year in rent, received the vote. In the counties, the £2 freeholder kept his vote, but copyholders (whose right to the land they possessed was written on copies of the manor records) who paid £10 a year rent, leaseholders for 20 years paying £50 a year rent, or 60 year leaseholders paying £10 a year rent, and tenants at will paying £50 a year rent, also received the vote.

In order to give these figures some meaning, we must remember that £2 rent would be paid for several acres of good agricultural land; a very large farm would be rented at £40 a year. Similarly, in the towns, a house could be rented for 7½p. a week, so a dwelling worth £10 a year would be a fairly rich man's property — a factory owner, for example.

Polling was reduced from 15 to two days.

As a result of this Reform Act of 1832, the influence of the land-owning nobles and the agricultural towns declined. The industrial middle class, with some half-million voters, now had power in Parliament, and the great industrial cities of the north and midlands became politically important. At last, Parliament had begun to move with the times.

Later reforms

It was, however, only a beginning. The workers still had no vote, and in their dissatisfaction, many turned to Chartism (see page 191). Another 26 years were to elapse before the next stage of progress, and the reforms which then followed we will summarise under three headings: (i) the distribution of seats; (ii) the extension of the franchise; (iii) the fairness of the elections.

The distribution of seats has been altered by various Acts from 1832 to the present day, so that the different electoral districts should each have more or less the same number of voters per candidate.

The franchise has been gradually extended. In 1867, the town worker received the vote, (i.e. all householders after one year's residence, as well as lodgers paying £10 a year) — another million voters. In 1884, the country worker similarly received the vote — another two million voters. In 1918, all males over 21 received the right to vote, and women similarly in 1928. Then, in 1969, the voting age was lowered from 21 to 18.

Wealth ceased to be an essential for a Member of Parliament. In 1858, the property qualification for M.P.s was abolished, and in 1911, M.P.s received a salary. When secret voting was introduced in 1872, corruption diminished, for in an open vote a candidate knew how each elector had voted, and could reward or ruin him accordingly. But in a secret ballot, this was not possible. By 1853, furthermore, polling was limited to one day only.

LOCAL GOVERNMENT

At the same time as Parliament underwent reform, the same influence spread to local government. This was another sphere which had long required improvement.

Before 1835, the old town councils had been elected by the freemen only, not by the mass of ratepayers, and in Cambridge, for example, there were only 118 freemen out of a population of 20,000. The council met in secret, revealed no account of its expenditure of public money, and naturally, in many cases, was utterly corrupt.

So the Municipal Reform Act of 1835 ordered that every town should have a council elected by all male ratepayers who had lived for three years in any of the wards. The councillors, who were elected for three years, chose aldermen who served for six years, and also chose a mayor. The council, furthermore, had to publish an annual, audited account of its expenditure.

In 1888, County Councils, and County Borough Councils for the larger boroughs of over 50,000 population, were both created. In 1894, another Act established smaller elected authorities — Urban District Councils for towns, Rural District Councils for country areas, and Parish Councils for villages with a population of over 300 — thus completing the framework of local government.

Chapter XXXII

Life in the
Nineteenth Century

Father sat in his chair by the fire — lord of the universe, ruler supreme. The whole of the family life revolved around Father, whose word was law and whose authority unquestioned. So great was the respect that surrounded him, indeed, that even his wife addressed him as 'Mr. Blank', instead of by his Christian name. His wife, as might be expected, was a meek and submissive woman. Her duty was to rear children and to manage the household—those were the limits of her existence. She possessed nothing of her own, for all her property, and anything she earned or obtained after marriage, was legally her husband's. She had no vote and therefore took no part in local and national government. The duty of the children was also to obey their father (always addressed as 'Sir')—the boys to study hard and enter the church or business, as decided by Father, the girls to learn household management and marry a suitable husband (again as decided by Father).

So Father sat in his chair by the fire — lord of the universe, ruler supreme, and the rest of the family were seated around him — six boys and five girls. The Victorians had large families — one reason for the increase in the population of England and Wales from nine million in 1801 to 33 million in 1901. The family were sitting because it was scarcely possible to walk about in a room that was so crammed with every possible piece of furniture — seven clumsy, comfortably-padded chairs, two sofas, a writing desk, two bureaux, six or eight tables, various stands, two china cabinets, a bookcase, several decorated folding screens and a small organ.

Amid all the furniture, indeed, you did have an occasional glimpse of the gaudy-coloured carpet, in the same way as you had a glimpse of the equally gaudy wallpaper amid the host of heavy gilt-framed pictures on the walls. All around were heavy velvet window curtains, thick dark-crimson door curtains, a plush valance round the mantel-piece, velvet tablecloths, antimacassars,* ribbons, bows, tassels, fringes — all in reds, greens, yellows and purples, until the eyes ached. And on every available space was the delight of the Victorian house — oddments, curios and bric-a-brac, wax flowers and vases of bullrushes, miniature articles of pottery, sea-shells, samplers, ornaments, books, etc., etc., etc., . . . and etc. Thus the whole room was as ugly as it was costly . . . and it was a very expensively furnished room.

Amid such a vast clutter of variety, it might seem difficult to select any one particular object for further comment. Nevertheless, there was one of the books upon the table, which for the moment takes our attention — a volume entitled *The Travels of Baron Munchausen*, a medium-sized, leather-bound work, written by E. E. Raspe. Now Baron Munchausen was undoubtedly the most remarkable adventurer in his own, or in any other time . . . and it must be remembered that the Victorian age of the 19th century was a period of very great adventurers . . . Let us, therefore, have a look at some extracts from his 'Travels' published in England in 1786 — extracts which easily prove his ability:

'Daylight and powder were spent one day in a Polish forest. When I was going home, a terrible bear made up to me at a great speed with open mouth ready to fall upon me. All my pockets were searched in an instant for powder and ball, but in vain — I found nothing but two spare flints; one I flung with all my might into the monster's open jaw, down his throat. It gave him pain and made him turn completely round so that I could level the second at him also, which, indeed, I did with wonderful success, for it flew in, met the first flint in the stomach, struck fire, and the bear blew up with a terrible explosion. Though I came safe off that time, yet I should not wish to try it again or venture against bears with no other ammunition!'

'It so happened on another occasion, that in a fine forest in Russia I came across a splendid black fox, whose skin was of too great value to allow a shot to spoil it. The fox stood close to a tree. In a moment I extracted the ball with which my gun was charged, and in its place put a good spike-nail. I then fired, and hit him so cleverly that I nailed his brush fast to the tree. I immediately went up to him, gave him a cross cut over the face with my hunting

---

*An antimacassar was a length of cloth placed over the back of a chair to protect the upholstery from the macassar hair oil of young gentlemen, when they leaned back.

knife, took my whip in my hand, and flogged him so vigorously that he actually leapt out of his skin'.

Once when driving towards St. Petersburg in a one-horse sleigh, the Baron was pursued by an enormous wolf:

'He soon overtook me. There was no possibility of escape. Mechanically I laid myself flat on the sledge and let my horse run for our safety. What I wished, but hardly hoped or expected, happened immediately after. The wolf did not mind me in the least, but took a leap over me, and falling furiously on the horse, began instantly to tear and devour the hind part of the poor animal, which ran the faster for its pain and terror. Thus unnoticed and safe myself, I lifted my head slyly up, and with horror I beheld that the wolf had eaten his way into the horse's body. It was not long before he had fairly forced himself into it, when I took advantage, and fell upon him with the butt end of my whip. This unexpected attack upon his rear frightened him so much, that he leapt forward with all his might, the horse's carcase dropped on the ground; but in his place the wolf was in the harness, and I on my part whipping him continually, we both arrived, in full career, safe at St. Petersburg, contrary to our respective expectations, and a very much to the astonishment of the spectators'.

Other adventures of this same Baron recalled how his ship was swallowed by an immense fish, in the belly of which he found 34 other ships and their crews.

It is thus quite obvious, as we have said, that Baron Munchausen was easily the most remarkable adventurer of his own, or any other, time. And no doubt, also the greatest liar.

On the same table as the literary work just mentioned, there was one solid, well-worn volume in particular — the Bible, the centrepiece of this Evangelical household (see page 158). At the beginning of every day, a brief service was held from it; before the commencement of every meal a reverent grace was repeated from it; while on Sunday, no other book was to be seen. Sunday, indeed, was a day of real religious devotion — family prayers in the morning, with all the servants attending, Church Service, dinner, Bible lessons, the reading of suitable religious literature, tea, Church Service, and family prayers at night.

A very heavy religious seriousness lay upon the entire household.

But it was this deeply religious spirit, resulting in hard work, thrift, soberness, and a high standard of morals and duty, which enabled Father to earn the wealth amid which he lived. Self-confident and self-satisfied the Victorians undoubtedly were, but their faith drove them to great achievements. They made this country the 'Workshop of the World', they clothed the world, they financed the world; there was no outpost of the universe that did not know their engineers, labourers, scientists, soldiers and missionaries. You are a fool if you scorn a faith which achieves results like this.

Across the books lay a newspaper. It was *The Times* and so it should have been, for *The Times* was *the* newspaper of the Victorian age, the supreme example of journalism. So effective and efficient was its organisation that it acquired news far ahead of the Government, and many a Minister was dependent for his information upon the favour of the Editor of *The Times* long before the facts could reach him through the normal official channels.

The Times was the newspaper which sent out a foreign correspondent when Crabb Robinson went to Portugal and Spain during the Peninsular War (1808-14), and was the first to issue news of Nelson's victory at the Battle of Trafalgar in 1805. It was the first to use the telegraph — when Queen Victoria's son was born in 1844. It was the first newspaper to send out a War Correspondent — Sir William Howard Russell who went to the Crimea during the war there with Russia (1854-6), and revealed to England the sufferings of our soldiers during the winter of 1854-5.

As news and information reached the headquarters of this great newspaper, more efficient methods of printing were introduced — the steam press in 1814, the rotary press in 1848. The result of all this activity and progress may be illustrated by remarking that in 1854 the circulation of *The Times* was 52,000; its nearest rival was the *Morning Advertiser* with 8,000.

But *The Times* was not to remain supreme for ever. In 1843 the *News of the World* was founded; in 1846, the *Daily News*. Later the *News Chronicle* commenced with Charles Dickens as its first editor; and in 1896, the Harmsworth brothers founded the *Daily Mail*, the first newspaper to reach a million circulation. The increased circulation of newspapers was one result of the ending of the newspaper and advertisement tax in 1855.

So Father picked up *The Times* and studied the advertisements. It was always as well to look at the advertisements; you never knew what bargain you might find. In 1833, at Portman Market, a man offered and sold his wife.

On other pages were details of sport and amusements, and it was at once clear that the Victorian age was very much kinder than the 18th century had been. The Royal Society for the Prevention of Cruelty to Animals was founded in 1824, bull-baiting became illegal in 1835, and cock-fighting in 1849. In 1866, Lord Queensberry drew up his rules for boxing,so that modern boxing replaced the old-style fisticuffs. The savagery of the old-style prize-fighting may be judged by the 18th century fighters who soaked their fists in a solution of caustic soda till they were as hard as oak.

Apart from the usual sports of horse-racing, hunting and shooting, there began the Football Association in 1863, and the County Cricket Championship in 1873 . . . at which we must pause for a moment.

Bestriding the cricket field in this century was the great figure, the powerful muscles and the dense black beard of Dr. William Gilbert Grace (1848-1915). At a time when the cricket pitch was not often mown except between the wickets, and the surrounding area was covered with stones, bottles and other obstacles, with the outfielders partly concealed in the long grass, his fame was all the more remarkable. Nor was he lionised in the press. A small headline 'Another good innings by Dr. Grace' sufficed to indicate that he had scored 243 not out in the first innings, and 301 in the second innings.

His records were as impressive as his personality. He toured America, Canada and Australia; twice he captained England. He was the first cricketer to score 2,000 runs in a season.He was the first to achieve the double of 1,000 runs and 100 wickets in a season. His best year was undoubtedly 1871, for his average was 78 — the next best average being 34, and the runs he scored in that season were not exceeded for 25 years. Altogether, he scored some 55,000 runs and took 3,000 wickets.

His cricket was aggressive. He hated defensive strokes, because, as he said 'You could only score three off them', and to prove his point, in an innings of 288, he hit every ball except four. For 41 years, his great cricketing career continued, before he retired at the age of 58, walking back to the pavilion after his last match, with a score of 74 to his credit.

Next, in 1874, lawn tennis was invented.

It might also be mentioned that in 1828, the London Zoo, founded by Sir Stamford Raffles, was opened. To us, no doubt, it would have seemed a very small and uninteresting affair, for it had less than 200 animals, and did not possess any giraffes, elephants, hippopotami, gorillas, orang-outangs or even a chimpanzee. Nevertheless, the Victorian public flocked in their thousands to see the various swans, peacocks and bearpits, and to gaze at the monkeys while asking exactly the same question as we still do now . . . 'and who does that one remind you of ?'

Around the room where Father sat were the family portraits. The Victorian age was certainly the age of photography. In 1839, the Frenchman, Louis Daguerre, invented his *daguerreotypes*, using a rectangular box with six inches between the lens and the plate. The plate was of silvered copper, covered with silver iodide. It was developed with mercury vapour, and the camera, plates and chemicals weighed about a hundredweight. By later Victorian times, the length of exposure was 10 minutes, so chairs were provided with hidden rests and clamps to keep the head still. This length of exposure also accounted for the rather strained and serious expressions on Victorian family portraits — it is somewhat difficult to maintain a fixed smile for ten minutes.

As Father was now feeling hungry, the family rose to make their way to the dining room. In front went Father — a dignified, possibly slightly pompous figure, self-confident and self-satisfied, but whose well-tailored, expensive suit, with gold watch chains and two gold watches, indicated again the success of hard work, thrift, soberness, and high standards of morals and duty. Behind him came mother, who managed the affairs of the household as father directed, then the boys who resembled their father, but were as yet more subdued. The four girls were all that Victorian girls should have been — vague, sweet and husband-hunting. They were all dressed in the latest article of fashion — the crinoline, introduced about 1850. The lower part of the silk dress was arranged over a circular framework of steel wires or bamboo at the waist, until it attained a circumference of 15 or more feet, and reached from waist to floor. The upper bodies of these girls were extremely slender, compressed by tightly-laced bodices of steel or whalebone, so that the whole figure looked like a flower stem rising out of a flower tub. Strangely beautiful that crinoline might have seemed however, but to sit down, to lie down, to walk, enter a carriage, shake hands or even to kiss someone, required time, tact and a skill at manoeuvring that was almost unbelievable. Elegant that slender upper body and waist might have appeared however, but already one of the daughters of that family had died as a result of the tight lacing of the steel or whalebone bodice.

So the males in dignity, and the females in full sail, entered the dining room where the servants had prepared the dinner, and this was indeed the great age for servants. They moved in regiments about the Victorian households, scrubbing, dusting, cleaning, polishing, cooking and carrying.

It was also the great age for meals. What a pageant of food travelled across that table! The first course consisted of soup, fish, turkey, beef, mutton, lamb, larks, partridges, wigeon, fowl, calf's ears and sweetbreads; then the second course of black game, hares, brussel sprouts, meringues, truffles, jelly, crayfish, sea-kale and apricots, and finally fruits, sweets and nuts. After dinner, Father returned to his study, where he put on a velvet smoking jacket and a tasselled smoking cap, and settled down to smoke a cigar or one of the new cigarettes which soldiers returning to England from the Crimean War (1854-6) had introduced.

As evening advanced, the lights were lit — a great improvement on the illumination of the previous century. Even the candles now had bent-over wicks which burnt away, instead of straight wicks which collected soot at the top and had to be cut off every so often with a pair of scissor-like trimmers. Gas, too, was in use, especially after 1887 when Welsbach invented his gas mantle — a cotton cylinder soaked in a solution of 99 per cent thoria and one per cent ceria.

But candles and gas had to be lit, and the lighting equipment was still the primitive flint-and-tinder method. You struck a piece of flint against a piece of iron so that sparks fell upon some tinder (usually rags), then carefully . . . very, very carefully . . . you blew the smouldering tinder to fan it into flames. The instructions were simple . . . the practice took perhaps half an hour. Then in 1827, Walker introduced matches coated with chlorate of potash, antimony, sulphide and gum arabic, which produced a flame, when rubbed on sandpaper. This was followed in 1855 by the Swedish invention of the Safety Match which used harmless red phosphorus on the side of the match box, not on the match head.

But the age of the candle, gas and match was to pass away when, in 1878, Sir Joseph Swan sent an electric current through a carbon filament in a vacuum, so that the glow gave a light. It was a light only equivalent to a present 25 watt bulb, but from this humble beginning came the substitution of a tungsten filament in 1907, and the use of inert (not active) gases (first argon, later argon and nitrogen) inside the bulb to make it last longer. Indeed, the use of different gases developed rapidly and no doubt you have all seen the electric lamps containing mercury vapour, sodium vapour or neon gas. You will also have seen the 1934 discovery of fluorescent lighting when ultra-violet rays are directed on to powders which fluoresce (give off coloured light).

Let us, however, return for a final moment to the Victorian household. The new methods of lighting — gas and electricity — passed from the inside of the Victorian house to the outside. The streets were now lit, and as the servants began to draw the heavy curtains, they saw in the light of the street lamps, a small and motley crowd lurching noisily along the pavement. These were the inhabitants of the other side of Victorian life — the life of the night clubs and gambling dens, places of drunkenness and debauchery, lairs that rang with ribald songs, oaths, screams and curses. These were the denizens of the slum areas, the men, women and children who sweated away their souls in factories, who hawked and begged and thieved in the streets, who swept the refuse from the gutters, who searched the sewerage for what they could find . . . whose heaven was hell.

Then the curtains were drawn together, and the two sets of lives were separated once more . . . the one to continue with its tragic wildness till the early hours of the morning, and the other to retire early to bed with its strict beliefs and morals.

Chapter XXXIII

The Consequences of
Two World Wars

It started on 28th July, 1914, and finished on 11th November, 1918. It scorched Europe, ravaged France, and involved America. It sent $22\frac{3}{4}$ million souls to meet their God or gods, and flung back the remains of the living to some sort of a civilisation. And the tears of Europe were barely dry by 1939. That was the First World War.

On 3rd September, 1939, a second great holocaust of strife blasted the world. It affected every one of the five continents; it was fought on mountains and on plains, across vast frozen wastes and deep in tropical jungles. The death roll has not even yet been fully totalled, but may well have reached 55 millions, not to mention a further 34 million wounded. That was the Second World War.

What then, were the economic consequences of these two universal wars? In what way did they affect England?

One very important result was the death blow to the idea of *Laissez faire*. During the wars, the Government had taken control of agriculture, industry and trade in order to defeat the enemy, but after the wars ended, however, the control was still continued. So let us first see what happened to agriculture, industry and trade in the period 1914-45, and after that we will consider these same three subjects from 1945 onwards.

Agriculture 1914-45

During the First World War, agriculture naturally experienced a boom. More food was urgently required, especially in 1917 when Germany bluntly announced that every merchant ship either leaving or approaching the shores of Britain would be torpedoed without warning. And the Germans meant what they said, for they possessed more submarines than any other country. From February to March of 1917, Britain lost an average of four ships per day; in April, 196 ships totalling 600,000 tons were lost, while one ship out of every four leaving the British Isles never returned. By the end of the year, no fewer than 1,271 ships — over $3\frac{1}{2}$ million tons — had been sunk.

274

The food situation became desperate, and the British farmers accordingly ploughed more land and kept more cattle to prevent the country starving. The Government guaranteed prices for the farmers' produce, and also fixed minimum wages to help the agricultural labourer. Thus agriculture prospered from 1914-18.

When the war was over, however, the hard times seemed likely to return once more, but the Government then assisted the farmer in six ways:

(i) by limiting foreign imports;

(ii) by giving subsidies (help in money) to aid beet sugar and beef cattle farmers;

(iii) by freeing, in 1929, farms and farm lands from the payment of rates;

(iv) improving compensation for disaster such as floods, disease, etc.;

(v) by setting up, in 1931 and 1933, Agricultural Marketing Boards for hops, potatoes, pork, bacon and milk, so that these foodstuffs could be better marketed, and

(vi) by scientific help.

In this last connection, the experimental station set up at Rothamsted in 1843 was extended, and science began to play a very great part in farming. For example, soils that were too acid to grow good crops could be treated with lime (calcium) or basic slag (manganese) to improve them. Hay could be preserved by passing through blasts of hot air in a drying machine, or by mixing with molasses in pits called 'silos'. New drugs and medicines prevented or cured cattle diseases.

More important still was the development of machinery, amid which we must particularly mention the combine harvester which reaped, threshed, sifted the grain and turned out bags filled with corn, so that work which took a man $1\frac{1}{2}$ days in 1830 could now be done in two hours.

Not only was the labour of man affected by the use of machines. By 1939, over 50,000 tractors had replaced the horse-drawn plough or cart on England's farms, thus causing a minor revolution in agriculture. The ploughman and his horses had toiled from dawn till dusk to plough an acre; a tractor did it in half-an-hour.

Another asset to farming was electricity, which gave light, operated machinery and milked cows, while experiments were even made to warm the earth by underground electric cables, thus enabling the more rapid growth of crops.

But all these efforts of the Government failed. England changed from ploughland to pasture, and pastureland meant that less labour was required. So the number of farmworkers decreased and the villages of England decayed. Fame and fortune now lay in the towns, and as the towns increased in size so in turn they swallowed up the beauty and the wealth of the countryside. Whereas in 1840 the British wheat crop supplied 90 per cent of the population, by 1940 it supplied barely 13 per cent . . . and England faced the Second World War.

When the 1939-45 war broke out, England's home food supply came under the energetic control of County War Agricultural Committees. These committees directed the farmers what to grow, and could remove from their farms those tenants who were inefficient. Every available area of grassland, including parks and golf courses, was ploughed up, until a total of over six million acres was added for food production. Fertilizers and machinery were also supplied to farmers. Nor was there a shortage of labour — agricultural workers were excused military service, the Women's Land Army was formed amid amusement and admiration, and any further requirements were met by prisoners-of-war. The gods help those who help themselves, and the efforts of all concerned were assisted by weather conditions which enabled record harvests in 1942 and 1943.

Now let us consider the fortunes of industry and trade during this same period 1914-45.

Industry and Trade 1914-45 — Depression and Crisis 1918-39

Even before 1914, industry and trade were facing difficulties. Then after the war, those difficulties increased and at an even faster rate, until we reached the worst economic crisis in our history. The Great War, indeed, had torn apart the world; it had smashed completely the old pattern of commerce; it had reduced the former value of money to comparative worthlessness. So it is not surprising that, amid such chaos, England suffered.

The root of the matter was clear — after 1918, we could not export nearly enough to pay for our imports. This was a most important and terrible realisation — we could not export nearly enough to pay for our imports.

The reasons for the lack of exports were quite clear, too.

It must be realised that two-thirds of our food supplies were imported, all our cotton, nine-tenths of our wool and timber, as well as one-third of our iron ore, so obviously we needed to export a tremendous amount of goods to pay for all that. Instead, however, England's once vast wealth-bringing export trade in textiles (i.e. cotton and woollen goods), coal, iron and steel, and shipbuilding, rapidly declined because when the war was over, other countries were either too poor to buy from us or had begun to make their own requirements. The new nation states of Europe, indeed — (Jugoslavia, Poland, Czechoslovakia, the new Russia, the new Austria and Hungary) — all wanted to be proudly independent, and not to have to rely on British supplies.

Even where there was a market beyond Europe for our exports, we had to face grim competition from Germany, Japanese and American business.

It was indeed most unfortunate for us that we had only four exports on which to depend — textiles, coal, iron and steel, and shipbuilding — and all of them declined together. Let us trace the sorry story in each case.

Cotton industry

To many it seemed incredible that the cotton industry could ever fail. After the inventions of the Industrial Revolution from 1730-1820, there were still further developments. In 1825, Richard Roberts invented a self-acting (i.e. automatic) mule, worked entirely by steam power, and about 1830, ring-spinning enabled the spindles to revolve at a terrific speed. These were followed by the Northrop Loom invented in America later in the century. Admittedly, there was a setback when cotton supplies were seriously interrupted by the American Civil War 1861-5, but the industry then obtained its raw material from India and Egypt, while in 1902, the British Cotton Growing Association was established to obtain supplies from India, Africa and the West Indies.

The industry was ideally situated in Lancashire, whose damp climate prevented the cotton threads from breaking as they did when too dry. The nearby rivers provided soft water for processing, and together with coal, ensured steam power for machinery. The high population of the area provided an ample supply of labour, increased by Irish immigrants if needed. Then, once the great factories of Manchester had manufactured the goods, they could be exported through the port of Liverpool, which also handled the imports of raw cotton.

With all these advantages, it seemed that England's cotton industry was in a strong position — but even so, it was still not strong enough to withstand the consequences of the First World War. The vast amount of cheap native labour to be found in the Near East, India, China and Japan, and the use of the most modern machinery, enabled these countries to make their own goods, and afterwards to sell elsewhere far more cheaply than we could. It was an almost hopeless situation for us when the Japanese could manufacture cotton goods in their homeland, pay the cost of thousands of miles of transport, and still sell them cheaper in England than Lancashire could.

Worse still, synthetic fibres appeared — nylon (made from benzine, and taking its name from the initial letters of New York and London where it was made), rayon (produced from wood pulp) and terylene (produced from coal by two British scientists, J. T. Dickson and John Whinfield, in 1941). All these rivals were far superior to cotton.

So the once great mills of Lancashire had to close.

Coal mining

Coal mining was no more successful than the textile industry, although just as surprising in its decline.

From 1850 onwards, mining had developed with amazing effort and energy. Coal was obviously a means of warmth and power, but as the century progressed, it proved an almost endless source of other benefits to mankind — explosives, plastics, waterproofs, textiles, artificial silk, synthetic rubber, dyes, varnishes, paints, drugs, aspirins, saccharins, disinfectants, fertilisers, perfumes, cosmetics, printing inks, ammonia, creosote, pitch and tar — all of these were obtained from coal. Then there were the later demands for gas and electricity.

So it is no wonder that whereas in 1830, only 23 million tons were mined in this country, by 1875 the amount had increased to 133 million tons; and by 1913, to 287 million tons. With the aid of coal-cutting machines and other appliances, tunnels up to two miles long and half a mile below the surface were made, and the chief coal mining areas became Northumberland, Durham, Yorkshire, South Stafford, Derby, Nottinghamshire and South Wales.

As the 19th century progressed, the Government, too, began to take a greater interest in the conditions of the mineworkers. By the Mining Act of 1842, no female or child labour was allowed underground, while in 1908, coalminers were not to work more than eight hours per day. To make their work even more bearable, by a law of 1862, every mine had to have two shafts. Fans created a draught of air up one shaft, with the result that a current of fresh air passed down the other shaft and along the galleries. Work was made much easier from 1880, when locomotives driven by compressed air were used to pull the coal tubs along the mine passages. Ten years later, electric winding motors pulled wire cables attached to the trucks.

But after the First World War, the coal industry suffered from foreign competition, particularly from the U.S.A., Germany and France, and also from the use of petroleum, oil and hydro-electric power. Amid the changing conditions of the 20th century, indeed, the demand for coal declined very rapidly — for example, the petrol-engined motor car was replacing the steam locomotive, the motor vessel replaced the steamship; while in furnaces, boilers and home firegrates, a more efficient construction enabled the same heat to be obtained from less fuel.

Even in our best coalfields, many of the good seams were already finished, and the machinery we used was out of date. As a matter of fact, only 1/7th of the coal we produced was cut by machines; the rest — about 240 million tons — was hacked out by human muscle power. This was a less expensive method in small mines with thin seams, but very costly in terms of human effort, disease and death.

So by 1925, the mines were facing a very serious situation.

Two Commissions of Enquiry had been set up to find out what help could be given. In 1919, the Sankey Commission, under Judge Sir John Sankey recommended that the Government should take over the mines (i.e. nationalise them), and in 1926, a Commission under Sir Herbert Samuel opposed such nationalisation. In any event, the Government took no action at all to improve the conditions in the mines, except to provide a State subsidy (a grant of money).

However, in 1926, this subsidy was withdrawn, and in order to sell more coal by lowering the price, the employers proposed to reduce the men's wages and extend the hours of work. The miners' reply was prompt and definite, 'Not a penny off the pay; not a minute on the day'. They went on strike, and the battle against the employers began. Even though a General Strike followed, the final result was failure, and coal mining continued as a depressed industry.

Metal industry

As far as iron, steel and shipbuilding were concerned, both the U.S.A. and Germany possessed vast quantities of iron ore, and the cheap price of iron and steel enabled these and other countries to build their own ships. Furthermore, the Governments of other countries helped the shipbuilders; the British Government did not. So most of the steel that England produced was used at home for engineering and motor cars instead of being sold more desirably abroad.

Financial problems

As well as the decline of our four main exports, we had other problems as well.

Financially, we were weak. Before 1914, we had had large overseas investments in new industries, and from these investments, we had received interest. But to get money for the four years of war, we had to sell some of these investments and thus lost the interest. In addition, countries which had previously paid us to act as bankers for them and to insure their industrial undertakings, no longer required our services.

We had also lost money from our carrying trade at sea. Before the war, most of the world's trade — as much as 70 per cent, indeed — had been carried in our ships, But after the war, there was much less trade to be done, and other nations had learnt to transport their own goods in their own ships . . . so we lost the income from our carrying trade.

In brief, therefore — after the Great War, England's industry and trade were hit hard (i) by a flood of foreign imports (until Free Trade was ended 1931-2); (ii) by a loss of exports because other countries were too poor to buy from us, and either made their own goods or bought them more cheaply elsewhere. (iii) Because our four main exports — textiles, coal, iron and steel, shipbuilding — all declined together. (iv) Because the war ended our overseas investments, our overseas banking and insurance services, and our seaborne carrying trade . . . all of which had earned us money.

Then, in 1929, came disaster. During the previous five years, wealthy Americans had been buying shares in their home industries, in the hope they would make a profit. Unfortunately, the ambitions of many of those firms were greater than their abilities, and in 1929, the inevitable happened. Firm after firm went bankrupt; the American Stock Exchange in Wall Street, New York, where shares were bought and sold, collapsed as people tried desperately to sell shares that were worthless. Suddenly and swiftly, thousands of people lost their money, some of them nearly every cent they possessed. In one most famous phrase — 'Millionaires became beggars in a day'.

In order to have money to carry on, America began to call back the gold and investments she had lent to England and the rest of Europe. As the crisis spread, other foreigners also wanted their money back. From July to September 1931, £200 million of gold was withdrawn from London, and under these circumstances, England had no alternative but to leave the gold standard in 1931, i.e. our banknotes were no longer able to be exchanged for gold. The value of the pound note thus fell to 60p.

The combined effect of these blows was catastrophic. The volume of England's trade became steadily less and less despite every effort that could be made to check the decline. Firms failed, factories fell silent, and the number of out-of-work persons began to increase. The sad story continued until the great depression reached its worst stage from 1929-33 — particularly including the year 1932-3, when the number of unemployed in England reached the appalling total of three million, i.e. one in every five workers was out of a job.

By 1933, indeed, the great manufacturing cities of England had become hollow mockeries of existence, with a funereal silence hanging over the closed-down, rusting factories and the boarded-up shops; with groups of idle men standing dejectedly about the quiet streets — men in whom the eager will to work had long been extinguished by the continued lack of opportunity — men without hope. True, there was the 'dole' — a weekly Government allowance to those out of work, so that no-one actually died of starvation — but even so, there was still a very real poverty, and men wanted work, not some form of Government 'charity'.

Improvements

Amid this depression, there came the almost revolutionary solutions of a brilliant Cambridge graduate, John Maynard Keynes (1883-1946) — the greatest economist of this country since Adam Smith.

Until his time, when a Government faced a loss of income during a depression, the usual remedy had been to save money — that is, to reduce costs — and to increase taxes as much as ever possible, so that the Budget would continue to balance. Indeed, this seemed a logical and sensible policy to follow, for the Government would not be spending more than its income.

But Keynes argued that in time of depression, the Government should spend money, not save it. Grants for public works, roads, education, housing, new business developments, and similar projects should be made. This would cause employment; the employees would earn money, which they would then use to buy goods, and thus in turn benefit industry. The Government should reduce taxes, not increase them, so that people had more money to spend on goods. The Government should lend money at low interest so businessmen could build new factories to provide more work. Admittedly, the Budget would not balance for some period of time, for the Government would be spending more than it received in income, but the money spent would lessen the suffering of unemployment during the depression, and afterwards, in due course, the public works and factories would show a profit, from which they could then repay the Government loans.

Furthermore, we lived at a time of world-wide trade, when grave uncertainties and great difficulties were bound to occur. To overcome the inevitable depressions, private enterprise should still be allowed to continue as far as possible, but the Government must always be ready to cope with the situation by its control of the banks who could lend money where and when it was needed.

Keynes, however, had to wait for recognition in this country. The ideas he put forward in his book *The General Theory of Employment, Interest and Money*, published in 1936, were not immediately accepted, and only when the Labour Government of 1945 came into power, were his views put into effect.

So during the 1918-39 depression, the situation was partly relieved in seven ways.

Firstly, it must be remembered that before the Great War, we had been a Free Trade country, and when the hostilities were over, there came a flood of foreign imports. The only way to protect our manufacturers was to limit these imports by imposing duties from 1931.

Secondly, new industries were set up — artificial silk, synthetic fibre, plastics, detergents, electrical engineering, motor cars. All these goods were intended for selling at home — exports were a side-line. But most of these new industries were set up in the south and south-west, where they found electric power, low rents and rates, a good transport system, and the great trading centre of London. Thus the industrial north did not gain any benefit. Indeed, the north still had 40 per cent unemployment when the south had only six per cent.

Thirdly, new processes cheapened costs, especially when Austin and Morris began to make cheap cars by mass production. Many of these new processes depended on electricity, and in 1926, the Electricity Act set up a national 'Grid' system to link the whole of the country together. Previously, each individual electricity station had to have enough machinery to cope with the maximum supply required, although this maximum was needed for only an hour or two per day. Also, reserve machinery had to be provided in case of a breakdown. Under the Grid system, a station which had a sudden call for more electricity could be helped by another station which was having a slack time. Breakdowns could also be overcome by help from other stations.

Fourthly to help the industrial situation, large firms were established, either on their own or by combining with others, for a large firm could withstand losses and defeat difficulties which would cripple a smaller business. Once companies had united, it was possible to pool their money and ideas, attract investments, reduce costs of production, determine output and prices, and so make profit. In this way, such great organisations as Imperial Chemical Industries (I.C.I.), were established in 1926; while the union of the Sunlight Soap firm with other margarine and vegetable oil firms resulted in the vast Unilever concern, with factories in over 50 different countries. Likewise, the Lancashire Cotton Corporation 1929; the Coal Mines Development Committee 1930; the Iron and Steel Federation 1934, were all formed. At the same time, firms which were no longer profitable, such as the Jarrow shipyards and several steel works, were closed down.

Fifthly, the Government tried to help the workers. Training schemes were arranged so that workers could learn new jobs; transfers of workers were arranged from one job or area to another where there were better prospects of employment. Government grants were given to undertake public works (road building, etc.), to establish new factories, to enable the completion of the world's greatest liner, the *Queen Mary* on Clydebank, and more particularly to help 'special areas' such as West Cumberland, Durham and South Wales, where the unemployment was worst.

These 'special areas' were certainly desperate for assistance. In 1934, six out of ten persons in Methyr Tydfil were unemployed, and in 1935, seven out of ten in Jarrow. In places such as these, not only industry, but men likewise decayed. Those who witnessed the great Jarrow 'Hunger March' of 1936, when 200 men walked 300 miles to London to present a petition, realised the suffering that unemployment can cause. Those were the times when, in Jarrow, 200 skilled craftsmen applied for one job . . . and that was as a road-sweeper.

During this depression, the money provided by the National Insurance scheme — which lasted for 15 weeks unemployment — was hopelessly inadequate. Men were out of work for years, let alone a few weeks. So the period of benefit had to be extended, the extra money being known as the 'dole'. The 'dole', however, proved expensive, and in an effort to reduce the cost, the Government in 1931 introduced a 'means test'. In future, the amount of the Government grant was dependent upon the total income which a family received. This, no doubt, seemed a fair and sensible decision, but unfortunately it involved a full enquiry into the financial circumstances of the family which applied for the dole, and the poor bitterly resented this intrusion into their private lives. It was, too, a deep humiliation for many an out-of-work father to have to reveal that the family was being supported by the earnings of his children.

Sixthly, we must take a full view of industrial England between 1919-39. The Depression, grim as it certainly was, nevertheless affected only certain classes in certain areas of the country. For a higher paid worker and the middle class, for those who lived outside the depressed areas and particularly those whose homes were in the south of England, life was a far better existence, not worse. They lived in inexpensive council houses. Their health improved through better food and sanitation. Wages increased, and became of still greater value owing to smaller families, and the lessening of working time to about 48 hours a week in general. These people could afford the pleasure of radio, concerts, the new sound films which began in England in 1927, railway excursions, or even the benefit of a small motor car.

Finally came the approach and declaration of the Second World War. Then, of course, many of the new industries ceased. People wanted bullet-proof vests, not artificial silks, but at the same time, the demand for munitions, weapons of war and ships brought new life once again to the north of England.

Agriculture, Industry and Trade from 1945

During the Second World War, the Government took control of agriculture and trade. It had to, in order to ensure a powerful centralised authority in England's struggle for survival against the Nazis of Germany. But what was to happen when the war was over?

In 1945, the Labour Government came into power, and brought with it the belief that nationalisation would help to solve the difficulties of the post-war world. By nationalisation is meant that the State would take over control of great undertakings for the benefit of the nation as a whole, instead of private enterprise having control for the chief benefit of a few individuals only. Also if the State took over, it would have the money to make costly improvements; and since there would be only the single great authority instead of a number of small independent ones, there would be a greater efficiency and consequently better results.

Thus in *agriculture*, though the war had ended, the County Agricultural Committees did not cease to exist. They continued to supervise the farmers and to have the power to remove those who were inefficient, so the first shadows of the nationalisation of the land began to fall. The farmer was to plough the land not as he thought best for his own personal benefit, but as he was told to do in order to benefit the nation. Not until 1958 did the Committees cease.

The Ministry of Food continued for a time to be responsible for rationing, price fixing, bulk purchases of produce and farming subsidies (grants of money to farmers). The cost of these farming subsidies, indeed, rose to some £300 million per annum by 1960, which meant that the English farmer depended heavily on Government help.

The main development in agriculture was 'factory farming'. This was the intensive control of livestock, whereby several thousand hens which never saw daylight were confined in battery cages in huge sheds for egg production, or kept in broiler houses for eating; where ducks that never saw water were reared in covered containers; calves penned in slatted cages were fattened for veal; and pigs were reared in 'sweat' boxes' where the natural heat of the packed animals created a temperature of 90°C.

But England is only a small country, unable to supply all her own food herself. Therefore we had to import, and we had to pay for these imports by our exports. To ensure our being able to pay, the Government took control of our *industry* and trade.

Coal, the source of industrial power, was nationalised in 1946, and the National Coal Board was established to get coal efficiently and cheaply. To encourage the miners, in 1947 they were even to receive six days wages for five days work! In 1948, the electricity and gas services were also nationalised.

But there was one form of power which ruled the postwar world, for History was once again on the threshold of a new age — this time, the atomic age. So an Atomic Energy Authority was set up in 1954 for the research and development of this form of energy.

Once the sources of industrial power had passed into Government control, the actual industries themselves began to be nationalised (i.e. taken over by the Government), commencing with iron and steel in 1949. Such industries as were not actually nationalised, were carefully investigated with a view to increasing their efficiency.

After that, the manufactured goods had to be transported, so attention turned to England's railway system. During the Second World War, the railways had deteriorated, and by 1945, the lines, engines and rolling stock needed repair. Only the Government could afford the cost, and also stop wasteful competition among the four great railway companies. Another consideration was that even if the railways could not be run at a profit (and thus attract private companies to organise them), they were nevertheless vital to the nation. So the Government took over the railways in 1947.

By 1960, however, British Railways was running at a very serious loss, largely due to road competition. So Dr. Reginald Beeching, a director of one of England's largest companies (Imperial Chemical Industries), an extremely capable organiser and business man, was appointed to try to make the railways more profitable. This he proposed to do by modernising all the equipment, improving the organisation, and reducing costs by closing down lines that did not pay.

His heroic efforts, however, failed to stop the losses, and by the 1968 Transport Act, the Government had to cancel most of British Rail's debts.

Meanwhile, the air services, also taken over by the Government in 1946, were divided into three organisations — B.O.A.C. (British Overseas Airways Corporation), B.E.A. (British European Airways) and British South American Airways.

As well as the road, rail and air transport, there was the question of sea-borne cargoes. The Second World War, 1939-45, had resulted in very heavy shipping losses, but when the hostilities ended these losses were made good by confiscating 46 per cent of Germany's merchant ships, and by vigorously building more of our own — so vigorously indeed, that by 1946 Britain undertook 50 per cent of the world's ship building. The chief centres of the industry were the broad banks of the River Clyde, Newcastle-upon-Tyne, the well-known firm of Cammell-Lairds at Birkenhead, and the yards at London, Portsmouth, Southampton and Plymouth.

In all these areas, there seemed to be no end to the size and speed of the ships which were made. Gigantic liners of 80,000 tons such as the *Queen Elizabeth* (83,673 tons) which could cross the Atlantic in three days, were launched, while even tramp steamers attained a size of 8,000 tons and could travel at 10 knots. Many of these new ships were driven by oil, a much better means of power than coal. Coal had to be hauled, heaved and stacked; oil flows easily and freely, and gives more power for the same weight. Also oil-driven ships do not need a stokehold and therefore have less labour.

The chief difficulty was to find cargoes for these newly constructed vessels. There is no doubt that England's *trade* had suffered very severely indeed as a result of the Second World War. Between 1945-60, our exports increased, admittedly, for instead of relying on textiles, coal, iron and steel, and shipbuilding, we had now changed to engineering (cars, aircraft, machine tools) and chemicals (plastics, detergents, drugs). But though our exports increased, it was still not enough to pay for our imports, as the following reasons show . . .

We had lost our trade with the Iron Curtain countries (Russia and her allies); we had lost our Empire. If we wanted to trade anywhere else, we had to compete with West Germany, Japan and America, and we were not in a good position to compete. Our machinery was out-of-date or worn out by war use. Such goods as we did export were costly, for the Trade Unions insisted on higher wages but not on increased production; the goods were often of poor workmanship and very late in delivery.

To quote but one instance that illustrates the way in which our production suffered, we have only to consider the requirements of the Trade Unions. In order to fit a navigation light on a ship, no fewer than five men were needed, each of them allowed by his union only to do his own job. First, the shipwright marked the position for the light. Then another union supplied a man who marked the central hole, while a third man actually drilled the hole. A fourth worker was then required to drill the other holes at the side of the centre one, and finally, the last of the quintet of workers fixed the light with bolts.

Let us also realise that by 1960, the motor car industry provided 1/6th of British exports — but three out of the four main firms were controlled by Americans, and the technical skill required for the engineering was mainly German.

Is it surprising, therefore, that our export effort was not as good as it should have, or could have, been?

Worse still was the fact that for years before the Second World War, we had been buying more goods from abroad than we sold in return, consequently we had spent more than we earned. The difference, however, had been made up by the interest we received on British money invested abroad in foreign industries. But in order to pay the crippling cost of a six year war, we were forced to sell 30 per cent of these overseas investments, and thus we lost the interest.

In addition, there were very heavy war debts to be paid off — a total of £3,400 million, to be precise.

Then as a final folly, though we had lost our status after the Second World War, we continued to act as if we were still a first-class power, spending large sums of money on military defence at home and abroad.

Bankruptcy lay ahead. So desperate was England's position that we had to borrow 5,000 million dollars from America and Canada in 1946, and to accept still further assistance in 1948. With this help, and by limiting British spending, the Government eased the situation, but by 1960, the trade situation was still not good.

Accordingly, fresh efforts were undertaken to ensure that the nation made the best use of its men and materials.

In 1962, a National Economic Development Council (N.E.D.C.), more popularly known as 'Neddy', was established to plan ahead the economic development of the country. Then, in 1964, a Ministry of Economic Affairs and a Ministry of Technology were appointed to organise the entire national economy.

These were followed in 1965 by a Prices and Incomes Board, to which every increase in prices or wages had to be referred for approval. This seemed very necessary, for between 1945-1960, prices had risen by five per cent each year, and wages by $7\frac{1}{2}$ per cent each year . . . but production per man had increased only two per cent per year. Such a rise in prices is called 'inflation', and may be illustrated by the example that goods which cost £100 in 1939, cost £350 in 1966.

In an attempt to overcome her trading problems, England applied to join the European Economic Community (E.E.C.). This organisation, better known as the 'Common Market', had been established by the Treaty of Rome in 1957, when six European nations — France, Holland, Belgium, West Germany, Luxemburg and Italy — agreed to form a community with a united industrial, agricultural, and later, political, policy. As a first step, customs duties between the six would be reduced, and heavy tariffs imposed on imports from the rest of the world.

The results were of such benefit to the six, that in 1961, England applied to join.

Our application, however, was not whole-hearted. We already had trade with the U.S.A. and the Commonwealth, which we would lose if we joined the Common Market. British agriculture would suffer because Common Market rules would not allow our Government to continue to pay subsidies to our farmers. We would have to adopt Continental units of measurement; — the old, familiar pounds, shillings and pence would be replaced by 100 new pence to the £, pints would become litres, and miles would be measured in kilometres. Also, many Englishmen feared that, in a European Parliament, we should lose our proud sovereignty.

In 1961, too, our economy was very weak indeed.

Thus the Common Market members, particularly France, were for a long while unwilling to admit so undesirable a partner (and it was not until 1973 that we finally joined).

Perhaps the most cheerful aspect of these troubled economic times was that, in the North Sea, drilling operations were finding rich supplies of natural gas, and even more importantly, vast quantities of oil.

K

Chapter XXXIV

The Second
Industrial Revolution

History is a continuous process. It does not exist as a series of separate, stagnant, watertight compartments, placed end to end in one long line. Instead it flows onwards like a river, each part moving and merging into the next.

So in the history of industry from 1700-1970, it is possible to realise that there has been not one Industrial Revolution . . . but two.

The first Industrial Revolution is the more familiar. Commencing in the 18th century (i) with the application of steam power to the former hand processes; (ii) it required the use of coal and iron, and (iii) owed its success to the heavy industries of textiles, coal, iron and steel, and shipbuilding; (iv) established mainly in the factories of the north; (v) it made England the 'Workshop of the World', whose greatness and glory were proved at the Great Exhibition 1851.

But then, from the 1880's, there developed a Second Industrial Revolution, worked by (i) new forces of power — electricity and the internal combustion engine; (ii) using different materials (such as steel, aluminium, bakelite, artificial silk, vinyls and silicones — to name but a few). These were required (iii) for the new light industries (artificial silk, synthetic fibres, plastics, detergents, electrical engineering, motor cars) with a new organisation of business; (iv) situated in the south and south-west of the country. And (v) as England passed into the Second Industrial Revolution, so we became a second class power.

Therefore, note very carefully the differences between the First and Second Industrial Revolutions which we have just mentioned.

And now, let us see, in greater detail, what happened in this Second Revolution.

Power
The later Industrial Revolution was powered not by steam, but by electricity. This force had long been known, for the wisdom of the

ancient Greeks, 2,500 years ago, was aware that amber, when rubbed, would attract small objects, and the Greek word for 'amber' was 'elektron'. But the man who found the answer to the problem of producing electricity in large quantities was the greatest genius in electrical history — Michael Faraday (1791-1867).

Michael Faraday was born in London. His father was a blacksmith, and he tried to give his son a good education despite his poor circumstances. The boy was then apprenticed to a book-binder, and in the course of his work, he read eagerly through all the books on science which he could find.

One day, a customer, seeing his interest, gave him a ticket to a course of lectures at the Royal Institution. Here he heard the great professor, Sir Humphrey Davy, and having made notes and illustrations of the lectures, he carefully bound and sent them to Sir Humphrey at the same time as he asked him for a job. He was appointed laboratory assistant, and from then onwards mounted rapidly the ladder of fame. His success was certainly well-earned, for no man could have toiled harder to solve the mysteries of his subject. He kept a very careful record of all his experiments, and this task filled several large volumes, all handwritten, with ink sketches, and each paragraph numbered and indexed. The last paragraph is numbered 16,041.

But it is his electrical discoveries which we must consider here. Already the Frenchman, André Marie Ampère (after whom a unit of strength of current has been named) had discovered that a coil of wire became a magnet if and while an electric current was passed through it. Therefore, wondered Faraday, since electricity could make a magnet, could a magnet make electricity? So in 1831, he placed a moving magnet in a coil of wire, and delightedly observed that an electric current was produced in the wire. From that discovery, he made the first dynamo — a copper disc, turned by hand between the poles of a horseshoe magnet On that same principle, too, are based the great power-producing dynamos of today, as well as the electric motors and the telephone.

Some 50 years later, indeed, in 1884, Sir Charles Parsons invented a turbine, where the continuous pressure of steam or water on the rim blades of a wheel caused the wheel to turn, and thus generate electricity by driving a dynamo.

Once electricity could be produced in large quantity, its uses became immeasurable.

Lighting was among the first of its benefits. In 1800, Sir Humphrey

Davy invented the arc lamp, where a powerful electric current flashed brightly between two charcoal terminals. In 1878, however, Sir Joseph Swan sent an electric current through a carbon filament in a vacuum, so that the glow gave a light. It was a light equivalent only to a present 25 watt bulb, but from that humble beginning came our modern illumination.

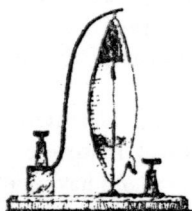

Swan's electric light bulb.

Electric power then entered the world in other ways. The telegraph, telephone, wireless and television depended upon it. Electric trams and electric trains, electric machines of every description, electric light and heat, all became part of the life of the nation — not forgetting to mention the host of electrical gadgets that freed the housewife from the drudgery of home chores, so that she could devote her time to children, to a career or to pleasure.

To assist these developments, the Government passed the Electricity Act in 1926, setting up a national Grid system to link the whole of the country together. Previously, each individual electricity station had to have enough machinery to cope with the maximum supply required, even though this maximum was needed only for an hour or so each day. Also, reserve machines had to be provided in case of a breakdown. Under the Grid system, a station which had a sudden call for more electricity could be helped by another station which was having a slack time. Breakdowns could also be overcome by help from other stations.

Yet despite the inventions for which England was responsible, this nation still failed to maintain her advantage. Too many people had their money invested in coal and steam; many people still preferred gas lighting. So while other nations developed the far better, far cheaper electrical power, by 1914 the only place in England using electricity on a large scale was Tyneside. Even by 1960, our development was still not very comparable to that attained abroad.

The ending of the Second World War in 1945 however, witnessed another form of power to rule the world. History was once again on the threshold of a new age — this time, the atomic age. It had been discovered that when a nucleus of uranium 235 was split, the energy which resulted could be controlled by using an atomic pile. And the amount of energy was enormous. If matter could be completely converted into energy, one cubic inch of uranium would produce the same energy as $1\frac{1}{2}$ tons of coal, or one ton of uranium would equal three million tons of coal. Just consider that, for a moment, and try to realise what it means; and what tremendous possibilities could thus lie ahead.

The first British atomic pile was built at Harwell, in Berkshire, in 1947, and used for research. Other factories were established at Springfield, near Preston, Lancashire, where uranium 238 was extracted from ore, and sent to Capenhurst in Cheshire where it was converted into plutonium — a substance which can be used similarly to uranium 235. Then, in 1956, England's, and the world's first atomic power plant used to make electricity, was opened at Calder Hall in Cumberland.

Even so, however, the cost of producing nuclear power in this country has reduced its value and profit, thus leaving nations wealthier than we are to make better use of it.

But electricity was only one source of power in the Second Industrial Revolution. Equally important was the internal combustion engine.

It was in 1860 that Etienne Lenoir, a Frenchman, produced the first really successful internal combustion engine, which worked by the explosion of coal gas and air in a cylinder. The use of such machines spread throughout France.

Development followed steadily. Nikolaus Otto of Germany made a four-stroke engine in 1876. Nine years later in 1885, Karl Benz of Germany used an electric spark to ignite the petrol vapour, in his three-wheeled car. The modern road vehicle had arrived.

Motor vehicles

To estimate the importance of the internal combustion engine, one had only to watch any section of the $11\frac{1}{2}$ million motor cars, 1 million motor cycles and $1\frac{1}{2}$ million lorries and goods vehicles which controlled the highways of this country in 1970. Their effect has been incalculable . . .

Horse-drawn vehicles became almost extinct, but of far greater importance, the railways began to suffer. It is obviously far more pleasant to travel by road than by rail in order to view the scenery; it is certainly much cheaper; and for the businessman it is far more convenient to have delivery from door to door instead of having to carry to and fro from a railway station. Indeed, by 1958, the roads carried 76 per cent of all goods traffic.

For the general public, road travel increased their pleasure. Areas of country too remote for their beauty or historic interest to be seen and appreciated, could now be visited. Distant relatives and friends could be met more easily. As far as work was concerned, it was now possible to live further from the grimy city or crowded town, travelling to and fro every day by car or bus (this type of travel is known as 'commuting').

Yet all was not well socially. The old village life — the old rural England that remained — suffered sadly. The youth of the village travelled by bus to enjoy amenities and amusements of the nearest town, and returned, discontented and rebellious, to their birthplace. The older generation saw the peace and tranquillity they had known and cherished, now rudely disturbed by busloads of tourists, or by town-dwellers seeking open-air relaxation from their work.

Town life altered also. Dense convoys of traffic passed along roads never designed for such congestion. The problems of traffic control and parking became almost insurmountable. And the toll of life increased, too. Every year, over 5,000 people were killed and 300,000 injured by road accidents. Yet to be added to this total are the deaths from air pollution caused by car exhaust fumes.

The strain on the roadways themselves became intolerable, and the old Turnpike Trusts had to close. The last of these Trusts — on the Anglesey section of the Holyhead road — ended in 1895. Instead, in 1888, County Councils were made responsible for road upkeep, with the aid of a Government grant. As costs increased, however, the Government in 1909 established a Road Fund obtained by taxing vehicles and petrol; while ten years later, the Ministry of Transport took over the responsibility for trunk roads.

Developments in road maintenance were inevitable. The old, rough-surface country roads, or the cobble stones or wooden blocks on town routes were ideal to prevent the iron-shod hooves of horses from slipping, but the coming of wheeled tyres necessitated new road surfaces altogether. The most suitable method found was to cover the macadam with tar, or to make the roads of concrete.

Economically as well as socially, the internal combustion engine had important effects.

The motorworks of Morris at Oxford, Austin at Birmingham and Fords at Dagenham provided employment for hundreds of thousands of workers. In addition, these firms affected other industries, particularly through their direct need of aluminium, rubber, machine tools and petrol. Indirectly, too, they provided work. Old occupations such as road and bridge building, revived; new occupations as in petrol stations or repair garages, were created.

Trade naturally benefited from the internal combustion engine. At one time before the Second World War, people usually walked to purchase their goods at a local shop. Here they were served by the owner or his assistant. They bought small amounts at a time, and often on credit. Motor transport, and the use of refrigerators, resulted in the development of supermarkets, where people served themselves, bought large quantities, and paid cash. Heavy goods could be delivered by van or lorry.

It was the export trade, however, which profited more than anything else. Even amid the worst of the 20th century depression, when other firms failed or faded, the motor car industry not merely survived, but even prospered. One-sixth of the value of our exports was cars.

At the same time, it is worth while to remember that three out of the four greatest car companies in England were American-owned, and the technical skill required for the engineering was mainly German.

So the Second Industrial Revolution progressed — powered not by steam, but by electricity and the internal combustion engine.

Materials

Likewise, the materials that were used were different in the two Industrial Revolutions.

The later Revolution was based not on iron, but on steel, which proved stronger and more reliable. For railways, shipping, bridges, machinery and armaments, this metal was used; and since the U.S.A. and Germany could produce far more steel than we could, we lost our leadership in the world.

The use of other materials developed. As we have already learnt, the motor car industry saw the development of aluminium, rubber, machines tools and petrol. Other industries extended the use of celluloid (discovered in 1861) and bakelite (discovered in 1907).

It was war, however, which provided the greatest spur to scientific progress in new materials. War required raw materials which could not be obtained as a result of enemy blockade. So science produced artificial rubber from coal, lime and hydrochloric acid. Artificial silk was made from wood. Not only did the scientists produce imitations of known things, but they also made entirely new creations. There was in 1937, the man-made fibre called nylon — literally obtained from coal, air and water — that is, from carbon, nitrogen, oxygen and hydrogen. The name came from the initial letters of New York and London where it was made. Terylene was produced from coal, by two British scientists, Dickson and Whinfield in 1941. From glass, the scientists made fibre glass, which could be manufactured into clothes, curtains, medical dressings, motor car bodies, fishing rods, etc. — an amazing substance, in all truth, for it was fire-proof, rot-proof, shrink-proof, stronger than steel, lighter than cotton, and as pliable as silk. Then came a group of creations called vinyls — man-made rubber-like materials made from acetylene and petroleum gases, and which were light, flexible, tough and long-lasting. Many of these new products could be coloured with synthetic dyes.

More famous were the silicones, made from sand, coal (or oil), salt and water, mixed together. By varying the amounts of each, it was possible to create substances which broke like glass or bounced like rubber, as well as paints and cosmetics.

It seems a terrible tragedy that it required war to bring all these benefits to mankind.

The nature of these new materials reveals the next difference between the First and Second Industrial Revolutions. The First Revolution was of heavy industries — textiles, coal, iron and steel, and ship-building — and situated in the north where there were convenient supplies of water, iron and coal. The Second Revolution was of light industries — artificial silk, synthetic fibre, plastics, detergents, electrical engineering, motor cars. All these goods were intended for selling at home — exports were a side-line. Most of them were established in the south and south-west where they found electric power, low rents and rates, a good transport system, and the great trading centre of London.

The new factories of the Second Industrial Revolution were very different from those of the first. The new industrial cities were not dark masses of grimy, filthy buildings, suffocated by the dense smoke from factory chimneys. Instead, there arose shimmering structures of glass, concrete and steel, surrounded by green lawns and shady avenues of trees.

20th century organisation

In the 20th century, the organisation of the Second Industrial

Revolution business companies followed four main developments: specialisation, machine labour, mass production and combination.

Specialisation: Ever since the first Industrial Revolution, industry has become more and more specialised. This means, for example, that instead of one man making a complete motor car engine, a large number of men each make some particular (or 'special') part — one man produces the carburettor, another man makes the fan, another the fan-belt, another the sparking plugs, and so on. While yet others in turn fit together all these individual pieces until the complete engine is ready.

Machine Labour: As time continued, however, an even greater change occurred. Most of the work in modern industry, was gradually undertaken by machines, for these proved far cheaper to employ, as well as more reliable and more accurate, than human beings. Indeed, the skill of machinery has been so developed that it can now control the complete process of manufacture from the start to the finish. Automatic factories have been built wherein machines convert the raw materials into the finished product, detect and reject faulty pieces, arrange everything in order, assemble, pack and label, without any human assistance whatsoever apart from a few machine operators.

Mass Production: Since the method of specialising and the use of machinery enabled work to be done so very quickly, we have what is called 'mass production'. Not just a few car engines or a few bicycles or a few of some particular article can be made . . . but millions of them. Thus these goods can be sold quite cheaply.

Combination: Another reason for cheap goods is competition. Firms try to sell their products by pricing them more cheaply than their rivals. This cut-throat competition, however, became too great, and rather than be ruined by each other, different companies began to join together. There was also another reason for such unity. Amid the chaos of two World Wars and the trade depression between them, one large company could withstand losses and overcome difficulties which would cripple any number of smaller businesses. Once companies had united, it was possible to pool their money and ideas, attract investments, reduce costs of production, determine output and prices, and so make a profit.

Thus firms began to combine, and in two main ways :-

(i) Companies responsible for different parts of a single product, e.g. in the making of a car, the steel companies, glass companies, chassis builders, nut-and-bolt manufacturers, tyre-makers, etc., all joined together.

(ii) Companies in the same industry joined together. One example is the Imperial Tobacco Company formed in 1902 by the union of 13 different tobacco firms.

The Government encouraged such amalgamations, and accordingly there arose such organisations as Imperial Chemical Industries 1926; the mighty union of the Sunlight Soap firm with margarine and vegetable oil firms to form Unilever in 1929, with factories in over 50 different countries; the Lancashire Cotton Corporation 1929; Coal Mine Development Committee 1930; and the Iron and Steel Federation 1934. At the same time, firms which were no longer profitable, such as the Jarrow shipyards and several steel works, were closed down.

Then in the same way as the wholesale manufactures formed large companies, so the retail trade saw the establishment of multiple stores, as, for example, Home and Colonial for groceries; Freeman, Hardy and Willis for shoes; Boots the chemists; Joseph Lyons for confectionery.

Chapter XXXV

The Welfare State

Laissez faire

In the 20th century, the idea of *laissez faire* ('leave it alone') was buried.

Two centuries before, the belief that the Government should not interfere in the economic life of the nation, had flourished. Everything would sort itself out, if only it was left alone to do so. If agriculture and industry were left alone, the price of goods would reach a proper price according to the law of supply and demand. If agriculture and industry were left alone, the wages that were paid would reach a correct level according to the number of people there were to be employed. If there were too many people trying to obtain work, some would starve to death, so those left would have the opportunity for employment. The problem of poverty would be solved by letting people die until the amount of food and money available could support the survivors. *Laissez faire*, then . . . leave everything alone . . . and that, of course, meant leaving the poor worker to his fate.

But for a long time — from the 1830s onwards, indeed — there had been an increasing belief that the poorer classes should no longer be 'left alone'. The great development of communications — roads, railways, telegraph, telephone, wireless, newspapers and postal services — made people more aware of the world further and further away from them. It made one half of the world realise how the other half lived — or, more accurately perhaps — failed to live.

The result was a genuine desire and determination to help the poorer classes. Indeed, the conditions of factory work, of poverty, health, housing, and education amid which they tried to exist were a disgrace to civilisation, and a sorry reflection upon the society that permitted such evils to continue.

Liberal Reforms 1906-1914

At the beginning of the 20th century, this stirring of the public conscience was urged on by the newly-formed Labour Party, and accordingly, the Liberal Government of 1906-1914, commenced the task of reform. In doing so, it laid the foundations of the 'Welfare State'.

Working conditions were improved first of all through the Workmen's Compensation Act 1906, by which compensation was extended to all accidents in all trades. Then, in 1908, the coalminers received an eight-hour day, to be followed by minimum wages in 1912. At the same time, the Government did not forget such neglected workers as the shop assistants, who, in 1911, received a half-day holiday per week. Attention was also directed to such industries as tailoring, shirt-making, boot-making, etc. which were outside the Factory Act of 1901, since the workers toiled in hidden back rooms or in their own garrets, and where the conditions were as grim as they could possibly be. By the 1909 Trade Boards Act, this 'sweated labour' was lessened by imposing minimum wages (the Trade Boards were replaced by Wages Councils in 1945).

Labour Exchanges were set up in 1909 to which those who wanted work, and those who had work to offer, could both apply, and so be put in touch with each other.

The Trade Unions were strengthened also, for at the very beginning of the 20th century, they faced two challenges to their existence.

First, there was the celebrated Taff Vale case. In 1901, there was a strike on the Taff Vale Railway in South Wales. During this strike, naturally the Company lost a lot of money, and therefore sued the Union for compensation; the Union had called the strike, so why should the Union not pay for any damage that resulted? The highest Court of Law, the House of Lords, agreed, and the Union was fined £23,000. Immediately the whole trade union movement rose up in alarm, for obviously, if they had to pay for any damage caused every time there was a strike they would soon be bankrupt. So the Labour M.P.s used their influence, and the 1906 Trades Dispute Act said that Unions would not have to pay for strike damage.

A second challenge was the Osborne Case. At the beginning of the 20th century, Members of Parliament received no salary, and therefore had to have a private income of their own. In order to pay the Labour M.P.s (who came from a class of people who were not likely to have a private income), the Trade Unions required their members to contribute to a fund. But in 1908-9, W. V. Osborne, a railway union secretary and a Liberal in politics, successfully objected to the political use of his money to benefit the Labour Party, and the practice was declared illegal by the Law Courts. The Labour M.P.s thus lost their income from the unions, and therefore went into action with an even greater determination. As a result, in 1911, Members of Parliament received a salary, while in 1913, the Trade Union Act allowed political funds to be collected by trade unions, but members could 'contract out' (i.e. not pay) if they wished.

The reforms of the Liberal Government, however, extended to those who had no trade unions to help them, — the young and the old.

In 1906, school meals for needy children, and in 1907, the school medical service began. By the Children's Act of 1908, children were not allowed to beg, enter public houses, or be sold tobacco. Equally important, the abuses of 'baby-farming' were stopped. This, indeed, was an appalling practice by which mothers who so wished, took their children to other women to be looked after. As payment was required, the practice resulted in the development of a profit-making business. In the worst cases, a number of unwanted neglected babies were crowded into a slum room, with little food, and no washing or attention. If the child-minder wished to go to the shops, the cinema or the public house, the children were left tied to the furniture. Many of them died.

Also by the 1908 Act, juvenile courts were established to deal with young offenders, together with remand homes for those either awaiting trial or to go to a suitable school.

The same year as the Children's Act, the Old Age Pensions Act was also passed, to benefit the over 70's on low incomes.

Finally, we must mention that in 1911, there came the National Insurance Act. Workmen had 2p. a week deducted from their pay for when they were ill, while the employer had also to contribute 1½p., and the Government 1p. The money went into a central fund which enabled a sick worker to have free medical attention, reduced price medicine, and a weekly illness allowance for a limited period. Also, by the same Act, a similar scheme of contributions by employer, workman and State enabled those in certain trades only (building, ship-building, engineering, etc.) to receive a weekly allowance for up to 15 weeks if they were unemployed.

No other Government in history has ever welcomed a new century with such a wonderful programme of reform. It was undoubtedly an excellent beginning.

1914-1945

But then followed four years of war, 21 years of depression and crisis, and six more years of war. In that total period of time, therefore, it is not surprising that any further progress was limited to three activities in particular.

In 1937, the Factories Act put all the previous laws together: those aged from 14-16, 44 hours a week; ages 16-18, and all women, 48 hours a week. A 'Factory' included almost anywhere where manual labour was employed for gain, e.g. garages, laundries, docks, wharves, quays, film studios, open-air premises, and the laws covered almost every aspect of work — health, welfare, safety, wages, etc.

After the First World War, the Government also attacked the problem of housing and slum clearance. Money was given to help private builders, while local authorities were authorised to build council houses and let them at a cheap rent, the rest of the cost being paid out of the rates. As a result, about $4\frac{1}{2}$ million houses were built between the two World Wars.

Education, too, was not neglected. By Fisher's Education Act of 1918, elementary school fees were abolished entirely, and also the 'half-time system' introduced in 1844, so that from 1918 onwards, all children had a free, full-time education to the age of 14.

Labour Government 1945-51

It was not until after the Second World War that the Labour Government of 1945-51 was able to usher in what was to be known as the 'Welfare State'.

This Welfare State, indeed, was to be the answer to the problem of the poverty and the suffering which the whole of mankind's previous history had failed to solve. From thenceforth, there need be no worry about unemployment and poverty; the State would look after every individual from before he was born until after he was dead.

In 1942, Lord William Beveridge, a British economist, wrote a very thorough report on the welfare of the nation, making a carefully detailed plan by which the State should be, and could be, responsible for the welfare of its people. In essence, there was to be *one* scheme of social welfare, which was to apply to *every* person. It was this plan, somewhat altered, that Aneurin Bevan, the Minister of Health, introduced after 1945, and its provisions were to prove of the utmost importance.

Firstly, in order to replace the losses of human life in war, Family Allowances were introduced in 1946 — so much money per week paid by the Government to parents for every child after the first, thus encouraging people to have larger families.

Then, to ensure that these larger families were healthy, a National Health Service was established two years later — expectant mothers and mothers received milk, orange juice and cod-liver oil at reduced prices, while health visitors and clinics were only too ready to give advice and assistance to those with babies. When the baby became a little older, nursery schools were available until the age of five, and throughout the rest of the school career, the child was provided with free milk, reduced price dinners, and the services of nurses, doctor and dentist free of charge. This, of course, was in addition to free education. When the child grew up, he entered a world where the Government gave subsidies (help in money) to keep down the price of such essential foods as bread, butter, meat, milk and eggs, so that everyone could afford to buy them.

In the case of illness, the State provided free medical, dental and optical treatment, as well as free or reduced price drugs, dentures and spectacles. Finally, when death came, the State would pay for a decent funeral if necessary.

It was quite obvious, of course, that the State would have to have money to pay for all these family allowances, reduced price foods, and the services of nurses, doctors and dentists, so the National Insurance Act was passed in 1946. By the terms of this Act, every employee had so much deducted each week from his wages; every employer had to pay so much a week for each workman; and local rates and the State paid so much. These contributions affected nearly all persons from 16-65 years of age, and so the National Health Service was paid for, as well as other benefits, e.g. Widows and Old Age Pensions, death grants, unemployment, etc.

After thus encouraging larger families by Family Allowances, and ensuring that they were healthy by the National Health Service, it was then necessary to educate this more numerous and healthier population. So in 1944 a national, universal scheme of education became law. The stages of education were to be as follows: nursery (under five), primary (5-7), junior (7-11). At the age of 11 plus, each child had to take an examination to decide whether it should go to a Secondary Modern School for less academic pupils, or to a Grammar School for the more academic, from either of which there might be a transfer to a Technical College. The school leaving age was raised to 15.

Then, after leaving school, the teenagers had to be found work. So the Government promised full employment — everyone was to be found work. Only the cripples, the deformed, and mental cases could not be covered by this promise, and so they would receive National Assistance, 1948. Unmarried or deserted mothers, and the families of those in prison, also received National Assistance.

The attempt of the Labour Government to build a larger, healthier and happier nation was one of the greatest efforts of its kind ever made. It was now clearly recognised that poverty was not necessarily a crime nor something to be assisted out of kind-heartedness. Poverty was a reflection upon the State — in other words, if there were a large number of poor people in a State, it showed that the State was badly organised. From now on, therefore, the State, not merely a few kind-hearted individuals, would look after the poor and try to prevent poverty.

But every system has its disadvantages, and there were real evils in the Welfare State.

In the first instance, the grant of Family Allowances encouraged people to have more children — not for love, but for money. Thus the extra income was not always spent for the benefit of the children, but was sometimes devoted to purchasing the two life-giving essentials of some of the British working class parents — 'beer and baccy'.

When a child was born, it entered the Welfare State. It received reduced-price food and every possible care and attention. The State did everything it could to help both child and parent. The result, of course, meant that the child began to belong, not to the parent, but to the State. Indeed, no longer need the parent be responsible for the child if unwilling to be so — it was the State nurse, the State doctor, the State dentist and State schoolmaster (and later, no doubt, the State policeman) who would undertake what had previously been regarded as the parents' duty to bring up their own children.

When a child was grown up, work was provided. But in order that everyone should have a job (i.e. full employment) three men might have to do the work of one, so men lost the ability to work hard since they had no need to.

Indeed, the benefits of the Welfare State reached such a generosity, that a married man with a large family found he would receive more from State assistance if he was unemployed than he could ever hope to earn by an honest day's hard work. An unskilled labourer, married, with five children of school age, when out of work received unemployment benefit, social security benefit, marriage allowance and family allowance, together with free school meals and uniform for his children. His rent and rates were paid, fuel bills paid, sheets and extra clothing provided, and he did not have to pay pensions, insurance or prescription charges. The total benefit he thus received was nearly three times the most he could earn when at work. So why get a job?

Above all, in a Welfare State, where the Government controlled everything, people tended to become less self-reliant — 'Let the Government do it. That's their worry'.

Meanwhile, the cost of all these social benefits steadily increased, reaching the tremendous total of £9,000 million per year in 1970. So it is not surprising that people began to question whether the expense was too great, and if the nation was obtaining 'value for money'.

Chapter XXXVI

The Emancipation
of Women

The Victorian Woman

Let us consider the life of a typical 18th century and Victorian woman of the upper class of society.

In her youth she learnt to read and to sew; she learnt how to embroider and how to darn. She was most carefully taught how to speak, smile, walk, sit, and dine at table — even the holding of a cup required the crooking of the little finger at exactly the right angle. Perhaps also she learnt how to play the piano, to sing or to recite. It was a very varied education indeed. But the object of every item in that curriculum was the same — to enable her to marry. Her sole aim, desire and career in life was to obtain a husband: the spinster, remember, was the mark of failure. If she did not succeed in her attempts — and her attempts extended to almost unbelievable effort — she knew she would be dependent upon her family, and if they failed her, she starved.

There was, however, another item in her education, and this was considered more important than any or all of the others. The chief subject of the feminine curriculum, indeed, was morals — for, quite obviously, no worthwhile Victorian husband-to-be would consider a bride whose character and conduct were not of the highest possible standard. The Victorian young lady, therefore, had to be educated most carefully in the right standards of behaviour; indeed, she had to have no contact with anything which could, in any possible way, affect the purity of her character. She must be shielded and guarded from all that might be even faintly vulgar. Even the legs of the table in her home had to be draped with frills for the sake of decency.

When she had to appear in public amid the gaze of vulgar men, she was often veiled and gloved, and her body concealed from head to foot by her clothes. Thus her hidden beauty would not attract the glances of undesirable males. If she was permitted to bathe in the sea, she undressed in a wheeled hut which a horse then pulled some distance into the water, and after that, in a bathing costume reaching from neck to ankle, she walked down the hut steps into the waves, thus showing as little as possible of herself to the view of male observers. Indeed, she was not allowed to have even portraits of young men in her bedroom.

Her conversation had to be above reproach. The word 'trousers', for example, was forbidden; they had to be referred to as 'unmentionables'.

Thus prepared, she entered the marriage market, but to the very last her morals were safeguarded. When finally a suitable young gentleman had been found, the couple were always accompanied by a chaperone — the girl's mother, aunt, elder sister or a paid companion — who studied carefully the character of the young man, and saw that nothing improper occurred while the courting was being carried out.

Once the young lady was married amid the church bells and the sighs of the relieved parents (an unmarried daughter was a reflection on the family), she entered a household ruled by her husband. She possessed nothing of her own, for until 1882, all her property, and anything she earned or obtained after her marriage, was legally her husband's. She had no vote, and therefore took no part in local and national Government.

In the upper class of society, she had no work to do either. In an age of servants for every purpose, she led a life of leisure in a beautiful home. She attended church regularly, paying the most devout attention to the sermon of the preacher and the dress of every other lady present. She undertook every good work that was possible for church and charity; she opened church fetes, and contributed regularly to church funds. She gave money regularly and advice even more generously to the poor and the lower classes, and in return she expected from them the utmost gratitude and respect.

At intervals, she would leave the mansion house, and travel in almost royal state to Bath or Cheltenham or Tunbridge Wells, where the mineral waters, called 'spas' were considered good for rheumatism and other ailments. Apart from bathing in, or drinking, the waters, she danced, played cards, and above all, gossiped.

Thus she spent her life — a life bounded by unquestioning obedience to her husband, and also by a strict code of conduct and behaviour.

Great Victorian Women

Admittedly there were some women who were not prepared to be thus bound. They wanted to be free — free to follow their own desires. So let us for a moment consider first those who wanted to be authors.

Jane Austen (1775-1817) belonged to the kind of upper class family which she wrote about in her novels. Her chief works were *Sense and Sensibility*, *Pride and Prejudice*, *Emma* and *Northanger Abbey* — all of them giving an accurate picture of the lives and feelings of the young people of her time. There is nothing sensational in the account, but there is a wonderful sense of humour. Those who dislike her works claim that they are narrow-minded, snobbish, and full of old-fashioned ideas, but despite these objections, she is still very widely read today. To some extent, too, she paved the way for the famous Brontë sisters.

There were three sisters in the Brontë family of Haworth, in York-shire — Charlotte (1816-55), Emily (1818-48) and Anne (1820-49). Their mother died when they were very young, and they lived in the care of their strict Puritan father, in a cold dismal parsonage set amid the bleak moorland of the chill north. The loneliness of their lives was not to last long — they all died before they were 40 — but in that short span of time, they enriched the literature of England. Charlotte died at the age of 39, but by then she had written a famous novel, *Jane Eyre*. Emily died at the age of 30, but over a century later, her story of *Wuthering Heights* was still well-loved and famous. Anne died at 29, but already she had written *Agnes Grey*. Not even the joyless lives they lived in Victorian England could prevent their genius from reaching its well-deserved fame.

Mary Anne Evans (1819-80) was born amid the countryside of Warwickshire. She studied ancient and modern literature, the German and Italian languages, music and science, and also she travelled abroad. But under the pen-name 'George Eliot', her greatest novels — *Scenes of Clerical Life*, *Adam Bede*, *The Mill on the Floss* and *Silas Marner* — were all set in the four Midland counties of England, and gained her a fame that spread far beyond even England itself.

But a few other Victorian women preferred deeds to words—women who wished to be active. There was Elizabeth Fry (1780-1845) who worked amid the lowest of humanity in Newgate Gaol. The real Victorian lady, remember, certainly helped the poor, but in the case of the lower ranks of humanity, it was charity from a distance, while criminals, of course, were a class too revolting even to be thought of.

At the same time as Elizabeth Fry, there lived another saint — Florence Nightingale (1820-1910). Restless and self-willed as a child, she rebelled against a life that was the best that Victorian society knew

— ease, elegance, luxury, travel abroad, opera and the spas. From all this, she turned instead to the problems of human wretchedness, to the misery and sickness that suffered in the hospitals of those days — hospitals that were full of lice and liquor. In face of the tremendous opposition of her parents, she turned to the career of nursing — considered the most undignified, distasteful and degrading career possible for a Victorian woman — and in that occupation, she found her happiness.

Then, in 1854, she found her fame. This was the year when the Crimean War broke out between England, France and Turkey on one side, and Russia on the other. To the icy wasteland of the Crimea in southern Russia, the British army went in an effort to capture the great Russian naval base of Sebastopol. In that Crimea, the British army died, and not from bullet and cannon ball, but from cold, cholera, lack of winter clothes and absence of medical supplies. It was one of the worst examples of sheer mismanagement in the whole of our history.

So Florence Nightingale and a band of nurses went out to the base hospital at Scutari. There they were horrified to find, in a huge building with over 5,000 casualties, that not only were there no anaesthetics, but there were not even bandages nor straw for beds. The screams and the moans echoed through the damp and filthy place; the bodies of 50 to 60 men were flung daily into a common grave.

Amid all this, only one person remained completely calm and unruffled. Steadily she organised the nurses; they scrubbed floors, sorted out blankets, bandages, operating instruments and clothes, prepared the meals, and attended to the sick and wounded soldiers. It was an effort that succeeded, but in a short account such as this, no words could describe what that effort meant... — an effort that left Florence Nightingale an exhausted, nervous wreck and a national heroine. But the Great Nurse lived on, to organise a new, improved medical service for the British Army, and to raise nursing to the rank of a respected profession. Thus it was she entered History.

The 18th and early 19th century theatres also had their heroines — although the profession of acting was regarded by society as certain to lead to immorality. Yet for 37 years, the great Sarah Siddons (1755-1831) held the English stage. In tragedy, she was superb, her greatest role being that of Lady Macbeth in Shakespeare's *Macbeth* — a scheming, ambitious, ruthless woman, who became insane — and there is no more difficult a part to act on the stage than the part of a mad person.

A different life was that of Lady Mary Whortley Montagu (1689-1762) who travelled to France, Italy and Turkey. The letters that she wrote from these lands were witty and often full of scandal, as well as containing accurate descriptions of foreign homes, clothing and customs.

Then, in 1849, the celebrated American, Mrs. Amelia Bloomer appeared, in her close-fitting sleeves, a shirt to just below the knees, and Turkish trousers . . . and the shocked, horrified, disgusted and appalled Victorian society avoided her type more carefully than a plague. On hearing that a woman was wearing trousers, the wittiest of English magazines, *Punch*, commented, 'So far so good. When does the lady begin to shave?' We still use the word 'bloomer' today, meaning 'to make an unpardonable mistake'.

But all these, it must be pointed out, were exceptional women, and cannot be used to judge the rest of the 18th and early 19th century females, who continued to live their quiet, well-ordered lives.

Emancipation

Yet a change was to come, a change in a world where women were ruled by men and had to obey strict rules of conduct. This change saw the freeing (or 'emancipation' as it is called) of women from these two conditions of life.

The reason for the change has amazingly, but seriously, been considered to be . . . the bicycle! Of the strange causes of many great events in History, this is surely yet another. A careful consideration of the matter reveals the following facts. The bicycle became popular — it was swifter than walking, and cheaper and more convenient than horseback or carriage. So women learnt to ride, and immediately a dress revolution occurred. Dresses reaching to the ankle did not permit pedalling, so garments had now to be worn shorter, and had to be made less clumsy in body fitting. Once she could ride a bicycle, the Victorian woman could, and did travel further afield, and her circle of friends and acquaintances, as well as her knowledge of life, increased. Thirdly, it was no longer possible for the elderly mother, the aged aunt or the paid companion to accompany, as chaperone, a young lady and a young gentleman when they conducted their courtship during cycle rides. Thus it must be admitted that the bicycle played some part in the freeing of women from the strict lives they had previously lived.

Another reason for the emancipation of women was an improved education. Reading, sewing, embroidery and music were hardly an 'education', and gradually girls began to be taught other subjects, and to a higher standard. It was an important event when in 1848, Queen's College, London, was founded in order to train women teachers. From this College came two star students — Mary Buss, later Headmistress of London Collegiate School in 1850, and Dorothea Beale, later Principal of Cheltenham Ladies' College in 1858.

Gradually, education for girls developed further, until in 1869, Girton College, and in 1871, Newnham College at Cambridge University were founded for women students. The first women's college at Oxford University was Somerville in 1879.

An educated woman, of course, was not prepared to accept the narrow life of Victorian times. A woman's place was no longer to be restricted to the home; instead, the women went out to become doctors, lawyers and office workers — occupations previously undertaken by men only. They began to take a real interest in local events, so that in 1888 they obtained the right to vote in the elections for County and County Borough Councils, and in 1907, they were permitted to become members of such councils — positions previously held by men only.

Indeed, it seemed that only one stronghold of power still remained in male control — the Central Government. Only men were allowed to vote in the General Elections; only men could become Members of Parliament; and the men were quite determined that this stronghold at least would remain theirs. They had seen their power and influence weakened by female success in many occupations formerly regarded as undertaken by men only. But the limit of female success had now been reached. Women were not to be allowed to reach the highest ranks of all — the Government of the country. So the battle began.

The spearhead of the female brigade was the redoubtable Mrs. Emily Pankhurst (1857-1928). Her second-in-command was her daughter, Christabel. As a start, the female forces prepared themselves by holding demonstrations, by marching in long processions through the streets of London, with banners proclaiming 'Votes for Women', 'Let women have the right to vote', 'Equal rights for Women', and by organising large public meetings.

Once the army was marshalled, the feminine warriors, known as suffragettes, went into battle. When a Cabinet Minister began to make an important speech, he was heckled and interrupted by feminine shouts and cat-calls. Glass from the broken windows of the houses of leading citizens littered the London streets, and as Mrs. Pankhurst directed her attacks skilfully over a wide area, it was almost impossible for the harassed London police to prevent or even to discover those actually responsible. When the police were not being called out, it was the turn of the fire brigade — to extinguish fires in pillar boxes. Further to draw attention to themselves and their cause, suffragettes would chain themselves to the railings outside the Prime Minister's house in Downing Street.

When arrested and sent to prison, the determined women went on hunger strike, and so gained a great deal of popular sympathy when they had to be forcibly fed. Liquid food was passed through a tube inserted into the nostril and so to the stomach. The Government finally decided to pass the 'Cat and Mouse Act', 1913, whereby hunger strikers could be released from prison, and re-arrested later when they had recovered their health.

By 1913, however, the battle had developed in earnest. Christabel Pankhurst withdrew to the safety of Paris, and began to conduct operations in England from there. Thus innocent-looking women would enter museums and art galleries, make their way quietly towards some valuable painting, and suddenly slash it savagely with a knife. Moving out at night, the suffragettes set fire to goods yards, railway stations and country houses, and on their way back would cut through telephone wires.

The fact that if caught they would be roughly handled, ill-treated and sent to jail did not hinder these women, many of whom had been brought up in quiet, comfortable homes. Courage they certainly had, and one of them, indeed, paid the supreme sacrifice. At the Derby Race at Epsom in 1913, Emily Davidson flung herself beneath the hooves of the King's horse, and was killed.

Nevertheless, the efforts of the suffragettes failed to obtain the vote for women. Determined and brave though they were, the violence of their activities lost them public sympathy, and also the support of many women who desired more peaceful efforts.

When finally women obtained the right to vote, the reasons had nothing to do with the suffragettes. When the First World War broke out, as many men as possible were required for fighting, and it was the women who enabled this to be done. Women became doctors, nurses, hospital attendants, drivers, telephonists, clerks, secretaries, store-keepers, munition workers and so forth, thus releasing thousands of men to go to the fighting line. After four years Germany was defeated, and England was saved from German rule. In gratitude, in 1918, the country gave to all women over 30 the right to vote, and they could become Members of Parliament (the first being Lady Astor in 1919); while in 1928, the age limit for voting was reduced to 21 — the same as for men.

Just thirty years later came the last stage, when, in 1958, women were allowed to become members of the House of Lords.

Results of emancipation

So the 18th century and early Victorian woman had finally disappeared, and with her passing there came a new social life and new customs for feminine society — an altogether different and an altogether freer feminine world. Let us briefly consider this new life and these new customs.

In the 18th centuries, the goal of a woman was marriage, for then her life was made secure by her husband. After this period, however, as women were in a position to earn their own living, they were not, therefore, so dependent upon a husband. For some women, a career became more important than marriage, and thus they entered nearly every occupation known — teachers, lawyers, police, post-women, farm workers, factory work, railway porters, business management, the armed forces, athletics, and many more.

There were yet other women who managed to combine a career and marriage. They were able to do this because the responsibilities of marriage were lessened by having fewer children to look after. (The Victorian mother had, on average, five children; the Elizabeth II parent only two). Furthermore, housework was made much easier by electrical cleaners, dishwashers, laundry and heating machines; no longer was it necessary to dust and sweep, to scrub, polish, scour and rinse, with aching muscles and reddened hands. Central heating, or gas and electric fires, meant that the old coal fire grates did not have to be cleaned, re-filled and lit every morning.

Catering, too, was a simple matter of telephoning for goods to be delivered to the door by the shopkeeper's van. Even those hardier people who preferred to go out for shopping, found that the great chain stores supplied everything 'from a pin to an elephant' under one roof. For cooking, a tin-opener, a sauce-pan and an automatic oven was the sole kitchen equipment required. Tins containing already prepared ingredients had only to be opened, and the contents placed in an oven which could be adjusted for heat and time, and automatically switched itself off when necessary. Washing up and laundry work were undertaken by machines, soap powders and detergents.

Another revolution occurred in respect of female customs — an important one — dress. Clothes were now designed to fit, not to disguise, the body, with the result that garments now weighed in ounces what they had previously weighed in pounds. Skirts rose to above knee level; necklines were lower; trousers for women became fashionable. To add to natural beauty, or to disguise its lack, cosmetics were freely used — and before 1918, this was the mark of the worst type of woman. Hair styles were altered, and hair dyes ranged from black, brown, blue and golden to white.

In brief, the emancipation of women had taken place.

Chapter XXXVII

The Popular Press

By the end of the 19th century, the English working class had received the benefits of the 1870 Education Act. At least, they were now able to read and write, even if they were not very well educated. By the end of the 19th century, too, the working class had received the vote — the town workers in 1867 and the country labourers in 1884, and so could take part in the Government of the country.

Ordinary people, therefore, had now a real desire for knowledge — a desire to learn of the world around them, and in a simple, easy-to-understand, interesting way. The usual source of information was the newspapers, led by *The Times* — but all of these were written for the upper and middle classes. To the Members of Parliament, the nobility, university professors, civil servants and lawyers, indeed, *The Times* was certainly the most learned and respected of publications; but to the lower classes it was dull, solemn and pompous.

The need had thus arisen for a newspaper which catered for the working class.

Accordingly, in the 20th century, the greatest name in the newspaper world became that of Alfred Harmsworth, later Lord Northcliffe (1865-1922), the founder of what has been called 'the popular press'.

In 1894, he bought the *Evening News*. For fourteen years, that paper had never shown a profit. In its first year under Harmsworth, it reaped a £5,000 gain. Two years later, Harmsworth started the *Daily Mail*, and the very first issue sold 397,215 copies — a far greater number than that of any other paper in a single day. Later, the *Daily Mail* became the first newspaper to reach a circulation of one million copies.

From then onwards, the Harmsworth newspaper empire developed, for he obtained the *Weekly Dispatch*, *The Observer*, the *Daily Mirror*, *The Times* and several magazines. Alfred Harmsworth died in 1922, but his successors continued his policy, so that in 1961 his nephew, Cecil King Harmsworth, controlled two national daily papers, two Sunday papers, nearly all the leading women's magazines and countless journals.

The principles of Alfred Harmsworth were continued, too. As he sold the *Daily Mail* for only ½d., (pre-decimal), he relied on money from firms who paid to advertise in it. This meant that the paper had to have a high circulation, for no firm would pay money advertising in a paper that no one read.

So the Harmsworth publications were intended to be read not by a very intelligent few, nor by some particular class or type of person but by the mass of the people. To attract the mass of the people, therefore, Harmsworth used sensationalism, scoops and scandal, and these were expressed in simple, easy-to-understand language, large print, cartoons and numerous pictures. He then made his newspaper even more attractive by offering generous free gifts to readers. Since the majority of people like thrilling accounts, news which no other paper has managed to obtain, the 'naughty side of life', and free gifts, the popular press triumphed.

The headlines of a typical paper thus proclaimed in tasteful capital letters of thick, black type, two inches in height — guaranteed to catch the glance of any passer-by at 40-foot distance from the news-agent's stall — the exciting words 'MURDER MOST FOUL'. Also on the front page was the picture of a charming young lady, guaranteed to rivet the attention of any passer-by at treble that distance. *The Times*, with its desire for straightforward truth and a straight-forward, accurate account of the facts — *The Times*, with its solid, sober writing — declined.

The Harmsworth example was followed by others, until the 20th century saw a clear division among the morning newspapers, usually on political lines. Of the older publications, *The Times, The Guardian* and *The Telegraph* continued in their serious way, though lightened by a more open lay-out, brighter illustrations and larger print. Of the popular press, *The Dail Mail* and the *Daily Express* were Conservative, *The Daily Mirror* and *Daily Herald* supported the Labour Party, the *News Chronicle* was read by the Liberals, and the *Daily Worker* was the mouthpiece of the Communist Party.

So the popular press triumphed.

Chapter XXXVIII

Population 1850 — 1970

The population of England and Wales in 1851 was 18 million. In 1971, it was 48 million. The obvious question, therefore is 'why?' — particularly since the birth rate fell continuously and drastically for some 70 years during that time.

There were many reasons, indeed, for the declining birth rate (i.e. why so few babies were born). Medical knowledge had now extended to birth control, and after 1876, the use of contraceptives increased. In 1921, Dr. Marie Stopes opened, in London, the world's first birth control clinic. The knowledge and practice spread rapidly. For as the 20th century progressed fewer and fewer people desired to have large families . . . as the following causes reveal.

In the first instance, the Factory Acts and Education Acts no longer enabled children to be wage-earners, thus deterring not only those parents who regarded children as an investment, but also those who could not afford the cost of a family unless the children themselves helped to offset the expense. Equally important from an economic point of view, the fewer there were in a family, the more there was for each.

Competing with children in the family budget were numerous other interests. As the period 1850-1970 developed, there arose more interesting ways of spending money — motor cars, radio, television, theatres, household gadgets, holidays abroad, and above all, the necessity to 'Keep up with the Jones's'. In some cases, these other benefits proved far more attractive than children.

Competing also with the natural feminine instinct to have children, was the desire for a career. The emancipation of women (see Chapter XXXVI), meant that life provided more opportunity for female work and pleasure than merely to bring up a family. Women could become secretaries, clerks, typists, telegraphists, teachers, shop assistants lawyers, and a host of other occupations. They could take part in local and national Government. They could enjoy a life of the theatre cinema, television and holidays, and to do so, they did not want to be troubled by family worries.

There were non-monetary reasons that reduced the birth-rate, too. In the 20th century, three major wars were fought, and all of them within a single life-span — the Boer War (1899-1902), the Great War (1914-1918) and the Second World War (1939-1945). In these wars, a total of 1,100,000 out of Britain's armed forces died, and it must be realised that, as always in war, it is the finest and the fittest who die in action, the men of marriageable age.

Not only that, but in the 20th century, even when war was not actually in progress, there was the constant threat of hostilities. In addition, there were 21 years of economic depression and crisis from 1918-39, and then there was the decline of England's wealth and power after 1945. In circumstances such as these, many people refused to bring children into the world.

The final result of all these reasons was that whereas the Victorian family had five or six children, parents in the reign of Elizabeth II had a family of two.

But why, then, in view of so low a birth rate, did the population increase?

There were two causes.

Firstly, there werer fewer deaths. Though not so many children were born, those who were born, survived. Indeed, by 1960, the death rate was only 25 out of every 1,000 births. Not only did these babies survive, but also they lived longer. The improvements in medical knowledge, public health, housing, conditions of work and education, together with the efforts of the Welfare State, increased everyone's prospects of longer living. In 1851, a man's expectation of life was 40 years; by 1960, it was 68 years.

Secondly, there was a flood of immigration. The Irish whose homeland held no hope, the political refugees who fled from elsewhere in Europe, the coloured peoples from the West Indies, India and Pakistan . . . all came to England to try to find better conditions and prospects.

It was these two reasons which really accounted for the two-and-a-half-fold increase in the population between 1851-1971.

The coloured immigrants in particular caused problems. By 1961, over a thousand a week were arriving in this country, to settle in London, the Midlands and West Yorkshire. Racial hostility developed in these areas as the white population feared loss of jobs, and a shortage of housing, while since many of the immigrants were poor, there was the additional cost to the Welfare State of helping them.

In 1961, therefore, the Commonwealth Immigration Act limited the numbers of those who came to live in this country, while in 1968, a Race Relations Board was set up to investigate complaints of unfair treatment of coloured immigrants.

APPENDIX A

Isambard Kingdom Brunel (1806-59)

There was nothing small about the genius of Isambard Kingdom
Brunel. His vision, his beliefs and his work were all great, and the
tragedy was that he was too great for his time. And Fate opposed him,
too.

The first step in his amazing career was when he undertook the
building of a tunnel under the River Thames. This was the first
underwater tunnel of its kind, and at the time Brunel was only nineteen
years old. Perhaps, however, it was as well that he commenced so
early, for he was to die young.

Under the nineteen-year-old genius, then, the work progressed. A
huge shield some 38ft. broad and 22ft. high was erected, and standing
on the cross-girders the workmen hacked away the earth in front of
them. It was, in truth, a slow process — a very, very slow process. The
shield advanced only as much as one inch in three hours, and as it
moved forward the tunnel was bricked round behind it. After two
years' hard labour from 1825-27, however, even this slow progress
could not be maintained, for lack of money brought the work to a
complete standstill. Seven years passed before the effort was resumed,
and finally, despite floods and disasters, the quarter-mile tunnel from
Rotherhithe to Wapping was completed.

A similar story of delay marked the history of the Clifton Suspension
Bridge. Work began in 1831, stopped, recommenced in 1836, ceased
again, and was not completed until 1864. Thus the great engineer
never saw the actual glory of the wonderful arch that spanned the
Avon gorge.

In the case of the Saltash Bridge in Devon, he was slightly more
fortunate. Twin spans, each 465 feet long and each 1,000 tons in weight,
crossed the swirling River Tamar, and in the year 1859 a train steamed
slowly across the marvellous work. In the coach behind lay Brunel, a
seriously sick man.

It was the Great Western Railway that marked yet another peak of
his fame. Formed in 1833, this energetic railway company had the
line opened for public use in 1838. The broad seven foot gauge followed
gentle curves and slight gradients; near Bath lay the great Box Tunnel,

L

3,000 yards in length, taking $2\frac{1}{2}$ years to build, during which it required a ton of explosives and a ton of candles for light per week; and at the end of the journey, Paddington Station, with its great glass roofing. And the route, the seven foot gauge line, the Box Tunnel, and the Station, were all the work of the same engineer, who even helped Sir Daniel Gooch design the famous 'North Star' locomotive as well.

But fate opposed Brunel. There is no doubt whatever that his choice of a seven foot railway gauge was far better than George Stephenson's 4ft. $8\frac{1}{2}$in. width — it could carry heavier loads faster and more smoothly. But a country could not have two different gauges in operation at the same time, and in 1846 the British Government came to a decision. The choice was the 4ft. $8\frac{1}{2}$in. gauge, which has remained to this day. Once again Brunel was too great for his time, and once again Fate was against him. It had to be realised that by 1845 there were some 2,000 miles of narrow gauge in existence, but scarce 300 miles of broad gauge. To convert from broad to narrow was easy — the addition of a third and central rail on the existing sleepers; to convert from narrow to broad involved track widening and fresh sleepers. So the Great Western Railway in 1868 had to add a third rail, and the last broad gauge train ran in 1892.

To overcome the steepness of the South Devon hills, Brunel next designed an Atmospheric Railway, 1847. Between and beneath the rail was a tube with a slot along its length and a piston fitting inside. The locomotive was attached to the piston by a metal plate passing through the slot. As a pumping engine pumped out the air from the tube in front of the piston, both piston and the attached locomotive were pushed forward by air pressure behind. The slot was closed by a leather flap which opened as the train approached, and was closed as the train passed over. Therein lay the cause of failure — the leather flap did not seal the tube effectively, and in course of time rotted.

From land, Brunel turned to the sea. His *Great Western* built in 1838, was of 1,340 tons and 400 horse-power — a splendidly-built vessel for the sea-route from England to America. Unfortunately, a fire broke out on board and though the damage was soon repaired, the delay robbed Brunel of the triumph of building the first iron steamship to cross the Atlantic. By only a few hours the little *Sirius* achieved the honour.

But Brunel's masterpiece — the greatest of the great — was the *Great Eastern*. There were 6,500 square yards of sail, borne by six masts; five funnels belched forth smoke from the engines that had to be sufficiently powerful to drive two paddle-wheels each 56 feet in diameter and weighing over 90 tons; and at the rear of the ship was a screw propeller. The *Great Eastern* was certainly a masterpiece of engineering, conceived on a truly gigantic scale for those days. Its gross tonnage was nearly 27,500; it was 680 feet long (and remained for forty years the largest ship in the world), so it is not surprising that it could store 15,000 tons of coal in its bunkers, and could carry 6,000 tons of cargo and 4,000 passengers. That is why it failed. It cost too much to run, and in the 19th century such a vast quantity of cargo and so large a number of passengers were not likely to travel on one voyage. The ship did indeed achieve some success in laying a telegraph cable across the Atlantic in 1865-66, but in 1890 it had to be broken up as a commercial failure.

Few ships, perhaps, seemed more ill-fated than the *Great Eastern*. At the very launching the ship slid suddenly forward out of control, the pull on the cables caused the braking drums to revolve furiously, and one of the flying handles killed one man and injured five others. The vessel then stopped and after a further two days of immense effort it had moved only four feet. It was three months before the ship was water-borne. Then, as it moved along under its own steam, one of the funnels exploded, killing five men. Shortly after, the toil and trouble killed the great engineer himself, at the early age of 53. But the mighty ship had not yet finished. At Southampton her captain was drowned as he was landing from her. On one trans-Atlantic crossing a storm wrenched away her paddle-wheels, and on another voyage she tore an 80 foot gash in her hull on a New York reef. Even to the very last she maintained her fatedness — even as she was being broken up in 1890, they discovered the skeleton of a workman who had been entombed between the outer and the inner walls of the hull when the ship was being built some 33 years before.

APPENDIX B

Factory Laws 1802-1937

1802: Pauper apprentices in cotton mills — 12 hours per day, no night work.

1819: All 9-16 year olds in cotton mills — 12 hours per day, no night work.
But no proper inspection.

1833: Althorp's Factory Act. Inspectors appointed for textile mills (except silk) to see that:
Under 9, no work; 9-13 — 48 hour week and two hours education per day; 13-18 — 69 hour week.
But no birth certificates.

1842: Ashley's Mining Act. No female or child to work underground. Safety regulations enforced.

1844: Peel's Factory Act. 8-13 — $6\frac{1}{2}$ hours per day and three hours education, or one day work and one day school alternately (half-time system). 13-18 and women — 12 hours per day. Factory machinery to be fenced.

1847: Ten Hours Act. Boys under 18 and all women, 10 hours per day. Hence shift work to avoid the regulations, until later Act laid down times of work. Extended to children 1853, allied trades (bleaching, dyeing, etc.) 1845-61, and non-textile industries (e.g. pottery, watch-making) 1864 and 1867.

1878: Factory defined as a place which used mechanical power.

1878 and 1901: Factory Acts codified the laws, with special regulations for dangerous industries, e.g. pottery (where workers suffered from pneumonia, bronchitis, lead poisoning), or match-making (phossy jaw).

1908: Coal Mines Act — Miners to have eight hour day.

1909: Trade Boards Act set up Trade Boards to lay down wages and conditions in 'sweated industries', (e.g. tailoring, boot-making).

1937: Employees aged 14-16 — 44 hour week; 16-18 and all women — 48 hour week.

APPENDIX C

Social Reforms 1906-14

Reasons: (i) Public conscience awakened; (ii) Labour pressure in Parliament.

1906: Workmen's Compensation Act.

1906: Trades Dispute Act. 1901 Taff Vale case gave damages against a Union for strike damage. So the Unions pressed their M.P.'s to pass the Trades Dispute Act 1906 by which a Union could not be required to pay for strike damage.

1906: Education Authorities to provide free school meals for needy children.

1907: Free medical inspection and treatment for school children.

1907: Women allowed to serve on County Councils and County Borough Councils.

1908: Old Age Pensions. Over 70s with under £21 a year had a weekly pension.

1908: Children's Act. Children not allowed to beg, enter public houses, or be sold tobacco. 'Baby-farming' abuses stopped. Juvenile courts and remand homes established.

1908: Coal Mines Act. Miners to have eight hour day.

1909: Trade Boards Act set up Trade Boards to lay down wages and conditions in 'sweated industries', (e.g. tailoring, boot-making).

1909: Labour Exchanges established.

1910: Budget. To obtain money to pay for the navy and social services, Lloyd George proposed to tax the rich heavily, in his Budget 1909. (i) Income Tax increased to 6p. in the £1, and Super Tax on very high incomes; (ii) death duties, tobacco, spirits and stamp duties increased; (iii) new petrol tax and motor car licences to provide a Road Fund to improve the roads; (iv) duty on land values, particularly when a profit was made on the sale of land.

1911: National Insurance. Workers (2p.), employer (1½p.) and Government (1p.) all contributed, while doctors formed a panel for free treatment and chemists provided cheaper drugs.

1911: Shop assistants to have half-day holiday a week.

1912: Minimum wages for coal miners.

1913: Trade Union Act. 1908 Osborne case said Trade Union
       members need not pay into political funds, so Unions pressed
       their M.P.'s to pass 1913 Trade Union Act allowing collection
       of political funds, but members could 'contract out' (i.e. not
       pay if they wished).

INDEX